The Art of Ancient Music

The Art of Ancient Music

David Leinweber

LEXINGTON BOOKS
Lanham • Boulder • New York • London

Published by Lexington Books
An imprint of The Rowman & Littlefield Publishing Group, Inc.
4501 Forbes Boulevard, Suite 200, Lanham, Maryland 20706
www.rowman.com

6 Tinworth Street, London SE11 5AL, United Kingdom

Copyright © 2021 by The Rowman & Littlefield Publishing Group, Inc.

All rights reserved. No part of this book may be reproduced in any form or by any electronic or mechanical means, including information storage and retrieval systems, without written permission from the publisher, except by a reviewer who may quote passages in a review.

British Library Cataloguing in Publication Information Available

Library of Congress Control Number: 2020945891
ISBN 978-1-7936-2519-9 (cloth)
ISBN 978-1-7936-2521-2 (pbk)
ISBN 978-1-7936-2520-5 (electronic)

Dedication
*In loving memory of my father, Ron Leinweber,
and to his great-grandson, Dawson.*

Contents

Preface ix

Introduction xi

1 The Voice: History's First Musical Instrument 1
2 Early Musical Instruments 23
3 The Bow of Music 47
4 Music and Storytelling 69
5 Festivals and Parties 95
6 Church Music as an Heir of Ancient Music 119

Epilogue: The Art of Ancient Music 141

A Select Bibliography 145

Index 163

About the Author 171

Preface

This text explores the idea of music as an "art," something that we make or do. It looks at the art of music as it arose and evolved in the ancient world. In this sense, a study of ancient music is much more than simply a history of music, per se. Music is the history of humanity itself. The story of music reminds us of how we have built our complex world from unfathomably rugged beginnings, a hardscrabble existence difficult for present-day people even to imagine. Along with the history of the Fine Arts, music played a critical role in technology and science, including the use of tools. Music helped drive the development of our rich traditions of literature, including storytelling. Music helped shape our languages with added eloquence and expressive power. Music complemented public life. It enlivened ceremonies, festivals, and parties. Music informed religious ideas and other worldviews. Music provided an important focus for philosophers and theoreticians of all stripes. Music has also helped the world's diverse peoples to form and define their respective identities. In short, it is hard to overstate the significance of music.

The Art of Ancient Music discusses the rich musical contributions early peoples made to later generations—the critical role of music as an agent of historical progress. It hopes to offer an interdisciplinary work of professional scholarship, without assuming advanced knowledge of history, foreign languages, or music theory. The text has a light sprinkling of world history. It also references present-day musical traditions, especially in earlier chapters dealing with broader themes regarding the formative periods of music in prehistory. The heart of the text, however, is a focus on Western music in the ancient periods. Western musical traditions continue to shape the music we hear each day, even as culture evolves going forward. The text focuses on the earliest historical eras, and then the flourishing of music in the Classical heyday of the Ancient world. Major areas treated are the Ancient Near East, the lands of the Bible, the Greek world, and the Roman Empire. *The Art of Ancient Music* also has some inclusion of the musical heritages of the ancient Germanic and Celtic tribes. A final chapter provides some brief discussion of how music helped bridge the divide between Antiquity and the Middle Ages, especially in the guise of Church music.

I owe many thanks to many people who supported me in writing this book. My wife Mary tolerated my preoccupation and frustration, encouraging me all the way. My mother, Ruth Leinweber, provided similar moral support. She reviewed drafts with her red pen, recalling earlier days when she taught AP English Lit. Courtney Morales of Lexington Books really helped navigate the process of getting this text ready for publication. Anonymous reviews of the manuscript also proved very helpful as I reworked and edited initial drafts. Jessica Robinson, on the amazing Oxford College Library staff, also proved an enormous help. She never failed to find those sometimes-forgotten articles, books, and entries. Jessica patiently aided me in my often embarrassingly inept, technologically challenged efforts at research in the digital age. My student, Apollo Robey, provided outstanding drawings to help illustrate the text. Other colleagues and friends at Oxford College of Emory University also helped in the development of this manuscript—friends with whom I have enjoyed years of worthwhile interactions. Maria Archetto provided an excellent eye and insightful comments. My long-term colleague Clark Lemons also offered helpful input.

The College also provided the physical resources without which this next would have been impossible—access to a fine office, travel, computer technology, and staff support. We should never take such things for granted. I thank all these valued friends and colleagues for their important contributions to my writing. To the extent I have succeeded in my goals, I owe them an enormous debt of gratitude. Conversely, the inevitable failings found between these pages are nobody's fault but mine.

Introduction

What is music? Music is the organized production of sound. We make music by manipulating sound. But why do we make manipulate sounds? People intentionally create sounds to reflect moods, shape some ceremonial purpose, or help convey some message. When they do so, they take a necessary step in the creation of music. Yet, music is more than just human-created sounds. A vacuum cleaner makes noise. So, too, does a lawnmower. Such noises, even ones we make intentionally, are not necessarily music. Similarly, the noise of a fire siren serves a very useful purpose. A fire siren intentionally makes an artificial noise. Except perhaps in some more contrived composition, however, most people would not regard a fire siren as music. The voice, too, can make artificial noise. Voices can make tones, rhythms, and strange syllabic sounds. We can scream. Animals also create artificial noise. They growl, call, chirp, buzz, and make any number of other sounds. Monkeys pound on things to amuse or intimidate. We regard such animal sounds as part of nature. But they are artificially produced noises, too. When an eagle caws or a dog barks, they artificially add sounds to our natural landscape of noises.

What, then, distinguishes "music" from any other artificially created sound? Sound happens when air molecules vibrate, as all molecules do. When something artificial makes air, molecules vibrate more than usual. They make sounds. Faster vibrations make higher sounds. Slower vibrations produce lower sounds. We call these sound variations "pitches." In nature, motion creates such noises, whether it be due to wind, water, other animals, tremors, or whatever. In this sense, all sound is artificially produced noise. After all, a motionless universe would produce no sound whatsoever. Music, however, is more than simply sound. Music developed long ago when people learned to manipulate air vibrations to express themselves. By different techniques and devices, they learned to make special sounds. They invented tools to manipulate sounds. We call these tools, including the human voice, "musical instruments." We call the artists who have gained the skill to manipulate the sounds "musicians." The role of musicians in history evolved slowly, over a course of countless centuries.

Because we make music by vibrating air molecules by artificial means, all musical instruments actually belong to the category of "percussion" instrument, a term we more commonly associate with rhythm. *Merriam Webster's Dictionary* notes that the term "percussion" comes from the Latin verb "*percutere*," meaning "to beat." Upon reflection, musicians use a number of percussive methods to create movement of air. They shake, pluck, strum, pound, and blow, among other things. To do this, musicians use hammers, fingers, picks, breath, bows, and many other devices. Today, we also use electrical impulses to vibrate speakers, an updated version of the same ancient principle. All such techniques accomplish the same task: making sounds by vibrating the air. Once we have made such sounds, we can further hone them by a number of other ingenious methods. We enhance the self-made sounds by the shape of the instrument, the nuances of our touch, and the materials used to make the tones.

THE IMPORTANCE OF PLEASURE IN HISTORY

Unlike other naturally occurring sounds, musicians create music specifically for giving pleasure to themselves and others. This impulse for pleasure animates us as much as basic needs for food, shelter, or clothing. Pleasure is not a mere frill. All people—indeed all animals—naturally seek pleasure. Because music gives us pleasure, creating music is a natural impulse. Throughout our shared histories, we have striven to make music. We do this because of the pleasure that music gives. We make pleasurable music for the same reason that we wear attractive clothes, invent delicious recipes, or design buildings that look as nice from the outside as they do on the inside. We do such things because they give us pleasure. Because music is pleasurable, we have evolved a cultural tradition to give ourselves these enjoyable sensations. This makes music part of the drive to make our lives pleasurable, not so different from the drive to have sex, enjoy sugar, or live in comfortable surroundings. Such things come from genuine needs, but transcend them.

Since music gives us pleasure, we usually think it is supposed to be good, by which we mean pleasing. *Merriam Webster's Collegiate Dictionary* defines melody as a "pleasing arrangement of single tones." However, not all melodies are pleasant. Some melodies are unpleasant, perhaps even on purpose. "Pleasant" is presumably a subjective term. Many conventional definitions of musical elements like melody, harmony, or rhythm emphasize music as beautiful. So is it true that the purpose of music is to beautify the world? It is a good question. Consideration of "Aesthetics"—the study of beauty—has long formed a critical part of philosophy. Is music beautiful? Usually, it tries to be. When music fails to be beautiful, plenty of people will call it "bad music." However, not all music necessarily seeks to make beautiful sounds. Not all music even seeks to be good. Indeed, some music is ugly on purpose. Musicians make music to convey messages or express emotions, including unpleasant ones.

Plenty of composers intentionally write unpleasant music. Horror movies use unpleasant music to create a sense of fear, nervousness, or to enhance gross, disgusting images. Some punk rock, among other genres, virtually takes pride in being bad. Punk rock typically entails loud, discordant music, often performed by bands who sometimes almost seem proud of their musical incompetence. Although thwarting conventional musical notions of quality, such bands take a kind of pride in what they stand for. They have, in their own way, true artistic integrity. Even serious music has experimented with sounds considered unpleasant by conventional standards—bizarre electronic sounds, or "atonal" compositions that defy conventional notions of beautiful melodies and harmonies. But such examples of "unpleasant" music still support the idea that music is, ultimately, a pleasant experience. Though undoubtedly an acquired taste, many people appreciate such music. They respect its intellectual curiosity. They enjoy its challenging palate of new sounds. Millions of people love horror movies, including the jarring, disturbing music that invariably accompanies them. And much to the chagrin of many parents, plenty of teenagers have found the most extreme forms of music, like punk rock or Gothic rock, to express their youthful feelings better than any other.

In short, as the old saying goes, there is no accounting for taste. If people did not like such "bad" music, there would be no market for it. That said, there do seem to be many musical conventions commonly defined as "pleasant." Some notions of pleasant music seem almost universal. Just as people seem to find certain landscapes or faces more attractive, certain musical conventions also seem attractive to practically everybody. All but the most determined curmudgeons enjoy happy songs in major keys, haunting minor-key melodies, or brilliant scales. Such musical conventions—call them clichés if you must—appeal to wide swaths of the population. Such music can be as beautiful as anything in the world. But do sounds that simply please people's ears define what music is?

Music and the other arts beautify our world—just as much as fine paint, carved woodwork, marble walls, or the finest bone china. A society that produces a healthy musical culture, and passes it on to its heirs, is a vibrant and constructive one. A healthy musical culture points to a healthy overall society. Music is also part of the distinctive human search for meaning.

Music is definitely one of the things that helps us create value and meaning in the world, beyond our material needs. Unlike other animals, presumably, we humans have knowledge of our own inevitable deaths. This most basic fact about human awareness prompts questions and theories about the nature of our short and hard lives.[1] When we experience music performed well, we experience a connection to that part of human consciousness that goes beyond our physical selves. This higher value music has explains why music has always had such a close connection to religious faith, in all its complex forms.

THE ART OF MUSIC

Traditionally, people define music as an "art." The British historian RG Collingwood (1889–1943) famously believed that that broadest definition of "art" was that it involved expressing emotion.[2] Popular colloquial language commonly equates art with the visual arts like painting and sculpture. Music is also an art. When musicians reach a polished level of command over their musical talents, we call them "artists." We call the expressive skill of fine musicians "artistry." When artists reach a truly superb level of excellence in their crafts, they become part of the "Fine Arts." Of course, every culture has its own ideas of excellence.

Music is an art. Music is a craft. The words "art" and the word "craft" stem from different languages but share very similar meanings. They are almost interchangeable synonyms. *Merriam Webster's Collegiate Dictionary* defines "craft" as a "skill acquired by experience, study or observation," derived from the Old English word *kraeft*, which means strength. Strength in this sense might mean literally a strong arm, as in the physical strength of a manual laborer. "Craft" could also imply competence, as in "craftwork." The term "craft" can also refer to smart, but sneaky, people, as in the term "crafty." The English word "art" comes from the old Latin *ars*, a Latinate word meaning "skill" or "craft." Just as the word "craft" can imply "crafty," the word art can also have a sneaky connotation as in "artful" or "term of art," a phrase implying obfuscation. In Greek, the term "art" most closely corresponds to the word *"techne,"* related to the English word "technique."[3] In his *Nicomachean Ethics*, Aristotle likened medicine to an art, *techne*, as well as shipbuilding, business, military strategy, and littler, humbler endeavors like making a bridle.[4]

In her 1937 book *The Trivium: The Liberal Arts of Logic, Grammar and Rhetoric*, Sister Miriam Joseph distinguished between science and art: art is something someone does.[5] Science is something someone knows. Pure knowledge does not necessarily have a practical application.[6] The Latin word for "knowledge" is *"sciencia,"* coming from the verb *"scio,"* that is, "to know." Properly understood, "science" refers to all knowledge, not just things that happen in a laboratory with test tubes and Petri dishes. Science includes all the things we know, as opposed to the things we merely believe. In Greek, the comparable word for knowledge comes from *epistēmē*, a word meaning "to stand near." As we learn when we study the scientific method, we gain knowledge by observation, by standing alongside something to learn about how it works. It is from the Greeks that we get our word "epistemology." Epistemology is the study of knowing things. How do we know what we know? That is the basic question posed by epistemologists.

In some senses, music is both an art and a science. Music is an art to the extent it is something that we make. But music is also a science in the sense that it is something that we know—something that we can observe and experience. We talk about people "knowing music," for example. We might say that someone "knows" how to play a musical instrument. We can also "know music" in the sense that we understand the physical principles it involves, or the role of music in culture and history. Still, at the end of the day, music is something that we make, not just something that we know. Even the audience plays a critical role in the making of music. When a thoughtful audience hears music and assimilates it into a larger cultural or emotional context, it plays a vital role in musical creativity. Music is an art.

MUSIC HELPS US MEET OUR NEEDS

As with all forms of art, music arose in history because of human needs. Indeed, many innovations in human history have arisen from need. Electric lights, cars, airplanes, the wheel, cooking and heating and seeing with fire, pots and baskets, shoes—all these innovations stemmed from basic human needs—from the goal of making life less brutal. Today, few in the developed world, indeed most of the world, could imagine life without electricity or so many other modern amenities. Yet for thousands of years, people lived without electricity, now deemed essential. Since what we now consider essential did not even exist for most of history, what critical role does music have? Will humanity outgrow the need for music, just as it did the horse and buggy?

For some, the significance of music in history might seem a bit hard to fathom. Many things considered more important than music can sometimes seem to dominate our world. Why does music matter at all in the grand scheme of things? Do we really need music? Humans have three essential physical needs: food, shelter, and clothing. After food, shelter, and clothing, music seems an afterthought—perhaps one relatively far down the list, at that. From an evolutionary perspective, the point of music seems hard to fathom, except perhaps as a device to attract mates, like a peacock's feathers. The psychologist Steven Pinker opined that—at least in the plainest terms of biological cause and effect—music was "useless."[7] Pinker's point was not that music is literally useless, of course. His comment, however, does raise the provocative question: From a strictly biological or evolutionary perspective, how does one account for music's amazing power as a historical force, along with other arts? If music is a frill, why bother? Why do people today spend billions of dollars each year on musical instruments, concerts, music lessons, and recordings? Is music simply a luxury, like a nice watch or an extra delicious steak—some sort of accoutrement?

Music in history has been far from useless. Music enhanced human communication, both verbal and nonverbal. By enhancing community and communication, music came to play an elemental, building-block role in culture and society, the twin pillars of all history, past, and present. It is hard even to fathom how powerfully music insinuates images, styles, and, often, ideas, into our thoughts. Sounds give cues that we learn to identify. We hear certain sounds or tonal intervals as "Middle Eastern" or "Latin" or "emo," or "fifties," for example. The styles and sounds of such music shape part of what we commonly call cultural identities. We can thus learn about the world with our hearing, just as we learn with our other senses. We learn with music. We relate to one another with music. Music is one of the most powerful learning tools people have created. It is hard to imagine a world without music. It is hard to imagine a society having no need for music.

MUSIC AND SOCIETY

Music exists in both a social and a cultural framework. The words "culture" and "society," though closely related, do not mean the same thing. The word society stems from the old Latin word for friend or acquaintance, *socius*. A society is a group of people. People absolutely require societies to survive. It would be impossible for the human race to survive if people lived solitary existences. By forming societies, humans provide for basic human needs or other wants. Today, societies exist for many purposes, some formed intentionally and some formed by the simple act of people living together, as they must do. Any sort of business enterprise is a society. People also form specific societies for all sorts of other endeavors, from the essential to the frivolous. Societies exist for everything from serious professions, to cooking, to pub-crawling, and practically every other possible human-interest in-between.

Music is a part of society, part of our social history. Music has played as a backdrop to human affairs from time immemorial. Like the soundtrack of history, music became the glue that oozed into the nooks and crannies of practically every society's essential events—all their respective traditions and beliefs and modalities. Because music was essentially a form of human communication, it played an especially powerful meaning in a social context. This is because music, at its best, involves an inherent social context. Hearing music entails a relationship between two parties, a musician and the listener. Sure, people can, and do, play music solely for themselves. Even the most solitary musician, however, must ultimately play music in a social context. After all, only a society can create musical instruments to play or languages to sing. Society creates this need for music or language. Then it meets that need.

MUSIC AND CULTURE

Along with society, music also closely relates to "culture." Culture is another oft-used word that has a confusing definition. The word culture relates to things that grow—as in words like "agriculture" or "cultivate." Culture is a human thing that grows when people form societies. Culture happens when we embellish the process of meeting our human needs. For example, clothes are a necessity—to varying degrees. Whether we live in the arctic, a forest, a desert or a swamp, we all need clothes to protect the body from the elements. As human societies, we all need clothes for survival. Beyond the mere functionality of clothes, all human societies have developed various ways of decorating the body—colors, fashion, jewelry, and fine tailoring. We call this aspect of clothing—the love of personal adornment—"fashion." We might say that clothes are a basic social need, but fashion is part of culture. If clothes, per se, have a social function, "fashion" is a cultural outgrowth of that function.

Consider how clothing fashions arose over the centuries—with all the wealth and colors they have entailed. All fashion grew from this basic, very mundane human need for clothes. That is how culture grows from society. Just as fashion and style evolved from the basic need for clothing, one could say the same thing about other major cultural heritages. In a similar sense, sophisticated endeavors like the culinary arts or architecture derive quite directly from the needs for food and shelter. As human beings, we have gone far beyond our bare, essential needs as we pursue greater comfort, security and enjoyment. In this way, there is a symbiotic relationship between society and culture.

Music is part of the cultural outgrowth that comes from society. Music helps meet basic human needs. We need to communicate. We need to form relationships, to congregate, and to deliberate. We need to share our thoughts and feelings in order to build communities, make decisions, and have sex. These are, at their most basic level, the simple social needs for human speech and communication—just as we have simple social needs for warmth and food. We could, one supposes, simply communicate these basic needs with grunts, poundings, gestures, or the most basic vocabulary. "Me want hamburger." Instead, however, we have built an elaborate *culture* that enriches communication. This culture includes the world of sound—speech and music. This wonderful cultural richness produced by our special sounds includes so much—beautiful poetry, emotive tones, heartfelt songs, epic narratives, and so much more. Such gifts of sound are among the most precious contributions a society can make to culture.

Beyond food, shelter, and clothing, human societies have other universal needs. All humans have a sex drive, an impulse arguably as powerful as the drive for food, warmth, or shelter, and just as essential, since the sex drive not only gives pleasure and companionship but also perpetuates humanity. All human societies have also found it necessary at some point to resort to violence, at the very least to defend properties, boundaries, or freedoms. In a similar way, all human societies have developed some sort of creative impulse—music and the other Fine Arts. All human societies have developed some set of broader beliefs that helps explain our place in the cosmos. Religion and philosophy in all their myriad guises fill this role. In a similar fashion, all human societies have recounted, and invented, stories. Music has played a central role in every single one of these human developments.

HUMAN NEEDS

Humans are a type of animal. We possess the same drives, needs, and limitations as other animals. Humans live, hopefully reproduce, and ultimately die—just like all other living things. Do humans have needs, however, beyond the most basic physical ones? For example, do we need—really *need*—love? Do we *need* beauty? Do we *need* entertainment? Do we *need* decoration? Are such needs just as essential, in their own ways, as the basic needs for food, shelter, and clothing? Music and the visual arts seem to fall into this category of less immediate needs. Yet the persistence of beauty, love, and diverting amusements throughout history suggests that such things play a critical role in our existence. The most materialistic and practical among us might see music and the arts as unnecessary frills, decorative features to provide some diversion when they have met other more essential needs. For others, music and the arts seem like genuine needs in the truest sense of the term.

The question of what drove humans to the quest for "sound production"—music, in all its myriad forms—is a fascinating one. The ethnomusicologist Jesús Salia Gumà has reasoned that the production of sound plays an essential role in human history at the social level, especially because of its ability to influence behavior. He argues that not only did music help establish cultures involving rituals—often focused on hunting or the seasonal cycles in those early days—but music also played an important role in sexual attraction, still another irresistible force of history.[8] Music thus helped groups form family units for reproduction. As it evolved, music became a tradition involving distinct sounds, rhythms, and, with time, word creations like poetry. Music allowed groups to transmit a culture from one generation to the next.

THE FUNCTIONAL THEORY OF ART

The idea that music arose out of necessity and practicality, as opposed to some loftier sense of artistic expression, has a long-standing pedigree. What some historians have called "The Functional Theory of Art" emphasizes the practical function of the arts. This again means that the arts fill a genuine need, not a decorative frill. A religious priesthood, for example, genuinely needs the arts. Liturgy in the Catholic Church truly needs music to function properly. If one assumes that the Catholic Religion meets a human need, not some exploitative frill, it follows that music is an essential thing, not just an afterthought.[9]

Real human needs drove the arts, including technology. In a chapter placed in the 1998 book *Creativity in Human Evolution and Prehistory*, Archaeologist Richard Bradley described creativity as a human endeavor that arises out of the intersection of invention and constraint, driven by tangible needs. He argued that the special challenges of the Neolithic (Stone Age) period posed a special impetus for human ingenuity in its earliest guises, for example, in architecture. The desire for buildings reflecting the religious cosmologies of the day helped prompt innovation. Structures like, say, Stonehenge, received a creative stimulus from straightforward challenges like working with massive stones. Meeting these challenges drove technology. Beyond technology, the establishment of such a landmark structure also furthered a culture of myth and religion, the myriads of mysterious associations that have surrounded the place ever since. The beliefs of Stone Age peoples, and the limitations facing them, resulted in this powerful creative incentive. Creativity thus drove the rise of the world's first megalithic monuments, forerunners of the world's many amazing buildings.[10]

This same sort of dynamic—challenge and response—also created music. How best to share feelings and ideas with friends, lovers, and the community at large? Music emerged as one of the most powerful ways to enhance our basic powers of communication. As we learned to speak, we learned to sing. As we learned to make tools, we learned to play instruments. Distinct traditions of music emerged—hymns, chants, and entire families of musical instruments. Our simple, relentless human needs for better communication drove the culturally enriching activities that would evolve into music. In the end, music became an indispensable part of the story of progress in human history.

If music arose as an outgrowth of human needs, it became so much more. At it evolved, music enabled people to store all kinds of knowledge. Music would play a key role in advancing the artisanal crafts. It became one of the most important vehicles of the language arts. Music fostered whole subsets of philosophical query. Music became a storehouse of learning unto itself, holding entire libraries made up of sound. Music served religion, the heart of the sacred experience. Music often doubled as prayer or meditation, the most intimate ways we express wonder, love, or praise. Music added romance and meaning to human relationships, sexual and otherwise. In short, as it evolved, music came to provide one of the main forms of human expression. Music helped to shape history even before history really began. And it is here, at the beginning of both music and history, that we begin our story.

NOTES

1. Barbara J. King, "When Animals Mourn," *Scientific American*, Vol. 309, No. 1 (July 2013), pp. 62–67, pg. 67.

2. R. G. Collingwood, *The Principles of Art* (New York, NY: Oxford University Press, 1958), pg. 151, as referenced in Ann Clark, "Is Music a Language?," *The Journal of Aesthetics and Art Criticism*, Vol. 41, No. 2 (Winter, 1982), pp. 195–204, pg. 195.

3. F. I. G. Rawlins, "Episteme and Techne," *Philosophy and Phenomenological Research*, Vol. 10, No. 3 (March 1950), pp. 389–97, pg. 389.

4. Aristotle, *The Nicomachean Ethics*, translated by J. A. K. Thomson (New York, NY: Penguin Books, 1953), I. 1; See also Tom Angier, *"Techne" in Aristotle's Ethics: Crafting the Moral Life* (New York, NY: Continuum International Publishing, 2010), viii.

5. Robert Pasnau, "Epistemology Idealized," *Mind*, Vol. 122, No. 488 (October 2013), pp. 987–1021, pg. 987.

6. Sister Miriam Joseph, *The Trivium: The Liberal Arts of Logic, Grammar and Rhetoric: Understanding the Nature and Function of Language* (Philadelphia, PA: Paul Dry Books, 2002), 5–6.

7. Steven Pinker, *How the Mind Works* (New York, NY: W.W. Norton and Co., 1997), pg. 528, as quoted in Henkjan Honing, Carel ten Cate, Isabelle Peretz, and Sandra E. Trehub, "Introduction: Without It No Music: Cognition, Biology and Evolution of Musicality," *Philosophical Transactions: Biological Sciences*, Vol. 370, No. 1664, *Theme Issue: Biology, Cognition and Origins of Musicality* (March 19, 2015), pp. 1–8, pg. 1.

8. Jesús Salia Gumà, *Etnoarqueomusicologia: La producción de sonidos y la reproducción social en las sociedades cazadoras-recolectoras* (Madrid: Consejo Superior de Investigaciones científicas, 2015), 14.

9. Carl Dahlhaus, *The Foundations of Music History*, translated by J. B. Robinson (New York, NY: Cambridge University Press, 1982), 20.

10. Richard Bradley, *Architecture, Imagination and the Ancient World, in Creativity and Human Evolution and Prehistory*, edited by Steven Mithen (New York, NY: Routledge, 1998), 227–40, 229.

Chapter 1

The Voice
History's First Musical Instrument

We will begin our discussion of music's important role in history with a look at the human voice, history's first musical instrument. Humans have the gift of speech, from which emerged our plethora of wonderful languages. Without a spoken language, people could nod the head, point the finger, pound the chest, stick out their tongues, or engage in or other similar gestures. Indeed, scholars since the nineteenth century have noted that along with humans, some animals, notably primates, use gestures of the hand to communicate.[1] Sure, such bodily movements get the point across well enough, as we can see in American Sign Language, for example. But the precision and nuance of a complex spoken language offer much more. Because nature endowed people with the amazing powers of speech, our human voice obviously played one of the most important roles in history. Before humans could develop the sciences or the Fine Arts, they first had to harness the awesome expressive powers of the human voice. This means that music, singing in particular, was one of the first art forms.

THE ROLE OF THE VOICE IN HISTORY

To consider the role of the human voice in history, we must go back to a time before buildings, or musical instruments—long before writing, or any other of the accoutrements of civilization. If we could go back far enough, many millennia before the advent of written records and actual historical details, we would arrive at a time when human beings lived without complex languages, at least in terms of having established vocabularies and grammar. People, no doubt, did have languages of sorts—sounds they made with their voices. But animals also make sounds. So when, precisely, can we say that actual language appeared? No one can ever answer this question with certainty. However, what does seem clear is that the same vocal impulses that led to music also led to the development of language—the ability to raise and lower the pitch of the human voice, to speak with dynamics, and to develop pleasing rhythmic cadences with the sounds coming out of the mouth. Such subtle vocal abilities made the human voice one of history's greatest change agents.

Upon reflection, it is hard to overemphasize the historical significance of the human voice. With the possible exception of hands, few human body parts connect more intimately to the human mind than the human voice. We think and we speak in almost one instantaneous action—sometimes too hastily, no doubt. For people fluent in a language, word and thought are hard to distinguish from one another, so intimately are our voices interwoven with our minds. With the human voice and language, people could communicate ideas and details in unprecedented ways that would establish the broad foundation for everything else that followed. Moreover, this ability for more advanced communication took many forms. For example, progress required teaching. Because it had superior communicative powers, the human voice helped transmit knowledge, as well as feelings and ideas. Without the initial impetus of vocal communication, there would be no Fine Arts, no science, no religion, and no philosophy. Thus, in the beginning of everything, the naked human voice played one of history's most critical causal roles. Devoid of established vernacular languages, the human voice began to build, slowly but surely, the foundations of communities.

So how exactly did what people today call vocal music help spawn all the changes that language and communication brought to the world? The term "voice," as conventionally used in colloquial English, has two meanings: an instrument, as in music, and a sound, as in the audible noises people make with their physical vocal apparatus.[2] Understanding the history of how singing evolved entails understanding both these basic components of the human voice—the instrument and the sound. All mammals can make sounds come out of their throats. It is the way that humans manipulate these vocal sounds, however, that gives people such a powerful means of communication.

THE PHYSIOLOGY OF THE VOICE APPARATUS

Part of what made the human voice special was no doubt the physiology of the voice apparatus, especially the lips, the mouth, the dental system, and the tongue. This embouchure could make more complex and subtle sounds than those made by other animals. All mammals share the anatomical quality of some sort of larynx. Like fingerprints or eye retinas, each larynx is different. In this sense, all mammals, including people, have distinct, individual voices.

Every person's voice is just as unique as everything else about that person. People commonly say that there no two snowflakes exactly alike. This is similarly true for everything else in nature, including people. Just as no two people are exactly alike, no two voices are exactly alike, either. The human voice made enormous contributions to culture because, among other things, it allowed for the development of individuality and personality. Indeed, the voice is one of the most readily obvious indicators of the amazing individuality and diversity that make up humanity.

Because the human voice comes out of the resonance chambers and cavities of the human head and chest/abdomen, it is an extension of human individuality. Its direct connection to the human brain adds distinct personalities to the physiology of the voice, a complex, inseparable dynamic.[3] This means that music, or what passed for it in the very beginning, helped shape individual personalities, friendship, and social connections—all things intimately related with basic communication. The human voice also helped differentiate people based on their talents and personal qualities. As human vocal abilities developed, they reflected the distinctive differentiations commonly made with voices still today. Some people had "good voices," others, presumably, not so good. While admittedly what constitutes a pleasing voice is a personal response, convention seems to favor certain kinds of voices as more pleasing or attractive than others, just as it does with physical beauty. People who can produce pleasing sounds with their voices, whether by natural talent and physical makeup or by training and conscious manipulation, often gain recognition and rewards in their respective societies. This would presumably be just as true in a simple tribal community as it remains today in the world of mass electronic communications and digital media. Because vocal music combines human beings' shared physiology with individuality, the best singers and voice teachers have always blended an emphasis on proper technique with letting artists find their inner voices, literally and figuratively.[4]

The human voice became one of the many characteristics—physical and otherwise—that seemed to distinguish people from the world of animals. Wielding their complex ability of vocal expression, humans had an exponentially greater power to communicate. Other animals obviously communicated with one another with their various calls, cries, growls, and howls. Indeed, scholars concur that virtually all mammals must communicate, at least to mate. Similarly, animals communicate to form their various communities—herds, packs, flocks, and so on.[5] But while animal behaviors and their communicative powers remain a subject of much research, it still seems safe and obvious to say that only humans have the power of language in the most direct sense—the ability to express ideas with a specific vocabulary and specific sentence structures. Common sense tells us that animal communication is limited in obvious ways.[6] Perhaps most importantly, humans have words that represent things—a vocabulary that describes not only objects and activities but also feelings and beliefs. This human ability to speak is, in its way, a divine gift.

THE VOICE BEFORE LANGUAGE

Before language really developed, human sounds were probably simply another part of the world of animal sounds. Along with simple "sounds," the ability to highlight tones and pitches—the rudiments of singing—with the voice played a critical role. The ability to add tonality and rhythm to the human voice, with increasing precision, laid the foundation for expressive talking and singing, and not necessarily in that order. In this sense, music was the first language, a view famously propounded by James Burnet, the father of linguistics. In 1773, Burnet advanced his famous theory that imitating bird sounds played a key role in the world's first language developments, a phenomenon that he saw as the first forays into both music and spoken language. In those earliest days, music and language were one and the same. Neither had yet developed into the distinct spheres of human expression, we tend to categorize them with today. This view was also touched upon by Jean Jacques Louis Rousseau in 1781.[7]

The role of imitating animal sounds for hunting purposes probably played an important role in the development of both speech and music. This is why some might say that "nature has musical sounds, but no music."[8] Vocal sounds could help attract animals, leading to a successful hunt. Thus, probably the most immediate impetus for imitating animal sounds had to do with using animal calls for hunting, or other decoy tricks in, for example, warfare. Still today, the native peoples on the Solomon Islands like Santa Cruz in the Pacific Ocean use bait along with a flute-like device to attract and hunt birds.[9] They also imitate bird calls with their mouths, something that remains a folk custom in many cultures, including North America. Such practices have made the peoples of Santa Cruz very effective hunters. But imitating animal sounds also probably had another component: imitating the beauty of some animal sounds, especially the beautiful natural music of birds.[10] However unintentionally, skilled "bird callers" imitated the beautiful sounds of nature, one of history's oldest musical impulses.

SINGING

The term "singing"—with all its powerful cultural and historical associations—seems less helpful when contemplating the vocal musicality of history's earliest human beings. For centuries, the idea of "singing" has connoted melody, lyrics, relative vocal precision in hitting notes and tones, and, often, standardized traditions of choral and solo performance. But while today's singing directly descends from all those things, the world's first vocal music was far more elemental—embryonic versions of singing, at best. In a primitive environment, concepts like tonality or pitch must have been elusive, though they certainly may have existed, at least in some elemental senses.

In misty prehistory, the beginning of singing was little more than a certain affectation done with the voice—a manipulation of the voice to create certain kinds of vocal effects. Today, we recognize some artists for their "talk-singing" style of performing. In ancient times, such lines of demarcation between singing, poetry, and speaking similarly blurred—indeed, given the lack instrumentation, undoubtedly far more so. Present-day styles such as rap, hip-hop, beat-boxing, and country talk-ballads harken back to an ancient tradition of using the voice in a way that is not quite melodic singing, but not quite talking either.[11] Today, some deride such singers as less than musical. In point of fact, however, they connect us to one of the oldest and most powerful forms of musical expression.

IS SINGING NATURE OR NURTURE?

With its expressive powers, singing music can elicit and shape all kinds of emotions, from delight to terror. But does singing come naturally to us? Is singing nature, or nurture? Who thought of it first, and why? Why would the art and artistry of singing evolve in the first place? Is singing a naturally discovered joy in life, like sex or laughing or sports? Or, alternatively, is singing something learned, a deep acculturation produced by countless hours of childhood ditties, popular favorites, and formal instruction? No one can really answer this question. In earliest times, subtle inflections in the voice enabled people to communicate with each other in a time still devoid of complex languages, a world presumably lacking in developed idioms, grammatical constructions, and vocabulary. In such a setting, vocal sounds could express sadness, joy, anger, or fear, often described as the four basic human emotions.[12] Admittedly, this ability to express emotions with the voice does not seem particularly unique to humans. Other mammalian sounds, like dogs barking, howling, yapping, or growling, likewise express some sort of response to a situation, emotional or otherwise. Humans, however, combined the ability to make expressive sounds with verbal language, a powerful synthesis.

The first human beings had very rudimentary languages, at best. Depending on how one defines language, they might not have had any language whatsoever. The world's first languages were probably nonverbal in the literal sense of not having actual words. In a world without language, singing-type inflections in the voice would aid in communication and the expression of feelings. Scholars widely surmise that many of the world's first languages involved simple inflections in the voice, such as tonal affections or clicking sounds. About thirty groups in Africa today still speak clicking languages, for example, often thought to echo some of the oldest forms of human communication.[13] Other surviving languages also make use of tones, with higher or lower pitches of the voice changing the meaning of the otherwise similar sounds. Linguists have identified such "tonal languages" in a number of settings, notably including West Africa, Asiatic Sino-Tibetan languages, and in some of the New Guinean tribes.[14]

THE PLEASURE THAT SINGING GIVES TO OTHERS

Upon reflection, it seems possible that enjoying music is a natural reflex. Pleasing musical intervals—happy major key sounds, for example—elicit basic responses from people, and not just in socially conditioned ways. Similarly, low sonorous tones seem naturally to evoke gravitas (think actor James Earle Jones). Other tones evoke casual or frivolous feelings, and still others evoke passion, sexual, and otherwise. Scholars have argued that these instincts in how people perceive language have similar counterparts in music. These responses to musicality are natural instincts.[15] The shared responses to sounds produced both in language and in music come from the basic chemistry of the brain. This would mean that responses to sounds, pitches, harmonies, and intervals are not just learned behaviors. Some researchers have even concluded that such common musical devices as major keys or minor keys were a kind of inevitable evolution, based on the natural responses they produced in all human beings.[16]

If some sounds please people naturally, like sweet food on the tongue or soft touches on the skin, hearing music involves a physiological response. The climax that characterizes some of the best music has an appeal that is every bit as basic as sexual sensations.[17] While the development of musical scales, along with melody and harmony, was thousands of years in the making, the same principle that some sounds and intervals naturally pleased the ear still apply. Some sounds please, some repulse, some provoke, and some excite. In the mists of prehistory, before either languages or music existed in their more developed forms, humans simply learned to make sounds in accordance with these basic, communicative responses they caused in other people.

LULLABIES

A good example of this nonverbal intersection of music and language comes from the theory that singing originated with the very intimate act of a mother coddling and cooing to a newborn child. Indeed, the way that human mothers speak, and coo to their children is a basic difference between mothering habits observed in chimpanzees and those of human beings, which might otherwise be comparable.[18] It makes some sense, since people learn communication from their parents. Musical exposure with things like lullabies plays a critical role in the formation of speech. Because such songs establish a close bond between the parent and the child, they encourage the development of communication.[19]

As the familiar term "native speaker" implies, we learn language from birth—from total immersion in the sounds of language spoken by our parents, our immediate friends and family, and our extended communities. The creation of a native speaker starts immediately upon birth. Music is a natural extension of these nonverbal modes of vocal communication we use with newborn babies. Even today, most verbal mothers naturally communicate with their children in nonverbal ways. They coo or make "baby-talk" sounds with exaggerated facial expressions. In this way, music becomes an important part of the history of not only language but also how humans form complex interpersonal relationships.[20]

Most languages have "nonsense sounds," gibberish with almost universal appeal. The French call such phrases *mots sauvages* (wild words), like the phrase *pim, pam, poum*.[21] Nonsensical syllabic sounds appear with great frequency in lullabies sung to babies who have not yet acquired the gift of language. (Not altogether counterintuitively, the songs sung by and for drunkards may run a close second to the pleasing gibberish of childhood rhymes and lullabies.) In English, such nonsense rhymes or phrases commonly appear in the anthology of children's songs and lullabies going back for centuries.[22] Such phrases were quite common, even if only remembered today in a few surviving popular songs. *Fa la la* endures in a number of English-language songs, usually of a festive nature. One of the oldest known lullabies in English, the Middle English "Harley Lullaby," features the recurring syllabic line "llolay, llolay," a baby-talk lullaby sound that today is today perhaps best associated with the Christmas tune "Coventry Carol."[23]

Like many aspects of pleasing a child, speaking to children involves finding the mysterious pleasure-zones of a newborn child, the things that give contentment and joy. This would imply that certain kinds of musical sounds inherently please us. Sigmund Freud famously argued that the sounds a mother makes with a newborn elicit a natural pleasure response. In his 1905 work *Jokes and their Relation to the Subconscious*, Freud argued that "phonic games" like rhymes cause pleasure. Parents instinctively use rhyming sounds or other phonically pleasing gibberish to pacify their babies. Babies, in turn, imitate these pleasing syllable sounds made by parents. In this way, infants begin to acquire language. This learning of language that begins in the bond between infant and parent sets the stage not only for the development of language in the maturing newborn child but also in society as a whole.[24] Numerous studies have indicated that newborns' sense of hearing plays one of the most important roles in child development.[25]

EARLY LULLABIES

Given the huge role of mothering and parenting in the history of both singing and language, there can be little surprise that some of the earliest known examples of singing songs come from lullabies.[26] Alas, lullabies often remained unwritten. Most ancient lullabies are lost forever.[27] We also struggle to distinguish between the many ancient texts that pray for children's safekeeping versus actual lullabies that featured music.[28] We often must guess. Some of the few extant ancient lullabies come from Babylon and Sumer. These areas formed the heart of ancient Mesopotamia, the area roughly equated with present-day Iraq, one of the oldest places of urban living on the planet. A clay cuneiform tablet from the Old Babylonian period (c. 1950 BC–1530 BC), currently on display at the British Museum, includes the lines of what were probably a lullaby, perhaps one of the oldest known songs—"Little one, who dwelt in the heart of darkness," the song says. Scholars commonly presume the lyric to refer to a newborn recently delivered from the darkness of his mother's womb.[29]

The theme of keeping children safe from evil, including demons, played a prominent role in the texts of many ancient lullabies.[30] Mesopotamian myth frequently focused on the theme of noise made by humans, disturbing the sleep of the gods. This theme frequently appeared in the "baby incantations" and lullabies mothers used to lull their newborn children, though presumably in a more lighthearted way.[31] In Mesopotamian myth, the gods' upset at the noise created by growing human populations prompted the Great Flood, though there is some debate that perhaps the ancient Sumerian word for noise (*rigmu*) meant something like the Hebrew idea of sin. Several Mesopotamian or Egyptian incantations also seem like lullabies designed to ward away something called the "evil eye" from children.[32] Sigmund Freud once applied his theories of about the significance of dreams and subconscious desires to ancient Mesopotamian incantations and charms. Freud saw in them the product of universal fears and desires. Though Freud possessed a limited knowledge of the vast body of Mesopotamian cuneiform texts, his ideas about how magical incantations functioned dovetailed with his notions of how certain syllable sounds and rhythmic vocalizations created a sense of pleasure and safety for newborns.[33] Singsong rhythms typically led to expressing ideas in repeated fashion, reinforcing the development of cultural beliefs. They also somehow made children feel safe and loved.

CHANTING

Ancient mothers probably chanted lullabies as much as sang them, in the proper sense of the term.[34] As language and speech evolved, almost all cultures seem to have developed some form of rhythmic chanting, an obvious forerunner of more complex musicality and singing. Chanting is the rhythmic use of the voice. It can employ melody, though not always. Across the world, chanting often played an especially prominent role in magic and its close cousin religion.[35] Chanting directly relates to the word "incantation," which in itself comes from the Latin word for sing, *cantare*. The word "charm" comes from the word *carmen*, which also means "song." Similar words in English for magic also derive from older works to "speak" or "intone." In English, the word "spell" comes from the Old English word *spellian*, "to talk."

The desire to obtain supernatural outcomes by harnessing the invisible magical powers of vocal sounds meant that early peoples tried to make things happen by manipulating their voices in ways that differentiated their magical speech from everyday communication. They deepened or raised their voices, creating evocative vocalizations. They spoke in affected tones. They created rhythms. Even in the Bible, God brings about creation through the power of the voice saying, "Let there be light."[36] Scholars have noted similar beliefs in "sound power" worldwide.[37]

The idea that the vocal affectations can affect outcomes has perhaps its best example in the idea of "magic words." Today, popular culture still recognizes the enduring power and delight of simply vocalizing magic words like *abracadabra, alakazam*, or "open sesame."[38] Some of these words or phrases are truly ancient. *Abracadabra*, for example, appears as early as AD 200.[39] Western culture commonly associates such phrases with Arabian tales such as *A Thousand and One Tales of the Arabian Nights* reflecting Arabic, Turkish, Near Eastern, or otherwise Semitic origin, though that is not always the case.[40] Practitioners of such "magic words" invariably speak them with sonorous affectations to their voice, as though deepening or otherwise intensifying the sounds of their voices will enhance their magical power. Such magic words, with their mystic qualities, feature prominently in the world of stage magic and theater.[41]

Chanting for magical or religious purposes seems a worldwide phenomenon. Scholars have noted the virtually universal appearance of such rhythmic chanting across a wide swath of cultures and periods, from Appalachian snake-handlers to Sufi Islam, among countless others.[42] Scholars also frequently see modern-day indigenous peoples' use of chanting as a window into the world's first societies. For example, some scholars have seen the rhythmic choral chanting practiced by the Boyas of Tekkalakota in India as direct surviving traditions from the Stone Age.[43] In North America, chanting and dancing among many native tribes would accompany the use of peyote, long ceremonies that induced states of delirium and ecstasy.[44]

SOME NOTABLE USES OF CHANTING

Archaeology has provided some examples of early chanting and its important role in ancient societies. *Book of the Dead* is an ancient Egyptian book that collected magical rites and spells, for over a period of many centuries. Many chanted prayers found in *The Book of the Dead* focused on the funeral culture surrounding the pharaoh and his familiars. Priests would have chanted these aloud, creating a hypnotic effect upon the listener that enhanced the chance of a favorable outcome for the spell, hopefully. The chanting and the dramatic affectation of the voice also powerfully, and perhaps subliminally, elevated the stature of the priests in the minds of those hearing such sonorous sounds. The Egyptians placed copies of the *Book of the Dead* in important tombs, though no one tomb contains all the known texts of the *Book of the Dead*. The *Book of the Dead* also reflected the growing professionalism of both literature and music. Scribes copied the hymns and prayers, creating fresh texts to sell bereaved individuals.[45]

Chanting featured prominently in the Classical tradition, too—a fixture of much magic, sorcery, and religion often seen in Greek and Roman mythology. Witches and sorcerers often seemed to use chanting to cast their spells. In Virgil's *Aeneid*, Book VI, the witch Circe spends her days singing (*resonat cantu*).[46] Chanting also seems to have played a role in ancient Greco-Roman medicine. Before the more developed traditions of diagnostic-medicine that later appeared, early Greek and Roman religion often combined folk remedies with magical formulae. In one Roman folk remedy for a dislocation, the healer was to hover over the injured person, chanting and cutting reeds with a ceremonial knife in a prescribed manner. This combination of ritual action and chanted ritual words supposedly healed the person.[47]

THE HYMN

If chanting led to the development of singing, it is closely associated with the hymn, one of the most ancient types of song. Early hymns were a natural outgrowth of the way that vocal talents helped create language, which, in turn, fostered early forays into magic and religion. *Merriam Webster's Dictionary* defines a hymn as a religious song, derived from the Greek, *hymnos*, yet another Greek term for a type of song. The word hymn specifically means "song of praise." The Greeks even had one of their muses entirely dedicated to hymns, Polymnia, a name meaning "Many Hymns." The early Greek writer Hesiod names her in his *Theogony*.[48] Because hymns often entailed a liturgical text as well as a role in more formal worship, their presence often connotes a more evolved approach to religion and public assembly, as well as a more developed language. This emphasis on a literary text is one of the things that distinguished ancient hymns from their close cousins, the chant.

Given the chance, today we would no doubt be hard-pressed to distinguish between an ancient "chant" and an ancient "hymn." Indeed, no doubt, so would many ancient contemporaries. We know that the Hebrews, for example, chanted many of their hymns. The word for a singer of hymns in a synagogue still today is "Cantor," a "chanter." The "Psalms" of the Bible are hymns. But ancient people probably performed them with a combination of speaking, chanting, and singing.[49] At the end of the day, it is hard to know what these early musical hymns sounded like. Clearly, however, chanting in ancient times clearly evolved into the tradition of singing, especially sacred hymn singing.

THE HYMNS OF ANCIENT EGYPT

Some of the earliest known hymns come from ancient Egyptian religion. The Egyptians laced their pyramids, underground tombs, and papyri with hymns to their deities. One of the most famous Egyptian hymns is the Hymn to the Solar Disc deity Aton, a unique ancient Egyptian god sometimes seen as a precursor to monotheism. Reportedly written by the Pharaoh Akhenaton (1353–1336 BC), the full text of this famous ancient Egyptian hymn appears on the wall of a tomb in Al-Amarna. The form, style, and aesthetic of the Hymn to Aton borrow heavily from other earlier hymns to the Egyptian deity Amon.[50] Scholars sometimes see the "Hymn to Aton" as having influenced the Hebrew "Psalm 104." The shared emphasis on a loving Monotheistic deity and the glories of creation make such a connection seem plausible, albeit unprovable. Both "Psalm 104" and the "Hymn to Aton" also emphasize a tradition of divinely sanctioned morality, "Ethical Monotheism" in embryo.[51] Researchers also discovered another hymn alleged to resemble a Hebrew Psalm in the text of the Armana Letters, clay-tablet inscriptions. American scholar William Albright (1891–1971) saw similarities between some passages of the Armana Letters and Psalm 139.[52]

Royal hymns for public processions also played an important role in Ancient Egypt. The texts of such pharaonic hymns survive on the walls of many royal Egyptian tombs, as well as some papyri. Some of the most famous of such pharaonic hymns include a hymn found carved on the wall of the tomb of a pharaoh named Unas (c. 2300 BC). Unas's tomb inscriptions include 228 lines offering a hymn for escorting the king on his journey to the underworld. From the time of Unas, the practice of inscribing hymns on the walls of pyramid tombs would continue for the many years to come. Ancient Egyptians usually placed these texts near the dead king's body.[53] Excavations similarly found a hymn to Ramses IV (1155–49 BC) written on papyrus. While these hymns appear today on the walls of tombs, they probably enjoyed a broad public audience during the heyday of Ancient Egypt.

MESOPOTAMIAN HYMNS

Along with Egypt, hymns also played a vital role in Mesopotamian religious traditions. Sumer, the southernmost area of Mesopotamia, has some of the oldest surviving hymns. Here, the development of the hymn seems closely related to the development of writing, as least in terms of our sources. Early Mesopotamian literature, written starting around 4000 BC in the world's first script known as cuneiform, remained mundane record-keeping for many centuries—ledgers, receipts, various lists, and instructions. Over time, however, literature of greater complexity developed, including hymns. Today, our ability to read some of these cuneiform texts greatly enriches our knowledge of Sumerian religious life.

The single largest group of compositions extant from early Mesopotamia is the "Sumerian Hymnal," a body of collected Sumerian religious songs once sung to the accompaniment of the lyre.[54] The hymns involve many themes. They provide important glimpses into everyday life so long ago. Along with hymns to deities, the *Sumerian Hymnal* also includes "building hymns" lauding the construction of monumental structures. The hymns referenced not only the buildings themselves but also the workers, engineers, and royal sponsors who made them possible.[55] There is also a rich tradition of "wisdom literature" closely associated with Mesopotamian hymnody. Such wisdom literature offers insightful adages foreshadowing the likes of biblical book of *Proverbs*. Scholars also often see Sumerian hymns as direct ancestors of the Hebrew *Psalms*.[56]

PSALMS OF THE BIBLE

Of all the Ancient Near Eastern peoples, the Hebrews no doubt left the most enduring legacy of hymns for posterity. A small and relatively obscure people in many ways, the Hebrews' amazing success at writing, preserving and handing down their legacy remains one of history's most powerful reminders that the pen is truly mightier than the sword, an adage that can often seem rather dubious. The Hebrew Bible also contains one of the most complete, and certainly by far the most famous, collection of ancient Hymns, the *Book of Psalms*. The *Book of Psalms* is a collection of 150 hymns, their lyrical texts being all that tantalizingly remain from what was once an obviously rich ancient musical heritage of hymnody. By tradition, King David wrote about half of the Psalms.

The *Book of Psalms* owes a lot to the ancient Jewish translators who produced a Greek Bible. According to tradition, seventy-two translators translated the scripture, thus giving it the name the *Septuagint*. Since the *Septuagint* used ancient Hebrew texts from the third century BC that no longer exist, scholars see it as an important window into the Hebrew Bible in its most original form.[57] It is actually from the *Septuagint* that the term "Psalm" gained its fame and popularity. The Hebrew Bible actually calls the *Book of Psalms Sepher Tillihim*, that is, *Book of Praises*.[58] Because the Hebrew hymns were closely associated with the lyre or harp, however, Greek-speaking translators instead called the book *Psalms*. They took the word "psalm" from the Greek verb *psallo*, meaning "to pluck" or "to strum." This made it clear that the book of *Psalms* did not just feature poetry or prayers, but actual music.

Unfortunately, one can only imagine what sorts of tunes and sounds the *Psalms* entailed. But at least we have the lyrics. Along with the lyrical texts, we have a few tantalizing cues in the *Psalms* that seem like they were musical instructions. The famous word "Selah" found laced throughout the *Psalms* still confuses scholars over its exact meaning. It seems some sort of musical instruction, perhaps something like a dynamic marking or a staging cue. "Selah" might have meant a refrain, or instrumental interlude. Selah might also have been a way of distinguishing between stanzas.[59] "Selah" appears seventy-one times in the *Book of Psalms* and three times in *Habakkuk*.[60]

THE ANTIPHON

The "Antiphon" was another important type of hymn singing in ancient Judaism. It would later play an influential role in Christian hymnody. The antiphon is a call and response type of musical chanting. In antiphonal hymn singing, the congregation sings a short response to the chanting of a cantor or priest. Scholars have also proposed antiphonal solo and response patterns as characterizing the singing of the women in Ancient Israel when David returns from the battle with Goliath.[61] The women's chant hints at a responsorial style of singing—"Saul has killed this thousands, and David his tens of thousands," a musical ditty of triumph that would later be set to outstanding baroque setting by George Frederick Handel in his 1739 oratorio *Saul*. Some scholars have also seen antiphonal elements in the lament of David over the death of his rebellious son Absalom recounted in *2 Samuel*.[62]

HYMNS OF THE SECOND TEMPLE PERIOD

The ancient Jews seem to have nurtured and honed their musical traditions during the "Post-Exilic" period after the Babylonian Empire had conquered Jerusalem in 587 BC. Not wanting their conquered subjects to revolt, Babylonians took leaders of the Hebrews to Babylon as prisoners. After a fifty-year period in exile, the Persian Empire, having conquered Babylon, allowed Jews to return to their ancestral homeland. A remnant, led by leaders like Ezra and Nehemiah, rebuilt the ancient temple and tried to revive ancient ways. Scholars sometimes call this period of the Bible the "Second Temple Period." Much of what people today associate with Judaism comes to us by way of the Second Temple Period. We would not even have the Bible today were it not for the efforts of those long-ago Jewish leaders who returned to the land of their ancestors. Among the legacies that come to us by way of the Second Temple Period appear many hymns and chants, often derived from older traditions.

During the Second Temple Period, the monastic Jewish group known as the Essenes maintained an especially vibrant heritage of the old chanting tradition. In particular, the Essenes left history with the Dead Sea Scrolls, the biblical manuscripts they lovingly preserved and stored in jars. Discovered in a cave in Qumran in 1947, the Dead Sea Scrolls have significance for many things, including music. The Dead Sea Scrolls contain some clues as to the liturgical music of this period, and, in particular, the tradition of the antiphon as it had developed from earlier times. One text known as *Saint Mark's Scroll of Isiah* contains markings and cryptic letters that seem to hint at antiphonal singing. Such hints at a chanting style of singing point to an important link between ancient singing—particularly in Judaism—and the monastic chanting that came to prominence in the Middle Ages. These markings in the Dead Sea Scrolls seem to connect the Essenes to what some scholars have called "Paleo-Byzantine" Christianity, a tradition that emerged during the days of the early Church.[63]

THE *PAEAN*

Hymns also played a major role in the religious life of Ancient Greece. The Theban poet Pindar (c. 518–438 BC) is closely associated with the development of the Classical hymn. Pindar's writings included the important early form of hymn known as the *paean*, still today an English vocabulary word meaning a "recitation of praise." Despite the term's unknown origins, many scholars feel that the term "paean" reflects an archaic name for the deity Apollo. *Paeans* also addressed other deities, however. They often have an association with healing, including also the Greek healing god Asklepios.[64]

The term "paean" has resonated beyond its original Greek setting. Scholars sometimes describe Latin texts like Vergil's *Aeneid*, in its entirety, as a "paean." The *Aeneid* in this sense becomes a vast hymn to Augustus or the Roman Empire. In Vergil, epic narrative, convoluted plotlines, and metered eloquence all combine into one huge *paean*, a hymn in praise of Rome.[65] When Aeneas visits the Underworld in Book VI of the *Aeneid*, he hears a chorus of heroes singing *paeans*.[66] Like most hymns, the *Aeneid* in its entirety has a powerful theological premise—fate, and our duty to it. Since Vergil's time, *paean* has become a word still sometimes used in English, especially for those with a fine vocabulary. In English, to give a "paean" means to offer a speech that highlights lofty and eloquent accolades, usually delivered in public.

THE HOMERIC HYMNS

The Homeric Hymns provide another important source of early Greek Hymns. This collection of hymns, attributed credulously to Homer, dates from the sixth or seventh century BC. The author (or authors) lauds a litany of the Classical deities, ranging from the major Olympic figures to lesser-known gods and goddesses. The Homeric Hymns also verge into the territory of narration and discourse. They give many important details about sacred teachings, stories, beliefs, and personalities of ancient times. They provide a window into aspects of daily life such as sex, gender issues, and the world of work. Each Homeric Hymn typically begins with a laudatory discourse on the deity praised in the hymn, ending with a prayer. These Homeric Hymns also reflect an Archaic, rustic, early Greek religion. There is relatively little in the way of monumental sacred temple architecture, statuary, a professional priesthood, or more institutionalized liturgies.

The Homeric Hymns provide a good example of how sacred lyrics provide details of what would later become the more evolved traditions of theology and philosophy.[67] Homeric Hymn #25 lauds Apollo, along with the Muses—feminine graces associated with learning and the Fine Arts. The Hymn sees the Muses as having given the gift of music to people, especially the bards who bless the world with their sweet singing and playing.[68] Some Homeric Hymns also depict a musical conversation of question and response between the singer and the muses—ostensibly both coming from the mouth of the bard, in two personages, one mortal and one divinely inspired. Some of the response-style elements that seem present in the Homeric Hymns not only would later influence hymnody in such things as the antiphon, a staple of chanting, but also the "choral responses" made famous in Greek theater, especially tragedy.[69]

THE ODE

Another important type of Greek hymn was the "ode." In Greek, the word "ode" meant something like "song." *Merriam Webster's Dictionary* reports that the word "ode" comes to English through Latin, by way of the Greek word "*aidein*, to sing." The word "singer," which Homer himself used, is *aoidos*, a word related to the word "ode." Scholars usually translate the Greek word *aoidoi*—singers—as "bards," but also sometimes poets. The "Pindaric Odes" of the Greek poet Pindar (c. 518–438 BC) and the "Horatian Odes" of the Roman poet Horace (65 BC–AD 8) are especially important bodies of ancient odes. They became almost archetypal literary forms in their respective languages of Greek and Latin.[70]

Odes were usually songs of praise, blurring the line with hymns or the paean.[71] The related literary genre of "ballads" tended to be longer and more story-based. Conversely, the "ode" was a shorter form, often giving a tribute, insight, or emotive response to someone or something. The ode was a snapshot—a fleeting moment of the feelings and the senses, captured into word or song. We remember the intimate nature of the "Ode" in the familiar theater-term "Odeon," meaning "Place of Song." Borrowing from the tradition of Greek theaters, a classic "Odeon" is usually a smaller theater, especially suitable for shorter, more intimate performances and productions.

Today, the term "ode" remains famous, almost as a figure of speech. Among the most famous common usages of the word "ode" today is the classic final chorus from Beethoven's Ninth Symphony, which commonly translates the German *An die Freude* as "Ode to Joy." John Keat's famous 1819 poem "Ode to a Grecian Urn" is another common title incorporating the concept of the ode into a popular poem. Some clever writers have twisted the elegance of the ode, which has indeed become something of a cliché, contrasting the refined aura of an ode with something earthy or mundane. The Chilean poet Pablo Neruda (1904–1973) became famous for his Spanish language poetry, especially his *Odas Elementales* (*Elemental Odes*), often translated into English. Neruda's many odes often juxtaposed the lofty airs of the traditional literary ode with mundane or even unappetizing images, like his famous *Oda a los calcetines*, that is, "Ode to My Socks," and "*Oda a un gran atún en el marcado*," "Ode to a Big Tuna in the Marketplace."[72] Like humorous limericks, or nursery rhymes, such uses of the "ode" create irony. They contrast the sublime with the mundane. Humorous odes frequently devolve into bawdry wit suitable mostly for the pub.

A FEW FINAL REFLECTIONS ON THE HUMAN VOICE

The voice is not the only means of human communication. Plenty of people cannot use their voices, for whatever reason. Yet they still find other ways to communicate, often with amazing efficacy. That said, the human voice nonetheless constitutes one of the crowning achievements of human expression. Because of our amazing voices, we developed the awesome power of speech, with its beautiful language forms and precise vocabularies. No one text could list all the immeasurable contributions the human voice has made. Human voices met physical needs by helping us build vital social institutions. Our voices also empowered abstract conceptual thinking beyond basic essentials. The human voice gave us unparalleled abilities to share thoughts, feelings, and beliefs. The ability to speak enabled us to become better teachers, lovers, leaders, and healers. Over time, the human voice helped disseminate the higher order of thinking humans possess, something that seems to differentiate us from other animals.

Of all the special qualities possessed by the human voice, singing is among the most special and wonderful. Combined with our human intellect and creativity, the singing abilities of the human voice gave people a way to blend language with music. Thousands of years ago, singing—however loosely defined—emerged as one of the world's first art forms. In singing, language and music created a potent mixture that would later result in not only songs but also poetry, literature, oratory, and prose.

The rudimentary chants that constituted the world's first singing contained the seeds of so many important human abilities, albeit in embryo. Singing shaped the growth of newborn babies, one of the most important tasks in any society. Singing became a primary vehicle for manipulating our environments, adapting them to our distinct needs and wants. Singing provided a way for the best and the brightest in early societies to establish critical leadership roles. The human voice's natural musicality drove progress in the arts and religion, as well political power and public life. Vocal music helped begin the traditions that later became science and medicine. Last, but certainly not least, singing created beauty. For all these reasons, we should never take singing for granted. As well as being one of our most enduring human abilities, singing is also one of history's most powerful forces. Today, when we all enjoy singing well-worn tunes beloved by hundreds of millions of people worldwide, we honor this legacy bequeathed to us by ancient musicianship, the gift of the human voice to history.

NOTES

1. Erica A. Cartmill, Sian Beilock, and Susan Goldin-Meadow, "A Word in the Hand: Action, Gesture and Mental Representation in Humans and Non-Human Primates," *Philosophical Transactions: Biological Sciences*, Vol. 367, No. 1585, *From Action to Language: Comparative Perspectives on Primate Tool Use, Gesture and the Evolution of Human Language* (January 12, 2012), pp. 129–43, at 129.

2. W. S. Drew, "Science and Singing," *The Musical Times*, Vol. 73, No. 1068 (February 1, 1932), pp. 115–17, pg. 116.

3. Rachael Gates, L. Arick Forrest, and Kerrie Obert, *The Owner's Manual to the Voice: A Guide for Singers and Other Professional Voice Users* (New York, NY: Oxford University Press, 2013), 205.

4. Christina Shewell, *Voice Work: Art and Science in Changing Voices* (Chichester, West Sussex: John Wiley and Sons, 2009), pg. 11.

5. J. D. Carthy, "Animal Language," *Journal of the Royal Society of Arts*, Vol. 115, No. 5128 (March 1967), pp. 296–98, pg. 296.

6. Daniel Cloud, *The Domestication of Language: Cultural Evolution and the Uniqueness of the Human Animal* (New York, NY: Columbia University Press, 2014), pg. 88.

7. W. Tecumseh Fitch, *The Evolution of Language* (New York, NY: Cambridge University Press, 2010), 394.

8. S. H. Kessels, "Is There a Highest Art?," *Music & Letters*, Vol. 12, No. 4 (October 1931), pp. 398–404, pg. 399.

9. David C. Houston, "The Impact of Red Feather Currency on the Population of the Scarlet Honeyeater on Santa Cruz," in *Ethno-ornithology: Birds, Indigenous Peoples, Culture and Society*, edited by Sonia Tideman and Andrew Gosler (New York, NY: Earthscan, 2010), pgs. 55–67, pg. 58, 69.

10. John Potter and Neil Sorrell, *A History of Singing* (New York, NY: Cambridge University Press, 2012), 29.

11. Elaine Richardson, "(Dis)inventing Discourse: Examples from Black Culture and Hip-Hop Rap Discourse," in *Disinventing and Reconstituting Languages*, edited by Prof. Sinfree Makoni and Prof. Alastair Pennycook (Buffalo, NY: Multilingual Matters, Ltd., 2017), pgs. 196–215, pg. 202.

12. Alexandra Zinck and Albert Newen, "Classifying Emotion: A Developmental Account," *Synthese*, Vol. 161, No. 1 (March 2008), pp. 1–25, pg. 1.

13. Elizabeth Pennisi, "The First Language?," *Science, New Series*, Vol. 303, No. 5662 (February 27, 2004), pp. 1319–20, pg. 1319.

14. Stefan Wurm, "Tonal Languages in New Guinea and the Adjacent Islands," *Anthropos*, Bd. 49, H. 3./4. (1954), pp. 697–702, pg. 697. See also Michael Barrie, "Contour Tones and Contrast in Chinese Languages," *Journal of East Asian Linguistics*, Vol. 16, No. 4 (December 2007), pp. 337–62, pg. 339.

15. E. H. Turpin, *Proceedings of the Musical Association 15th Sess.* (1888–1889), pp. 19–34, pg. 21.

16. Norman D. Cook, *Tone of Voice and Mind: The Connections between Intonation, Emotion, Cognition and Consciousness* (Philadelphia, PA: John Benjamins Publishing Company, 2002), pg. 255.

17. Kent Nagano and Inge Kloepfer, *Classical Music: Expect the Unexpected*, translated by Hans-Christian Oeser (Chicago, IL: McGill Queen's University Press, 2019), pg. 201.

18. Dean Falk, *Finding Our Tongues: Mothers, Infants and the Origins of Language* (New York, NY: Perseus Books Group, 2009), pg. 5.

19. Albert Doja, "Socializing Enchantment: A Socio-Anthropological Approach to Infant-Directed Singing, Music Education and Cultural Socialization," *International Review of the Aesthetics and Sociology of Music*, Vol. 45, No. 1 (June 2014), pp. 115–47, pg. 118.

20. George F. R. Ellis, "Biology and Mechanisms Related to the Dawn of Language," in *Homo Symbolicus: The Dawn of Language, Imagination and Spirituality*, edited by Christopher Henshilwood and Francesco d'Errico (Philadelphia, PA: John Benjamins Publishing Company, 2011, pgs. 163–85, pg. 175.

21. Jean-Louis Aroui and Andy Arleo, *Towards a Typology of Poetic Forms: From Language to Metrics and Beyond* (Philadelphia, PA: John Benjamins Company, 2009), pg. 23.

22. Sam Foster, *Hey Diddle Diddle: Our Best-loved Nursery Rhymes and What They Really Mean* (Chichester, West Sussex: Summersdale Publishers, 2008), pg. 11.

23. Kathleen Palti, "Singing Women: Lullabies and Carols in Medieval England," *The Journal of English and Germanic Philology*, Vol. 110, No. 3 (July 2011), pp. 359–82, 360–61.

24. W. A. Thorpe, "The Comparison of Vocal Communication in Animals and Man," in *Non-Verbal Communication*, edited by Robert A. Hinde (New York, NY: Cambridge University Press, 1979), pgs. 27–49, pg. 38.

25. Manny Brand, "Lullabies That Awaken Musicality in Infants," *Music Educators Journal*, Vol. 71, No. 7 (March 1985), pp. 28–31, pg. 29.

26. Sigmund Freud, *Jokes and their Relation to the Unconscious* (New York, NY: W.W. Norton and Company, 1960), pg. 143–44. See also Rennata Gaddini, "Lullabies and Rhymes in the Emotional Life of Children," in *Winnicott Studies*, No. 11, Spring, 1996 (London: Karnac Books, 1996), pgs. 28–41, pg. 34.

27. Alice Sterling Honig, "The Language of Lullabies," *YC Young Children*, Vol. 60, No. 5 (September 2005), pp. 30–36, pg. 31.

28. Kristine Henriksen Garroway, *Growing Up in Ancient Israel: Children in Material Culture and Biblical Texts* (Atlanta, GA: SBL Press, 2018), pgs. 133–34.

29. As quoted in Walter Farber, "Magic at the Cradle. Babylonian and Assyrian Lullabies," *Anthropos*, Bd. 85, H. 1./3. (1990), pp. 139–48, pg. 140.

30. Doja, "Socializing Enchantment," 115–47, pg. 134.

31. Yağmur Heffron, "Revisiting 'Noise' (rigmu) in Atra-ḫasīs in Light of Baby Incantations," *Journal of Near Eastern Studies*, Vol. 73, No. 1 (April 2014), pp. 83–93, pg. 83.

32. John H. Elliot, *Beware the Evil Eye; The Evil Eye in the Bible and the Ancient World: Volume One - Introduction, Mesopotamia, and Egypt* (Cambridge, United Kingdom: James Clarke and Co., 2016), pg. 88.

33. Freud M. J. Geller, "Magic and Mesopotamia: How the Magic Works," *Folklore*, Vol. 108 (1997), pp. 1–7, pg. 2.

34. Edwin E. Gordon, *Music Learning Theory for Newborn and Young Children* (Chicago, IL: Gia Publications, 2013), pg. 7.

35. Edith Gerson-Kiwi, "Religious Chant: A Pan-Asiatic Conception of Music," *Journal of the International Folk Music Council*, Vol. 13 (1961), pp. 64–67, pg. 64.

36. *Genesis* 1:1–13.

37. Janis B. Nuckolls, "The Case for Sound Symbolism," *Annual Review of Anthropology*, Vol. 28 (1999), pp. 225–52, pg. 227.

38. F. Ohrt, "Abracadabra," *The Journal of the Royal Asiatic Society of Great Britain and Ireland*, Vol. 1 (January 1922), pp. 86–88.

39. H. S. Versnel, "The Poetics of the Magical Charm: An Essay on the Power of Words," in *Magic and Ritual in the Ancient World*, edited by Paul Mirecki and Martin Meyer (Boston, MA: Brill, 2002), pgs. 105–59, pg. 109.

40. Dorothea Bedigian, "History and Lore of Sesame in Southwest Asia," *Economic Botany*, Vol. 58, No. 3 (Autumn, 2004), pp. 329–53, pgs. 345–46.

41. Arran Stibbe, "Abracadabra, Alakazam: Colonialism and the Discourse of Entertainment Magic," *Soundings: An Interdisciplinary Journal*, Vol. 88, No. 3/4 (Fall/Winter, 2005), pp. 413–25, pg. 413–14.

42. Lynne Hume, *Portals: Opening Doorways to Other Realities Through the Senses* (New York, NY: Berg, 2007), 15–16.

43. M. S. Nagaraja Rao, "Survival of Certain Neolithic Elements among the Boyas of Tekkalakota," *Anthropos*, Bd. 60, H. 1./6. (1965), pp. 480–86, pg. 481.

44. Hugh B. Urban, *New Age, Neopagan, and New Religious Movements: Alternative Spirituality in Contemporary America* (Oakland, CA: The University of California Press, 2015), pg. 26.

45. Kathleen Kuiper, *Ancient Egypt: From Prehistory to the Islamic Conquest* (New York, NY: Britannica Educational Publishing, 2011), pg. 128.

46. Vergil, *The Aeneid*, VII. 1–15. Cf. Veerle Stoffelen, "Vergil's Circe: Sources for a Sorceress," *L'Antiquité Classique T.*, Vol. 63 (1994), pp. 121–35.

47. Pliny, *Natural History*, VIII. 267. See also H. S. Versnel, "The Poetics of the Magical Charm: An Essay on the Power of Words," in *Magic and Ritual in the Ancient World*, edited by Paul Mirecki and Marvin Meyer (Boston, MA: EJ Brill, 2002), 105–59, pg. 106.

48. Hesiod, *Theogony*, 75–78.

49. John Arthur Smith, *Music in Ancient Judaism and Early Christianity* (New York, NY: Routledge, 2011), pg. xvii.

50. Kazi Zulkader Siddiqui, "The Problem of Similarities in Ancient Near Eastern Religions: A Comparison of the Hymn to Aton and Psalm 104," *Islamic Studies*, Vol. 40, No. 1 (Spring, 2001), pp. 67–88, pg. 71.

51. Jan Assmann, *Moses the Egyptian: The Memory of Egypt in Western Monotheism* (Cambridge, MA: Harvard University Press, 1998), pgs. 28–29.

52. W. F. Albright, "An Archaic Hebrew Proverb in an Armana Letter from Central Palestine," *Journal of Near East Studies*, Vol. 89 (1943), pp. 29–32, as quoted in Emmet Sweeney, *Empire of Thebes, or Ages of Chaos Revisited* (New York, NY: Algora Publishing, 200), 75.

53. Harold Hay, *The Organization of the Pyramid Texts* (Boston, MA: E. J. Brill, 2012), 1–2.

54. *The Literature of Ancient Sumer*, translated and edited by Jeremy Black, Graham Cunningham, Eleanor Robson, and Gabor Zólyomi (New York, NY: Oxford University Press, 2004), 246.

55. *Mesopotamia: The World's Earliest Civilization*, edited by Kathleen Kuiper (New York, NY: Rosen Educational Services, 2011), pg. 60.

56. Samuel Noah Kramer, "Immortal Clay: The Literature of Sumer," *The American Scholar*, Vol. 15, No. 3 (Summer, 1946), pp. 314–26, pgs. 321–22.

57. Clyde Weber Votaw, "The Septuagint Greek Version of the Old Testament," *The Biblical World*, Vol. 16, No. 3 (September 1900), pp. 186–98, pg. 186.

58. W. Derek Suderman and Timothy J. Sandoval, *Wisdom, Worship, and Poetry: Fortress Commentary on the Bible Study Edition* (Minneapolis, MN: Augsburg Fortress Publishing, 2016), pg. 547. See also W. Emery Barnes, "Selah—Some Facts and a Suggestion," *The Journal of Theological Studies*, Vol. 18, No. 72 (July 1917), pp. 263–73, pg. 263.

59. James A. Montgomery, "Stanza-Formation in Hebrew Poetry," *Journal of Biblical Literature*, Vol. 64, No. 3 (September, 1945), pp. 379–84, pg. 381.

60. Barnes, "Selah—Some Facts and a Suggestion," 263–73, pg. 263.

61. *I Samuel* 18:6–8. See also Curt Sachs, *The Rise of Music in the Ancient World* (New York, NY: Dover Publications, 1971), 92.

62. *II Samuel* 18:33. See also John D. Spilker, "'Oh My Son!': The Musical Origins and Function of King David's Lamentation," *College Music Symposium*, Vol. 49/50 (2009/2010), pp. 427–50, pg. 427–28.

63. Eric Werner, "Musical Aspects of the Dead Sea Scrolls: For Curt Sachs on his Seventh-Fifth Birthday," *The Musical Quarterly*, Vol. 43, No. 1 (January 1957), pp. 21–37 (see pages 21–22).

64. Ian Rutherford, "Et Hominum Et Deorum … Laudes (?): A Hypothesis about the Organisation of Pindar's 'Paean,'" *Zeitschrift für Papyrologie und Epigraphik*, Bd. 107 (1995), pp. 44–52, pg. 44.

65. Frederick Ahl, "Proemion: Translating a Paean of Praise," in *Tradition, Translation, Trauma: The Classic and the Modern*, edited by Jan Parker and Timothy Mathews (New York, NY: Oxford University Press, 2011), pgs. 29–39, pgs. 30–31.

66. Vergil, *The Aeneid*, VI. 642–62. See also Lauren Curtis, *Walking through Elysium: Vergil's Underworld and the Poetics of Tradition* (Toronto, Canada: The University of Toronto Press, 2020), 187.

67. Diane J. Rayor, *The Homeric Hymns: A Translation, with Introduction and Notes* (Berkley, CA: The University of California Press, 2014), pg. 16.

68. *The Homeric Hymns*, Hymn to Apollo and the Muses, #25.

69. Steven H. Lonsdale, "'Homeric Hymn to Apollo': Prototype and Paradigm of Choral Performance," *Arion: A Journal of Humanities and the Classics*, Third Series, Vol. 3, No. 1, *The Chorus in Greek Tragedy and Culture*, One (Fall, 1994–Winter, 1995), pp. 25–40, pg. 25.

70. Robert Manson Myers, "Neo-Classical Criticism of the Ode for Music," *PMLA* (i.e., "Publications of the Modern Language Association"), Vol. 62, No. 2 (June 1947), pp. 399–421, pg. 402.

71. Susan Stewart, "What Praise Poems Are For," *PMLA*, Vol. 120, No. 1, *Special Topic: On Poetry* (January 2005), pp. 235–45, pg. 236.

72. Pablo Neruda et al., *The Wilson Quarterly* (1976), Vol. 22, No. 2 (Spring, 1998), pp. 113–18, pg. 118. See also Pablo Neruda and Robin Robertson, "Ode to a Large Tuna in the Market," *Poetry*, Vol. 190, No. 1, *The Translation Issue* (April 2007), pp. 16–20.

Chapter 2

Early Musical Instruments

Having looked at the beginning of vocal music, we now turn to the development of early musical instruments. If singing is closely related to the human voice's role in history, musical instruments involved the use of the hands. While we sing with our voices, we play music with our hands. We also make musical instruments with our hands. Musical instruments are handcrafted devices, part of the history of toolmaking. Our human ability to fashion tools, including musical instruments, shaped cultures in very basic ways.[1] Key inventions like the wheel (actually, it was the axle), cooking, or the fabled "inclined plane" played critical roles in building civilization. As inventions, musical instruments equaled any of these other iconic innovations. Part utilitarian artisanship and part an aesthetic art, musical instruments are part of the countless tools that have improved human lives.

As tools, musical instruments have evolved over the centuries. In our world today, amazing musical instruments like Steinway pianos, Martin guitars, Stradivarius violins, and Fender Telecasters set a standard for excellence few in earlier periods could have even imagined. Electronic music and digital technology offer even newer possibilities. Yet the amazing music and musical instruments available today owe their excellence to the simple instruments of prehistoric times, the forebears of all the music to come.

ART AND CRAFT

The making of musical instruments is both craft and art. The word "art" comes to us from the Latin *ars*, meaning something you make, like a *craft*. Since the Industrial Revolution, the idea of "arts and crafts" has come to connote hand-made items produced with a folksy charm and aesthetic. "Arts and crafts" items usually contrast with items produced by the more efficient but less romantic factory-system. Today, we often relegate arts and crafts to quaint gift-shops, living-history reenactments or special-interest hobbies. In reality, arts and crafts played a central role in the development of many essential human endeavors, including music. Before the Industrial Revolution, handcrafted items were the norm. At their best, such tools combined utility with aesthetic charm. They were art pieces as much as technology.

There are many examples of crafted tools that doubled as works of art. Rudimentary stone tools such as arrowheads, for example, led societies down the long path from simple stone chippers to the awesome stonecutters of later ages. Few scholars who have studied indigenous peoples past and present would deny the inherent beauty and artistry of a culture's stone projectile points, objects often reflecting superior craftwork.[2] Over the centuries, however, simple stone chipping grew more complex. With time, early stone chipping techniques fostered the ability to cut stone. Stonecutters developed the ability to make refined statuary or grandiose buildings. Just as history's most sophisticated examples of stone-cutting go back to the simple but important skill of chipping away at suitable stones to make rudimentary tools, so, too, musical instruments also possess a legacy dating back to a long-ago set of seemingly simple arts and crafts.

TOOLS

Music, with all its amazing subtleties and complexities today, could not have evolved without tools—without the tradition of the arts and crafts and the tools it created. From their earliest appearance in history, human beings distinguished themselves by their ability to manipulate their environment—by their ability to make tools, thereby improving daily lives. The amazing human hand, with its opposable thumb, empowered human intelligence and creativity in a way that distinguished people from other animals. The crafts we made with our hands helped make our world more amenable to human habitation. Because artisans provided a vital service to the community, the arts and crafts also came to reflect the intrinsic human needs for love, creative expression, service, pride in work, and communication. It is truly hard to overemphasize how much the arts and crafts have shaped some of the most significant developments in human history—necessary things, to be sure, but also wonderful and beautiful things.

Because they were both beautiful and useful, tools added wealth to ancient economies. This was certainly true in the case of musical instruments. Musical instruments often rank as among the most valued works of art produced in any given society. Some periods or places, like the Arab world, Renaissance Italy, Ancient Egypt, or Greece, have become especially famous for the exquisite care and artistry with which they fashioned their musical instruments.[3] As handcrafted tools, they invariably developed high valuation in their respective societies. The rise of big cities in the Ancient world furthered a vibrant marketplace for the arts and crafts. Handcrafted objects helped create bustling economies based on culture and art.[4] A growing relationship between the arts and wealth thus furthered progress in history.

If one goes back far enough, humans had little in the way of tools they could make by hand. Indeed, making tools required tools. Some tools had no real function of their own except for making other tools. Basic tools like the wooden wedge, used to split other pieces of wood, were probably some of the most important contributions to the world of "secondary and tertiary tools"—tools used to make other tools.[5] For example, a rock used as a weapon to hit somebody on the head is a primary tool—an object used for a purpose, but which requires no alteration. A secondary tool is an object modified for its final use, for example, a rock sharpened into an arrowhead. A tertiary tool exists solely to make other tools, not having a purpose in and of itself. Making a sewing needle—out of, say, bone—that then makes clothing is an example of a tertiary tool. The Fine Arts in all their forms seem to have required the development of tertiary tools. Tertiary tools reflected the growing ingenuity of human beings, as well as people learning how to use their hands in more delicate, careful ways.[6]

MUSICAL INSTRUMENTS AND TOOLS

Ancient artisans made musical instruments with tools. For that matter, musical instruments *are* tools. Some musical instruments, like simple drums that one pounded, were secondary or even primary tools. Others, however, required greater skill and craftwork—tools to bore holes or to decorate. The obvious limitations of the prehistorical world naturally prohibited complex musical instruments. Despite the many admirable efforts of Stone Age peoples, it would be naïve to downplay the difficulties of life during these earliest periods. Challenges in the Stone Age made devoting much time and energy to the Fine Arts a frill. Nobody in the Stone Age was going to make a Steinway Grand Piano, with its subtle shadings, complex pedal and hammer mechanisms, and finely honed wooden sounding board. Still, human creativity found a way. Lacking complex materials, tools, and knowledge, early human communities fashioned many of the world's first tools out of natural materials. They used stone, wood, bone, or ivory implements to scrape, grind, groove, and polish. They made tools to make other tools.

Among their other inventions, Stone Age peoples made the world's first musical instruments. These they usually created from materials readily available in nature, too—often bone. A very primitive flute, fashioned from a bear bone, found in Dijve Babe Cave in Slovenia, perhaps Neanderthal, provides one of the oldest examples of an early musical instrument ever found by archaeologists.[7] Because they emphasized beauty and creativity, such rudimentary musical instruments connote not only the first forms of music, but also the development of higher-order thinking, including symbolism and cosmology. Jewelry and other comparable items of decoration or personal adornment similarly reflect the development of a culture of the arts, as well as more specialized skill sets.

THE FOUNDING MYTHS OF MUSIC

Mythological accounts of the founding of music usually focus on the invention of musical instruments, technological innovations on a par with harnessing the awesome power of fire, inventing the wheel, or basic crafts like weaving and pottery. The founders of music have a significant place in many ancient legendary narratives. In Ancient Greece, the fifth-century BC historian Herodotus says that music in Greece came from the city of Argos.[8] The city of Argos was part of the Mycenaean area, made famous in so much mythology, most notably in Homer's *Iliad* and *Odyssey*. We sometimes still describe the Bronze Age in Greece (circa 2000 BC–1200 BC) as the "Mycenaean Age." Some of the early Greek period's finest specimens of musical instruments known to archaeology come from Mycenae. In this period, the large U-shaped lyre known as the phorminx appeared. The Greeks seem to have borrowed this type of lyre from abroad.

The Bible also has something to say about music's origins. According to the Bible, music was one of the first sophisticated cultural endeavors humans developed. *Genesis* 4 lists music as one of the foundational cultural advancements after the famous Fall of Man, along with shepherding and metalsmithing. Jubal was the biblical founder of music.[9] *Genesis* cites Jubal as having developed the musical tradition associated with the harp and the pipes. Biblical scholars often cite Jubal's half-brother Tubal-Cain as the father of metallurgy, things made out of brass and iron. The Bible also provides here what seems like the preserved lyrics of a song, the Song of Lamech, Jubal's father.[10] Historians usually consider these lines as an early form of poetry because of the repeated constructions they employ in the original Hebrew, as well as their placement in the text alongside the story about the creation of music.[11]

RHYTHM INSTRUMENTS

Perhaps the oldest "family" of musical instruments is the percussion family, with the drum being its most important contributor. When considering the history of how people began making musical instruments, it makes sense that the drum would come first. Rhythm is one of music's most essential components. The Australian musicologist Andrew Ford described all music as a "synthesis of intellectual design and bodily urge."[12] Rhythm, along with hummable melodies and ear-catching harmonies, are part of this bodily urge—the physical part of music that makes people tap their feet. Musicians today call this a musical quality a "groove"—the feel of music that is physical in nature, not just technical. A good groove starts with the rhythm. Thus, it makes sense that the oldest type of musical instrument on the planet is the drum, ancestor of all percussion instruments. Rhythm is also closely associated with dance, a more essential ingredient to moving the body in time than either melody or harmony. For this reason, in his *Poetics*, Aristotle argued that dancing employed rhythm, but not harmony.[13]

Drums are some of the oldest human-made artifacts found. Archaeologists have identified early flutes from as long ago as 35,000 BC, probably Neanderthal. Even earlier, excavations have unearthed rhythm devices resembling the Latin American *guiro* in Belgium, dating from as long ago as 70,000 BC.[14] Bone pendants found in the Ancient Israel, probably dating from around 15,000 BC, probably once pounded against each other, producing rhythmic sounds.[15] In southern India, scholars have found the presence of "rock" or "ringing rocks," piles of stones designed to be hit to produce a sound that has some sense of tonality, as well as the ability to be played like a drum. These "rock gongs" usually involve a pile of stones, sort of a little stone tower with a hollow center. The piling of the stones creates a natural resonance chamber.[16] These rock gongs represent an important branch of musical instruments called "lithophones"—a musical instrument made of one or more resonant rocks.[17]

In time, other, more sophisticated drums appeared. They involved honing an instrument with good acoustics, say by strapping an animal hide across a hollow wooden chamber. Scholars call such drums "membranophones." Membranophones appear early in both Mesopotamia and Egypt. Surviving specimens of such ancient membranophone drums are relatively rare. They connote the superior craftwork entailed in manufacturing a fine drum with a proper animal-skin drumhead.[18] A good membranophone emphasized resonance and balance, just like a good drum today.

Rattlers and shakers also appeared as early forms of rhythm instruments. Such musical devices served as sleep-inducing devices with children, like sleeping rattles today. Rattles appear in many ancient bedtime settings around the Mesopotamian and Egyptian worlds, again reflecting the great universality of impulses to soothe crying children to sleep. Such rattles often double as toys. Some of the most important children's rattles date from the Bronze Age, found in ancient Israeli sites like Megidoo or Gezer.[19] Egyptian wall paintings found in tombs often showing many types of musical instruments, including rhythm instruments that involved shaking, rattling, or pounding. The Egyptians had round-frame drums that influenced the Greek style of drum called the tympanum.[20]

Today, we might make too hard and fast a categorical distinction between "rhythm instruments" and "wind instruments." Ancient instruments often lacked such finer distinctions, especially in the earliest ages of prehistory. The limited tonal capabilities of some of the world's first flutes, horns, and reeds probably made them more like rhythm instruments than melodic ones—almost like the noisemakers people today blow on New Year's Eve. Another important musical instrument that blurred the line between rhythm device and tonality was the bell. In the Bible, God instructs Aaron to wear bells on his "ephod," part of the special sacred clothing worn by the priests.[21] The sounds of these ringing little bells would follow the priest as he entered the holy spaces of the tabernacle, perhaps warding off demonic attack, like charm ornaments.[22] *Exodus* 39 describes these bells as made of pure gold.[23]

THE TIMBREL AND THE SISTRUM

One of the most famous percussion instruments of the Ancient World was the timbrel, a tambourine-style device that allowed for a wide range of rhythmic possibilities. When the Bible's King David brought the ark to Jerusalem after capturing the city, a small orchestra played merrily during the procession. *II Samuel* described several rhythm instruments here, including almost certainly the timbrel, as well as cymbals.[24] In *I Chronicles*, the Bible reports an orchestra that provided festive, loud accompanying sounds for the Ark of the Covenant as the Hebrews brought it into the recently completed Temple of King Solomon. The timbrel was one of the instruments featured prominently.[25] After the Children of Israel successfully crossed the Red Sea and escaped pharaoh's army, the prophet Miriam leads a retinue of women in a dancing, singing procession. As she leads the women, she shakes a timbrel.[26]

The *sistrum* was another rhythm instrument associated with the dancing and rhythm. The *sistrum* was a rattle-like instrument, often wielded by women in a rhythmic procession. It appears widely across many lands in the Ancient Near East, the Greek world, and the Roman Empire, as far north as Britain. A famous pair of bronze *sistra* found at Pompeii rank among the most valuable items from that treasure-trove of ancient artifacts. The British Museum also has some superbly preserved Egyptian *sistra* from the later period.[27] The Bible probably references a *sistrum*-type of instrument in *II*

Samuel as David brings the ark into Jerusalem, along with the timbrel and other instruments.[28] The word used in the Bible is *mean'an'im*, translated in the Greek *Septuagint* as *kymbala* (cymbals) and the Vulgate as *sistra*, the Latin plural of sistrum. The *Revised Standard Version* translation equates the term with the modern-instrument—the castanet.[29] Another ancient rhythm instrument associated with women and religious processions is the *thyrsus*. Along with *sistra*, the *thyrsus* was yet another rattle-like device prominently featured. The worshippers are especially famous for their use of the *thyrsus*. Devotees shook the *thyrsus* as they paraded, adding audible notes of frenzy and passion to their cult's activities.

WIND INSTRUMENTS AND FLUTES

In conjunction with rhythm instruments, the world's first artisans also began to make wind instruments. A wind instrument is any instrument that you blow into to produce sound. In ancient times, wind instruments included flutes, reed instruments, and horns. Of all the wind instruments, the flute—in all its various forms and guises—is no doubt one of the most ancient instruments in the world. Seeing how the wind makes a haunting sound when whipping through a cave, or some sort of chimney, probably helped foster the idea of using wind to make musical sounds.[30] Thus, this beautiful instrument, the flute, which would become one of the most familiar and well-loved instruments in world music, had its origins in the Stone Age. Whistles made of bone appear in numerous Stone Age sites, including the Magdalenian Cave sites of France.[31] These artifacts probably date back to 17,000 BC.

Still today, the haunting, breathy tones of a flute evoke images of misty Antiquity. In the United States, flute music is especially closely associated with many Native American societies. Hollywood often uses the flute to provide soundtrack tones for films dealing with Native American tribes living in their indigenous modes. Scholars sometimes lament the "Native American Exoticism" in which films use the haunting and sparse sounds of flute to evoke a desert or prairie setting.[32] One of the most important images of Native American/Pre-Columbian flutes are the hunchbacked "kokopelli" flautist found in Native American petroglyphs found throughout the Southwest—a crouched figure playing the flute, carved into the sides of mountains and cliffs.[33] Beyond Native American images, the flute also appears in much mythology worldwide. Among the many works that highlight the cultural and geographical legacy of the flute, the 2013 work by Dale A. Olsen highlighted the almost uncanny global ubiquity of worldwide "flutelore," including the appearance of the flute in the most ancient tales from Africa, the pre-Columbian Americas, Europe, and Asia.[34] In Japan, flutes were typically made of bamboo.[35]

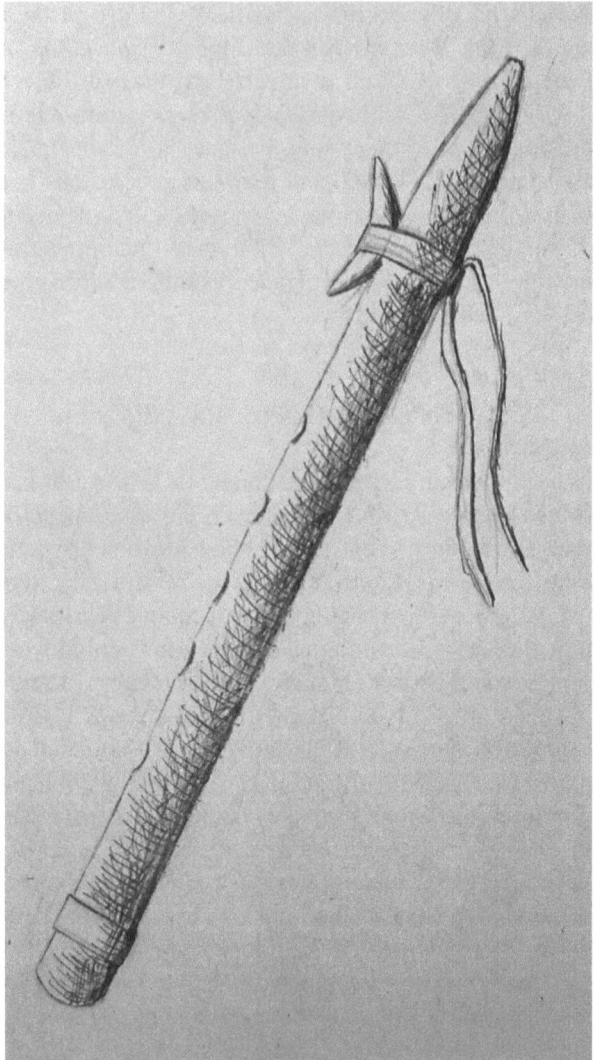

Figure 2.1   An ancient flute.

To produce sound in a flute, one blows across the opening of the tube, or a special slotted hole. Many flutes were made of bone or wood. Long hollow tubes were a common type of flute. Flutes of this nature also reflected early forays into the more complicated musical realm of intonation and the ability to play specific notes in specific pitches, higher or lower. A longer tube produced a lower note when the player blew into it. A shorter tube produced a higher note. Artisans made holes in the tube to create the effect of lengthening or shortening of tube, the world's first example of fingering for a musical instrument. Most early flutes were open-ended. Others had a stopped end. The first flutes often had three or four holes bored into the tube. China, Sumer, and Egypt each entered into the age of recorded history with these types of flutes already well established in their prehistorical cultures. We find early bone flutes widely throughout prehistoric Europe. Three or four holes bored into the tube usually reflected the common use of the pentatonic scale, a five-note scale still commonly used in much music, including blues and folk.[36]

THE OCARINA

Another early style of flute was the ocarina. Familiar to late-twentieth-century people because of the popular Nintendo video game *The Legend of Zelda and the Ocarina of Time*, the ocarina is actually an extremely ancient musical instrument. Merchants have sold cheap plastic or ceramic ocarinas as toys to children for many generations. Though its flat shape distinguishes it from the long cylindrical tubes more commonly equated with flutes, the ocarina is nonetheless a type of flute. An ocarina's hollow space produces sound when somebody blows into it, or across one of its holes. The ocarinas widely familiar to people today especially harken back to the nineteenth century and the mass manufacturing of children's toys. However popular a feature in children's playthings worldwide, the ocarina is a truly ancient musical instrument.

The ocarina appears in numerous settings around the world. Ocarinas have been used by the Bantu peoples of southern Africa.[37] Ocarina flutes also appear in the archaeological record of the Shang dynasty peoples in Bronze Age China.[38] Some of the most familiar primitive ocarinas were made of clay, widely used for many centuries. These clay ocarinas featured prominently in medieval Italy as carnival whistles.[39] By the late nineteenth century, souvenir hawkers were selling ocarina whistles in the fair markets of Paris, accurately marketed as one of the world's most ancient musical instruments.[40]

THE PIPES OF PAN

In the Greek world, the pipes of pan—called the *syrinx* in Latin—became one of the most famous types of ancient flutes. A Homeric Hymn of Pan (#19) says the pipes of pan were made of reed, from a family of stout plants that feature a hollow, tube-like stalk. The Greek pipes of pan used rudimentary principles of intonation. Artisans fashioned a series of tubes in a row, fastening them together according to their lengths, from shorter to higher. This made it possible for the player to play high and low notes. A fine *syrinx/panpipe* was highly valued as a gift by the Greek and Roman cultures, a gift coveted by both the gods and the humans.⁴¹ Another Hymn to Pan (#19) cites Pan's pipes as contributing to the sounds of nature on a hillside.⁴² Pan plays his pipes along with singing birds, joined by mountain nymphs. Ironically, Pan, with his overt and base sexuality, along with his hooves and goat bottom half, often seems to foreshadow medieval imagery of the devil. But Pan also presages medieval saints like Saint Anthony of Padua or Saint Francis of Assisi. Art and iconography often depicted such saints as communing with nature, especially singing birds.

Figure 2.2   A musician playing a *syrinx*, sometimes called the "Pipes of Pan."

The pipes of pan also appear elsewhere in the world, including the Incan tribes of Peru.[43] Here, the early Andean tribes often made panpipes out of clay, part of their craft of pottery. Panpipes in the Andes employed the ceramic process, an innovation in pottery sometimes erroneously attributed to Europe in the eighteenth century.[44] Nascan sites have provided many examples of whistles and panpipes. The Nascan process of "slip painting" these devices has received praise for its artisanal excellence. Slip paint involved putting the resin-tinctures on the clay before firing. It represented a major innovation in the chemical process, something like producing a glaze. Some of the Andean panpipes thus produced date from as early as 1800 BC.[45] Excavations also discovered a panpipe in the Hopewell Indian Mounds of New Castle Indiana, excavated between 1965 and 1972, identified as such in 1989.[46] Scholars have also observed panpipes used in the Solomon Islands, among numerous other places.[47]

MUSICAL INSTRUMENTS AND ANIMALS

Musical instruments typically came from natural organic materials—animal parts, clay, metals, or plants. It made sense that instruments fashioned from the earth would thus evoke the sounds of nature. The flute was especially associated with the care and company of animals. The early ancients saw music as a pastoral device, especially flutes played while herding—an image especially associated with Pan. There are several interesting points about the use of music in such pastoral settings. Animals seemingly enjoy and respond to music, though perhaps some more than others—just like people.[48] Thus, the image of an ancient shepherd passing away the long hours with his herds while playing some sort of a musical instrument makes good sense, for several reasons. It whiled away otherwise idle hours, no doubt. David reportedly played his lyre for the sheep in the Bible. The use of calming, attractive music by shepherds probably had a functional aspect, as well. Music kept the animals calm. It even helped gather them back to the herd in case they wandered away.

Some of the impetus for musical instruments may have been the domestication of animals. The famous 1697 poem "The Mourning Bride" by the English literary figure William Congreve opined that "music hath charms to soothe the savage beast," and he was actually right, in both the literal and the figurative sense.[49] In this sense, instruments like the flute had a practical use as a tool for animal husbandry. Along with famous examples like those of the Bible or Ancient Greece, pastoral settings have also featured music as part of the shepherd's toolkit to soothe the herds, notably Ethiopia, where Abyssinian shepherds still to this day play to their herds with traditional instruments like the Ethiopian lyre, the *Masonquo*, or the special Ethiopian flute known as the *Shambukaw*.[50]

While David's lyre has an ancient and extremely famous association with herds, the flute actually seems more commonly associated with shepherding than the lyre. For one thing, it might have been more portable, since many ancient lyres were quite large. Lyres also involved more care and maintenance. The lyre would also become closely associated with recited verse. This made the lyre a perfect instrument for entertaining and musing, as opposed to charming the beasts of the field, better suited for flutes. In Plato's *Republic*, the philosopher says that the lyre is for the city, while the flute is for shepherds in the country.[51] Ancient sources mention a flute tune called "Hippotharus" that herders played because they thought it induced stallions to mount mares.[52] The Scythians used to use some sort of a reed-like tube instrument to blow air into the vulva of a mare because they believed it to improve the quality of the milk produced.[53]

THE REED

Beyond flutes, reed instruments comprise another important member of the wind instrument family. Today's reed instruments include such instruments as clarinets, saxophones, oboes, and bassoons. There are different kinds of reeds, especially the single-reed type used in an instrument like a clarinet or a saxophone, and the "double-reed" used in an instrument like a bassoon. A reed instrument today usually has some sort of mouthpiece holding the reed and connecting it to a hollow tube that then produces the song. Holes for fingering are bored into the instrument, which allows the musician playing a reed instrument to play with decent intonation, playing high or low notes. Reeds also would come to play an important role in the history of the organ, as in reed organs.

Ancient artisans made reeds from thin slices of wood, or the stalks of certain plants. Early peoples also used the reed pipes commonly associated with the pipes of pan to make reeds. The grassy, stringy hollow tube stalks that characterize this family of reed plants also including the type of reed used to make papyri, as well as many baskets. One especially significant ancient reed instrument was the *aulos*, in Latin *tibia*. Most *auloi* unearthed by archaeologists are fragments, at best. Several examples of *auloi* survive intact from Antiquity, with perhaps the best specimens being four *auloi* excavated at Pompeii.[54] Excavations have also unearthed decently preserved *auloi* at Meroë in Egypt.[55] Surviving specimens of *auloi* include many variations in terms of size, the number of holes bored into the instruments, among other differences.

In Western myth, one of the most famous reed players was Marsyas. Marsyas played the *aulos*/flute, praised in Plato's *Republic* as able to charm the souls of listeners. The music of his reed virtually induced a state of divine possession. In fact, Plato feared the intoxicating sounds of the reed, banning it from the ideal state he envisioned.[56] Marsyas's mastery of the reed contrasted with Apollo's mastery of the lyre. In a popular myth, Marsyas and Apollo competed to see who had the superior musicianship. In one version of the story, when Marsyas lost the contest to Apollo, the god skinned him alive.[57] Subsequently, the flaying of Marsyas became somewhat unlikely subject of many fine statues, mosaics, paintings, and other artistic renderings.[58]

THE KHALIL

Another important, and closely related, ancient reed instrument was called the *khalil*. The *khalil* is especially associated with the Bible, though it doubtless also featured prominently in neighboring cultures. The *khalil* used a double-reed pipe comparable to a modern-day oboe, only typically often played with two tubes simultaneously. The double-reed sound production gave the instrument a droning sound, a quality still associated with much Middle Eastern music to the present day. In fact, most scholars regard the modern-day traditions of Arabic music as an inheritance handed down from the venerable traditions of the truly ancient biblical and Mesopotamian musical traditions.[59]

The ancients used the *khalil* for celebration more than solemn worship. *Khalils* helped herald the ascension of Solomon as the King of Israel.[60] The prophet Isiah referenced the *khalil* as a musical instrument associated with party settings.[61] This would again point to the images of Middle Eastern music up to the present, where double-reeded wind instruments like the Lebanese *mijwiz* are usually associated with men, leisure activities, celebrations like weddings, and rural, traditional Arab social settings.[62] The musical sounds enjoyed in such traditional Arab outlets still today reflect a truly ancient musical heritage.

HORNS

Wind instruments also included horns. The most important instrument in this regard was the trumpet, another truly ancient instrument. As with flutes, though, the fact that there were no standardized forms for instruments entails a wide variety of instruments lumped into this category. Today, most horns belong to the "brass family" of instruments. As the name implies, brass instruments are made of brass, an alloy like bronze, made by blending copper and zinc. However, the use of brass for instruments did not really emerge until Roman times, when brass horns became among the most important forms of musical instrument. Before instruments were made of metal, "trumpet tubes" appeared in many cultures, especially in tropical areas. The player made sound by blowing into the instrument through tense lips.[63]

Before metal trumpets, peoples made horns from wood, seashells, or animal horns. Pre-Columbian peoples in both North and South America made trumpet-like horns out of tree bark.[64] Conch trumpets also appear in many other early cultures worldwide, including ancient India and the Peruvian Andes.[65] In Greek mythology, Poseidon's son Triton played a horn made of a conch shell. The Roman poet Vergil recounts how the Trojan hero Misenus had once bested Triton at playing the conch horn, a bold act for which Triton saw Misenus drowned.[66]

With their blaring sound, trumpet-tube instruments often featured prominently in public life. Many tribal societies used trumpet-tube instruments to mark landmark events, especially initiation into adulthood, and funeral-related ceremonies.[67] To this day, loud sounds like horns, buzzers, sirens, and bells have important crowd-control functions. Like a bullhorn, early trumpets provided loud and dramatic ways to get people's attention. For this reason, trumpets have a long association with the military and politics. In a world that lacked the benefits of electrically powered public-address systems, loud instruments helped give signals to the crowd.

Perhaps the most famous ancient trumpet was the Hebrew *shofar*, made of a ram's horn. Like many comparable uses of trumpets in ancient times, the *shofar* frequently had a function of calling the people to assembly or war. God instructed Joshua to have the trumpet players play the *shofar* during the siege of Jericho, an event destined to become one of the Bible's most enduring tales.[68] The biblical Judge Ehud used the *shofar* to summon the people as a call to arms.[69] Congregations in Israel still today blow the *shofar* in conjunction with the Jewish New Year, Rosh Hoshanah.[70] The tradition of blowing a *shofar* on Rosh Hoshanah predates rabbinical Judaism, going back to the Lord's command to ancient Israel to blow the trumpet on the first day of the seventh month.[71]

The Bible contains many other examples of trumpets used as a summoning device. When Moses brought the Ten Commandments down from Mount Sinai, a loud trumpet blast heralded his giving of the law to the Children of Israel.[72] Horns in *Numbers* 10 called the people to assembly. God told Moses to use different bugle blasts to alert people—one blast for summoning people from the east, another for people from the south, and so on. There was also a special blast for summoning people to war.[73] The prophet Joel also mentions trumpet sounds calling the Israelites to assembly in times of peril.[74] Similar images appear in *Hosea* and *Jeremiah*.[75] In *Daniel*, the Babylonian king Nebuchadnezzar used trumpets, along with other musical instruments, to give the signal for the masses to bow down to his golden idol statue.[76]

HORNS AND METALLURGY

The history of the trumpet closely corresponds to the history of metallurgy. As with all musical instruments, the first trumpets came from organic materials found in nature, especially animal parts. However, the new technology of alloying bronze (copper and tin) around 4000 resulted in bronze trumpets. Thus, while animal-horn trumpets remained popular, especially in myth and legend, trumpets made out of various workable metals appeared early in the Bronze Age. Before the brass trumpets of Roman times emerged, artisans usually made trumpets from bronze or even gold and silver. In the Bible, the trumpets God commanded were to be made of silver.[77] These silver trumpet tubes in the Bible recall the silver and bronze trumpets found in the tomb of Egyptian Pharaoh Tutankhamen, c. 1325 BC. Tut's trumpets were nearly two feet in length. They were probably hard to play, especially higher notes.[78] Scholars once regarded King Tut's silver trumpets as the oldest metal trumpets known to exist. However, recent scholarship has argued that numerous metal trumpet-like items found in eastern Iran are much older, dating them as early as 2200 BC.[79]

The Romans also popularized a number of brass trumpet tubes. Vergil describes the Trojan Misenus as having played the *lituus* alongside the Trojan hero Hector. The *lituus* is a forerunner of the tuba, a long metal trumpet used in battles like a bugle. Still another brass trumpet-type horn the Romans used for military purposes was the *tubicen*, the long trumpet that would have often doubled as a banner-holder, especially at ceremonial functions. Along with wartime battlefield calls, athletic events often featured the playing of the *tubicens* to herald victories and dramatize the entry of athletes onto the field. Still another Roman horn was the *cornu*, forerunner of the modern-day coronet.[80] The Romans used another trumpet called the *bucina*. The *bucina*'s long, curled tube horn suggests a rudimentary version of a Sousaphone, or a curlicue shape similar to the French horn. Musicians playing all these instruments used their trained embouchure to affect tones, much in the style of a military bugle today. Valves for brass instruments did not appear until the nineteenth century.

Armies have used many musical instruments in war, ranging from drums to even fifes and bagpipes. However, few instruments played a bigger role in shaping the outcome of warfare than the ancient trumpet. The Romans used trumpets in naval battles. Horns in this context probably had the dual purpose of arousing the martial spirit of the sailors and communicating between ships at sea. The Roman politician Octavian used signal horns to direct his fleet at the Battle of Actium when he fought the combined forces of Mark Antony and Cleopatra.[81] Mark Antony reportedly had no less than 500 ships in his fleet. Communication between such a substantial group of ships, and sailors, would have been no mean feat.[82] The Greeks used trumpets in the naval battle of Salamis, a decisive fight fought in 480 BC between the Greeks and the invading forces of Persia.[83]

PYTHAGORAS AND TUNING

Early instruments had crude methods of tuning, at best. Over time, however, better systems of intonating instruments evolved. By apocryphal tradition, the Greek Pythagoras developed the system of ratios that enabled tuning musical instruments. Unfortunately, Pythagoras left no writing of his own. He was born around 569 BC on the island of Samos. His father was reportedly a gem engraver.[84] The adult Pythagoras became a numerologist and a musician, supposedly the discovery of the famous "Pythagorean Theorem" that used right triangles to measure distance. By tradition, Pythagoras acquired his sacred knowledge of geometry and math during travels to Egypt.[85] Though mostly a mythic figure, Pythagoras's ideas about tuning instruments reflect genuine improvements in music making.

Pythagoras supposedly understood the relationship between musical tones and ratios.[86] His ideas applied to both stringed and wind instruments. For example, a string that was exactly twenty-four inches long would have a certain pitch when strung across a lyre. If a musician somehow shortened the string by exactly half, the string would sound an octave higher, a ratio of 2:1. Other intervals featured other ratios. Today, many stringed instruments feature a "neck" that can accomplish the lengthening or shortening of a string by having players press their fingers on the string at certain points.[87] Having strings of different widths also affects intonation. The same principle of tuning ratios applies to wind instruments. Wind instruments typically feature some sort of hollow tube with holes bored into it. Valves (as in a trumpet), or a sliding device, as in a trombone, also use similar properties. Pythagoras's ideas about the ratios and their role in playing intervals and intonation represented a major advancement in music. Instruments with more precise tuning could play together more harmoniously. Slowly but surely, ensemble playing began to be a possibility in music.

MUSICAL NOTATION?

Another important chapter in the development of music theory involved the long process of creating a useful system of musical notation, the ability to "read music." The musicians of Antiquity had no real way to read or write music. The fact that music existed so long without any way of preserving it—either in written notation or, even later, in audio recordings—helps explain the huge importance of music theory. The lack of musical notation made it exponentially harder to preserve an increasingly rich heritage. Today, both written music and audio recordings jointly contributed to a vast heritage of well-loved music, shared by us all. Just imagine, however, a world without either written music or audio recordings. That was the world of music prior to musical notation.

Early systems of musical notation before the Middle Ages were extremely limited, to the extent that they existed at all. In 1923, the eminent scholar Curt Sachs proposed a theory of a Babylonian musical notation system to account for a mysterious series of numbering and lines on the clay tablet known as *siglum CBS 10966*. Later scholarship largely discredited Sach's idea.[88] Other theories surmised that these tablets found in Mesopotamia involved designated strings and intervals. Scholars sometimes surmise that a tablet found in Syria dating from around 1800 BC contains musical notation. The notation, however, takes the form of verbal instructions as opposed to a designated system of indicating notes and rhythms. The passage does seem to reflect, however, an increasingly common use of the seven-note scale.[89] The exact nature of the tables found in the clay tablets remains the subject of much discussion.[90] As seems typical, we will never really know for sure.

GREEK SYSTEMS OF MUSICAL NOTATION?

Some Greeks did attempt, however unsuccessfully, to develop a system of musical notation. These were probably too complicated and inaccessible to be of much use as anything other than a novelty. Anyway, even if the Greeks had invented a very practicable system of musical notation, the relatively limited access to paper/papyri would have resulted in a continued reliance on memorization and improvisation. Simply put, few decent alternatives to memorizing music existed.[91] Another problem is that the Greek notation system seems almost exclusively equated with a few ancient philosophers or musicians. They were the idiosyncratic theories of maverick individuals. The lack of a larger context of music theory makes their ideas seem even more jumbled and obscure.

The fourth-century philosopher Aristoxenus is probably the most important figure in Greek music after Pythagoras. Aristoxenus had little use for any Greek system of musical notation. For him, notation would make little contribution to musical artistry. Aristoxenus seemed to care little that music in his time lacked a notation system. He had, nonetheless, a very technical approach to music. He wrote a complex treatise on the "science of music," including lengthy discussions of pitch, harmony, the motion of music, intervals, and other music theory considerations. Since ancient music was primarily melodic, concern over intonation and scales constituted some of the most important considerations of music theory.[92] Much of Aristoxenus's writing discusses scales, including the diatonic scale, roughly the familiar seven-tone scale of modern Western music, as well as the chromatic scale.[93]

MODES

Along commonly cited featured of ancient (and medieval) music involved the "modes." Each mode built off an eight-note scale, starting at a different point and consequently following different tonal intervals. The word "scale" comes from the Latin *scala*, which simply means "ladder." A mode actually draws on the scale. By starting at different point, it creates different subsets. Modes therefore provided the rudimentary basis for scales and chords. Musicians today still sometimes use modal feelings and special intervals to write songs. The Greeks probably borrowed the modes from Ancient Near Eastern music, centuries older than the Greeks. The familiar names of the modes come from the Greek language—*Ionian, Dorian, Phrygian, Lydian, Mixolydian, Aeolian,* and *Locrian*. The *Ionian* mode roughly corresponds to the familiar "Major Scale" of Modern Western Music, while the *Aeolian* Scale (the minor sixth), would be the relative minor. Plato's *Republic* similarly assigns certain qualities or musical characters to the modes. The Lydian and Ionic modes are sad, most suited for laments. The Doric and Phrygian modes evoke bravery and heroism.[94] These Classical ideas about modes would heavily influence medieval church music.

SOME FINAL REFLECTIONS ON THE WORLD'S FIRST MUSICAL INSTRUMENTS

In the first chapter, we studied the important role of the voice in human history, especially as it developed into the traditions of singing. In this chapter, we discussed the further development of music, especially as it relates to the world's first musical instruments. Musical instruments were tools. By inventing musical tools, ancient peoples learned how to create special sounds that became the basis of instrumental music going forward. The world's first musical instruments reflected basic qualities of rhythm and tonality, the two primary features that would continue to define music on down to the present day. Along with rhythm instruments like drums and rattles, early musicians also invented the tradition of wind instruments—the flute, the reed, and the horn. If singing closely related to the history of the human voice, musical instruments involve the story of our amazing human hands, one of our species' most special physical attributes.

Musical instruments added a powerful new component to human culture. They enabled ancient peoples to create soundscapes that came to play a vital role in both public and private life. Musical instruments appear prominently in the history of everything from herd grazing to official assemblies. Originally made from materials readily available in the outdoors, musical instruments created new sounds that both reflected nature and transcended it. Ancient artisans fashioned many of the world's first musical instruments from animal parts or from simple pieces of wood or stone. With time, however, musical instruments made from metals appeared—part of the history of metallurgy. Early metal instruments often used gold, silver, or electrum, later followed by important alloys like bronze, or its cousin brass. Like finely made items still today, the best made musical instruments emphasized beauty, artistic excellence, and elegance. They doubled as works of art as well as functional tools.

The world's first musical instruments tended to make raw sounds, both tonally and rhythmically. Over time, however, musical instruments developed the capacity for more precise intonation, something that musicians take for granted today. Traditions of scales and modes developed that would come to shape musical compositions going forward. There was no real system of musical notation, for all practical purposes. As melody and harmony advanced, musicians usually emphasized a combination of memorization and improvisation.

While rhythm and wind instruments made enormous strides forward in music, perhaps one of the most important innovations in musical instruments was still to come. That was the invention of stringed instruments, notably the harp and the lyre. Stringed instruments would prove especially powerful at complementing the expressive power of human speech, both in terms of singing and poetry. With stringed instruments, musicians could sing and play at the same time, something usually hard or even impossible to do with wind instruments. Stringed instruments thus became important considerations not only in the history of music but also in literature. It is to stringed instruments that we will next direct our attention.

NOTES

1. Edward L. Troxell, "The Thumb of Man," *The Scientific Monthly*, Vol. 43, No. 2 (August 1936), pp. 148–50, pg. 148.
2. Douglas B. Bamforth, "Flintknapping Skill, Communal Hunting, and Paleoindian Projectile Point Typology," *Plains Anthropologist*, Vol. 36, No. 137 (November 1991), pp. 309–22, pg. 309.
3. John Leyland, "Musical Instruments as Works of Art," *The Decorator and Furnisher*, Vol. 12, No. 3 (June 1888), pp. 87–89, pg. 87.
4. Allen J. Scott, *The Cultural Economy of Cities* (London: Sage Publications, 2000), 2.
5. Roy Underhill, *Woodwright's Shop: A Practical Guide to Traditional Woodcraft* (Chapel Hill, NC: The University of North Carolina Press, 1981), pg. 81.
6. George Grant MacCurdy, "Proof of Man's Cultural Evolution," *The Scientific Monthly*, Vol. 21, No. 2 (August 1925), pp. 138–40, pg. 139.
7. Francesco d'Errico et al., "Archaeological Evidence for the Emergence of Language, Symbolism, and Music—An Alternative Multidisciplinary Perspective," *Journal of World Prehistory*, Vol. 17, No. 1 (March 2003), pp. 1–70, pg. 36.
8. Herodotus, *The Histories*, translated by Aubrey de Sélincourt (New York, NY: Penguin Books, 1954), III. 125–40.
9. *Genesis* 4:19–22 (RSV).
10. *Genesis* 4:23–24.
11. J. A. Smith, "The Language of Primitive Man," *The Hebrew Student*, Vol. 2, No. 7 (March 1883), pp. 193–200, pgs. 199–200.
12. Andrew Ford, *Earth Dances: Music in Search of the Primitive* (Collingwood VIC, Australia: Black Inc., 2015), 2.
13. Aristotle, *Poetics*, translated by Anthony Kenny (New York, NY: Oxford University Press, 2013), I. 1. 25–30.
14. Matt Dean, *The Drum: A History* (New York, NY: Scarecrow Press, 2012), 9.
15. Dana Shaham and Anna Belfer-Cohen, "The Natufian Audio-Visual Bone Pendants from Hayonim Cave," in *Not Just for Show: The Archaeology of Beads, Beadwork and Personal Ornaments*, edited by Daniella B. Bar-Yosef Mayer, Clive Bonsall, and Alice M. Choyke (Philadelphia, PA: Oxbow Books, 2017), 97.
16. Nicole Boivin, Adam Brumm, Helen Lewis, Dave Robinson, and Ravi Korisettar, "Sensual, Material, and Technological Understanding: Exploring Prehistoric Soundscapes in South India" *The Journal of the Royal Anthropological Institute*, Vol. 13, No. 2 (June 2007), pp. 267–94, pg. 273.
17. Catherine Fagg, "What Is a Lithophone—And What Is a Rock Gong?," *The Galpin Society Journal*, Vol. 47 (March 1994), pp. 154–55, pg. 154.
18. Marcelle Duchesne-Guillemin, "Music in Ancient Mesopotamia and Egypt," *World Archaeology*, Vol. 12, No. 3, *Archaeology and Musical Instruments* (February 1981), pp. 287–97, pg. 290.
19. Garroway, *Growing Up in Ancient Israel*, 103–4.
20. Daniel Sanchez Muñoz, "The South Face of the Helicon: Ancient Egyptian Musical Elements in Ancient Greek Music," in *Current Research in Egyptology*

2016: Proceedings of the Seventeenth Annual Symposium, edited by Julia Chyla, Joanna Debowska-Ludwin, and Carl Walsh (Philadelphia, PA: Oxbow Books, 2017), pgs. 173–86, pg. 177.

21. *Exodus* 28:34–35.

22. Theodore C. Foote, "The Ephod," *Journal of Biblical Literature*, Vol. 21, No. 1 (1902), pp. 1–47, pg. 34.

23. *Exodus* 39:25. See also C. Houtman, "On the Pomegranates and the Golden Bells of the High Priest's Mantle," *Vetus Testamentum*, Vol. 40, Fasc. 2 (April 1990), pp. 223–29, pg. 223.

24. *II Samuel* 6:5.

25. *I Chronicles* 13:8.

26. *Exodus* 15:20.

27. Duchesne-Guillemin, "Music in Ancient Mesopotamia," 287–97, pgs. 289–90.

28. *II Samuel* 6:5.

29. Ovid R. Sellers, "Musical Instruments of Israel," *The Biblical Archaeologist*, Vol. 4, No. 3 (September 1941), pp. 33–47, 44–45.

30. Anthony Baines, *Brass Instruments: Their History and Development* (New York, NY: Dover Publications, 1993), 37.

31. Gordon Childe, *What Happened in History* (New York, NY: Penguin Books, 1946), 35.

32. Nina Perlove, "Inherited Sound Images: Native American Exoticism in Aaron Copland's Duo for Flute and Piano," *American Music*, Vol. 18, No. 1 (Spring, 2000), pp. 50–77, 55.

33. Richard A. Rogers, *Petroglyphs, Pictographs and Projections: Native American Rock Art in the Contemporary Landscape* (Salt Lake City, UT: The University of Utah Press, 2018), 166.

34. Dale A. Olsen, *World Flutelore: Folktales, Myths and Other Stories of Magical Flute Power* (Chicago, IL: The University of Illinois Press, 2013), xiii.

35. William P. Malm, *Japanese Music and Musical Instruments* (Rutland, Vermont: Charles E. Tuttle Company, 1959), 25.

36. Anthony Baines, *Woodwind Instruments and their History* (New York, NY: Dover Publications, 1991), 181.

37. John Blacking, "Problems of Pitch, Pattern and Harmony in the Ocarina Music of the Venda," *African Music*, Vol. 2, No. 2 (1959), pp. 15–23, 16.

38. Kin-Woon Tong, "Shang Musical Instruments: Part Two," *Asian Music*, Vol. 15, No. 1 (1983), pp. 102–84, pg. 131.

39. Baines, *Woodwind Instruments*, 324.

40. "The Ocarina," *The Scientific American*, Vol. 51, No. 14 (October 4, 1884), p. 216.

41. Theocritus, *Idylls*, VI, 43. See also A. H. Fox Strangways, "The Pipes of Pan," *Music & Letters*, Vol. 10, No. 1 (January 1929), pp. 58–64, pg. 59.

42. "Homeric Hymn to Pan," IXX.

43. Joerg Haeberli, "Twelve Nasca Panpipes: A Study," *Ethnomusicology*, Vol. 23, No. 1 (January 1979), pp. 57–74, 57–58.

44. Lawrence E. Dawson, "Slip Casting: A Ceramic Technique Invented in Ancient Peru," *Ñawpa Pacha: Journal of Andean Archaeology*, Vol. 2 (1964), pp. 107–11, pg. 107.

45. Donald A. Proulx, *A Sourcebook of Nasca Ceramic Iconography: Reading a Culture through its Art* (Iowa City, IA: The University of Iowa Press, 2006), pg. 14.

46. Beth A. Cree, "Hopewell Panpipes: A Recent Discovery in Indiana," *Midcontinental Journal of Archaeology*, Vol. 17, No. 1 (1992), pp. 3–15, pg. 3.

47. A. M. Jones, "Panpipes and the Equiheptatonic Pitch," *African Music*, Vol. 6, No. 1 (1980), pp. 62–69, pg. 62.

48. Edward Ellsworth Hipsher, "Do Animals like Music?," *The Musical Quarterly*, Vol. 12, No. 2 (April 1926), pp. 166–74, pg. 174.

49. Michael Hicks, "Soothing the Savage Beast: A Note on Animals and Music," *The Journal of Aesthetic Education*, Vol. 18, No. 4 (Winter, 1984), pp. 47–55, pg. 47.

50. Harold Courlander, "Notes from an Abyssinian Diary," *The Musical Quarterly*, Vol. 30, No. 3 (July 1944), pp. 345–55, pg. 353.

51. Plato, *The Republic*, translated by Alan Bloom (New York, NY: Basic Books, 1991), III. 399d-3.

52. Plutarch, *Conjugal Precepts*, 1.

53. Herodotus, *History of the Persian Wars*, translated by Aubrey de Sélincourt (New York, NY: Penguin Books, 1954), IV. 2.

54. Stefan Hagel, "Re-evaluating the Pompeii Auloi," *The Journal of Hellenic Studies*, Vol. 128 (2008), pp. 52–71, pg. 52.

55. J. G. Landels, "The Reconstruction of Ancient Greek auloi," *World Archaeology*, Vol. 12, No. 3, *Archaeology and Musical Instruments* (February 1981), pp. 298–302, pg. 299.

56. Plato, *The Republic*, III. 399e.

57. Ovid, *Metamorphoses*, translated by David Raeburn (New York, NY: Penguin Books, 2004), VI. 382–412.

58. Ellen Van Keer, "The Myth of Marsyas in Ancient Greek Art: Musical and Mythological Iconography," *Music in Art*, Vol. 29, No. 1/2, *Music in Art: Iconography as a Source for Music History, Volume I* (Spring–Fall, 2004), pp. 20–37, pg. 20.

59. "The Sound of Arabian Music," *Music Educators Journal*, Vol. 49, No. 5 (April–May 1963), pp. 89–90 + 92, pg. 90.

60. *I Kings* 1:39–40.

61. *Isaiah* 5:12.

62. Ali Jihad Racy, "A Dialectical Perspective on Musical Instruments: The East-Mediterranean Mijwiz," *Ethnomusicology*, Vol. 38, No. 1 (Winter, 1994), pp. 37–57, 38–39.

63. Curt Sachs, *The History of Musical Instruments* (New York, NY: Dover Publications, 1940), 47.

64. Jeremy Montagu, *Horns and Trumpets of the World: An Illustrated Guide* (New York, NY: Rowman and Littlefield, 2014), 15.

65. Jeremy Montagu, "The Conch in Prehistory: Pottery, Stone and Natural," *World Archaeology*, Vol. 12, No. 3, *Archaeology and Musical Instruments* (February 1981), pp. 273–79, pg. 280.

66. Vergil, *The Aeneid*, VI. 162–74.
67. Baines, *Brass Instruments*, 37.
68. *Joshua* 6:4–5.
69. *Judges* 3:21.
70. Malcolm Miller, "Ancient Symbols, Modern Meanings The Use of the Shofar in Twentieth- and Twenty-First-Century Music," in *Qol Tamid: The Shofar in Ritual, History, and Culture*, edited by Jonathan L. Friedmann and Joel Gereboff (Claremont, CA: Claremont Press, 2017), pgs. 165–220, pg. 165.
71. *Numbers* 29:1.
72. *Exodus* 19:16.
73. *Numbers* 10:1–10.
74. Joel 2:1. See also Emma Wasserman, *Apocalypse as Holy War: Divine Politics and Polemics in the Letters of Paul* (New Haven, CT: Yale University Press, 2018), 53.
75. *Hosea* 8:1; See also *Jeremiah* 4:4–5 and 6:1.
76. *Daniel* 3:5–6.
77. *Numbers* 10:3.
78. Percival R. Kirby, "The Trumpets of Tut-Ankh-Amen and Their Successors," *Man*, Vol. 49 (February 1949), p. 19. See also Jerry Montagu, "One of Tutankhamon's Trumpets," *The Galpin Society Journal*, Vol. 29 (May 1976), pp. 115–17, pg. 117.
79. John Wallace and Alexander McGrattan, *The Trumpet* (New Haven, CT: Yale University Press, 2011), 10.
80. Cristina-Georgeta Alexandrescu, "The Iconography of Wind Instruments in Ancient Rome: Cornu, Bucina, Tuba, and Lituus," *Music in Art*, Vol. 32, No. 1/2, *Music in Art: Iconography as a Source for Music History*, Vol. III (Spring–Fall, 2007), pp. 33–46, pg. 39.
81. Cassius Dio I. 31
82. Plutarch, *Mark Antony*, 61. 1. See also G. W. Richardson, "Actium," *The Journal of Roman Studies*, Vol. 27, Part 2 (1937), pp. 153–64, pg. 154.
83. Aeschylus, *The Persians*, 386, as referenced in N. G. L. Hammond, "The Battle of Salamis," *The Journal of Hellenic Studies*, Vol. 76 (1956), pp. 32–54, pg.46.
84. Diogenes Laertius, *Lives of the Eminent Philosophers*, 8. 1, as referenced in Nancy Demand, "Pythagoras, Son of Mnesarchos," *Phronesis*, Vol. 18, No. 2 (1973), pp. 91–96, pg. 91.
85. O. R. Sellers, "Intervals in Egyptian Music," *The American Journal of Semitic Languages and Literatures*, Vol. 41, No. 1 (October 1924), pp. 11–16, pg. 16. See also Herodotus, II. 81. See also Truesdell S. Brown, "The Greek Sense of Time in History as Suggested by Their Accounts of Egypt," *Historia: Zeitschrift für Alte Geschichte*, Bd. 11, H. 3 (July 1962), pp. 257–70, pg. 265.
86. Kyle Gann, *The Arithmetic of Listening: Tuning Theory and History for the Impractical Musician* (Champaign, IL: The University of Illinois Press, 2019), pg. 27.
87. Richard L. Crocker, "Pythagorean Mathematics and Music," *The Journal of Aesthetics and Art Criticism*, Vol. 22, No. 2 (Winter, 1963), pp. 189–98, pg. 189.

88. David Wulstan, "The Earliest Musical Notation," *Music & Letters*, Vol. 52, No. 4 (October 1971), pp. 365–82, pg. 356–56.

89. Mark Gaare, "Alternatives to Traditional Notation," *Music Educators Journal*, Vol. 83, No. 5 (March 1997), pp. 17–23, pg. 17.

90. Curt Sachs, "The Mystery of the Babylonian Notation," *The Musical Quarterly*, Vol. 27, No. 1 (January 1941), pp. 62–69, pg. 63.

91. Dionysios Politis, Dimitrios Margounakis, Spyridon Lazaropoulos, Leontios Papaleontiou, George Botsaris, and Konstantinos Vandikas, "Emulation of Ancient Greek Music Using Sound Synthesis and Historical Notation," *Computer Music Journal*, Vol. 32, No. 4, *Parametric Piano Synthesis* (Winter, 2008), pp. 48–63, pg. 49.

92. R. P. Winnington-Ingram, "Aristoxenus and the Intervals of Greek Music," *The Classical Quarterly*, Vol. 26, No. 3/4 (July–October 1932), pp. 195–208, pg. 195.

93. Aristoxenus, *The Harmonics of Aristoxenus*, edited and with a translated notes by Henry Macran (Oxford, England: Clarendon Press, 1902), 65–70.

94. Plato, *The Republic*, III. 398e. See also Leo Samama, *The Meaning of Music* (Amsterdam: Amsterdam University Press, 2016), pg. 196.

Chapter 3

The Bow of Music

Stringed instruments formed another part of the musical instrument families coming from the ancient world. Stringed instruments typically feature strings pulled tight over a hollow space. Plucking the string produces a sound that the hollow-space echoes and amplifies. The instrument's hollow space would echo and amplify the tones made by the instrument, projecting them out to listeners. Musicians caused the strings to vibrate, usually either by plucking or strumming. The nuances of stringed instruments took acoustic music to a new level of development. Stringed instruments involved different technological knowledge than wind instruments or rhythm instruments. They involved more working parts. The process of making a stringed instrument entailed more steps. All stringed instruments today—from the violin, to the guitar, to the harp or piano—descend from the stringed instruments of the ancient world.

THE RELATIONSHIP BETWEEN ARCHERY AND STRINGED INSTRUMENTS

Stringed instruments reflect the somewhat unlikely pairing of music with warfare—the Bow of Music and the Bow of the Hunt.[1] An ancient Hymn to Apollo has a telling allusion to the way ancient peoples thought of stringed instruments—as the "bow of music." In the Hymn, Apollo equates the bow of music with the bow of hunting. He says, "May the lyre and the curved bow be dear to me," swearing by the powers of both music and the hunt.[2] This is Apollo's linkage of the musical bow and the hunting bow as part of the same innovation. In the poet's eyes, the stringed bow becomes one of the founding technologies of human civilization, on a par with writing or metallurgy.[3] The bow of the hunt provided for people's physical needs—security and nourishment. The bow of music provided for the soul. The bow of music and the bow of the hunt thus represented the dichotomy between the base and the cerebral—between the physical and the spiritual.[4]

The link between the bow of music and the bow of the archer seems especially illustrated in Homer's *Odyssey*. In the famous scene of the "Cleansing of the Hall," Homer includes the famous detail about Odysseus stringing-up his old bow upon his return to Ithaca, ready to cleanse the palace of the suitors harassing his long suffering wife Penelope. Homer compares Odysseus stringing his mighty bow with a musician stringing a lyre—a balance of tension and release. Upon stringing the mighty bow, Odysseus gave the string a pluck. The telltale twang made by the bow meant it was ready for business. Homer says that Odysseus, after "examining the mighty bow carefully—inch by inch, as easily as a skilled musician stretches a sheep-gut string around a lyre's peg and makes it fast," strung the old bow, which none of his competitors could string. Upon stringing the bow, he plucked the string, which "sang like a swallow's song."[5]

THE BOWING EFFECT

Like archery, stringed instruments involve a natural bowing effect. Roman writer Horace describes the lyre as curved.[6] This is because bows involved the subtle art of bending wood, key to creating a springboard effect. The trick was to achieve the bowing effect without weakening or breaking the wood. Pull the string too lax and the bow loses functionality. Conversely, if the string is pulled too tight, it will break the instrument. This bowing effect seems to have fascinated ancient poets and philosophers. Plato (c. 375 BC) saw the tension between the strings and the bow as representing how unity and harmony could come from tension between opposing pressures.[7] The second-century AD Greek writer Plutarch also compared healthy living and healthy minds to the art of finding the right tension in a lyre, or a bow. Just as a harp or bowstring could be either too loose or too tight, so too could *psyches*—the Greek word that meant something like soul or psychology.[8] As in archery, a well-strung lyre required the perfect balance of tension.

Like stringed weapons, stringed instruments appear relatively late. In North America, the bow and arrow appears in the Canadian Artic, sometimes between around 3000 BC and 1500 BC.[9] Excavations in Stellmoor (northern Europe) unearthed slotted arrows dated from around 9000 BC. Similarly, archaeology has discovered prehistoric bows in Denmark dating from around 6000 BC.[10] The use of strings pulled taut to make music comes even later. Stringed instruments' presence in earliest Antiquity seems limited to the Ancient Near East—Mesopotamia, Israel, and Egypt. The oldest surviving stringed instruments come mostly Mesopotamia or Egypt.[11] From there, they later passed on into the worlds of the Bible and the Greeks, becoming some of the most important musical instruments known to history.

LYRES AND HARPS

Ancient history's two main stringed instruments were the lyre and its close-cousin the harp. Lyres and harps are often confused. They share a common stock that can make them hard to differentiate, especially in their earliest guises. The principle difference between a lyre and a harp is that a lyre has a bridge. A harp simply holds the strings tight between two posts. With a lyre, a bridge supports the strings tight over a hollow sounding box, usually wood or some other resonant material. Because an instrument with a bridge could have an acoustical chamber for amplification and ambiance, they created more powerful and varied sounds. With time, the bridge would also make possible a neck for stringed instruments, or even some sort of a fingerboard. Over the centuries, these basic music-making technologies with strings, a sounding box, and a bridge appeared in countless guises and variations, ranging from obscure and unwieldy devices to some of the world's most widely recognized musical instruments.

The term "harp" is an English term, from the Old English *hearpe*. The term "lyre" is a Greek term, passed into later Western languages through Latin. As words, both lyres and harps deeply influenced the English vocabulary. Still today, people talk about "playing the harp," even when they refer to the harmonica, which is a reed instrument and not a harp at all. On a seemingly unrelated note, we still today say someone who nags "harps" on someone. The common noise-making instrument once called a "Jew's Harp"—today often marketed more thoughtfully as a "Mouth Harp" or a Jaw Harp—provides still another example of how the word "harp" has morphed.[12] The term "lyre," with its murky origins, gave us the term "lyric," testimony to the power of stringed instruments to enhance almost exponentially the expressive communicative power of words.

Lyres are closely associated with refinement, with the culture of aesthetes and the learned. The familiar phrase in Latin *"asinus ad lyram*—like an ass to the lyre," juxtaposed the image of one of nature's purportedly most stubborn, base and tone-deaf creatures with one of humankind's most elegant and charming musical devices, an ancient Latin proverb lampooned by the Renaissance humanist Erasmus, among others.[13] In English, a lyre is also a type of little music-holder used in marching bands. Marching-band lyres are

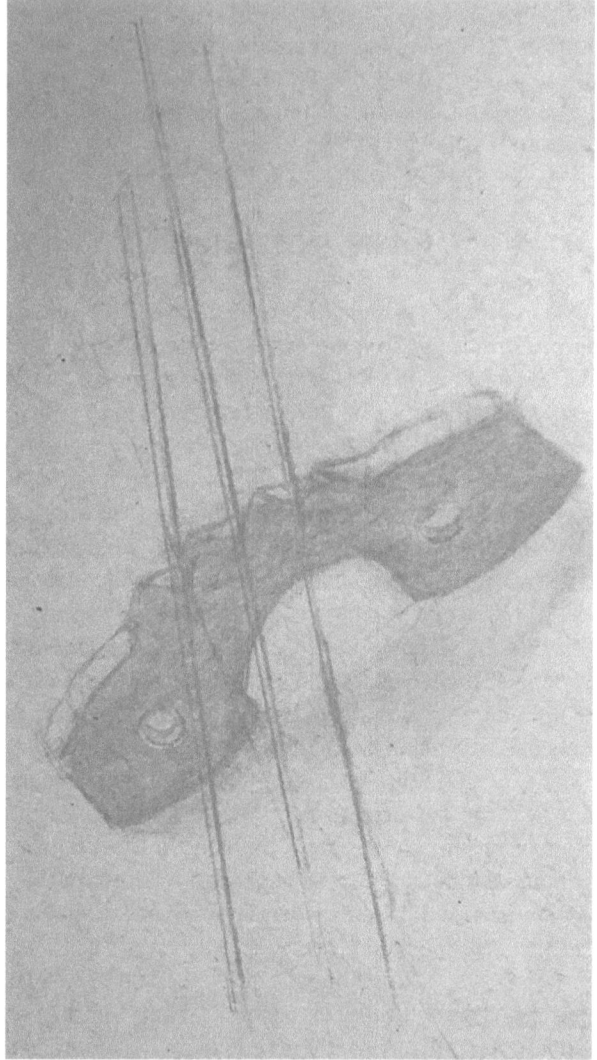

Figure 3.1 The bridge on a stringed instrument, suspending the strings taut.

usually colored silver or gold. The charming little ionic scrolls that grace the traditional marching-band lyre reflect the Classical aesthetic of the lyre. The scrolls remind us how the lyre intersected music and language. The lyre and the scroll decorative combination have also featured close associations in other architectural ornaments, notably wrought-iron fencing.[14]

With its bridge, the lyre had numerous advantages over the harp. Nonetheless, the harp retained its popularity as a relatively simple instrument with distinct charms. For its part, the lyre appears in a smaller geographical area than the harp. Lyres feature prominently in the culture of the Fertile Crescent, that is, the lands in and around the worlds of Mesopotamia, Egypt, and the Bible. The lyre also played a huge role in the Aegean world, where it became a prominent feature of Greek, Classical culture. Instruments like harps have a broader appearance in early times, though still not a universal one. They appear prominently in European history, as well as some areas of Africa and Asia.

EARLY STRINGED INSTRUMENTS

The ancient world featured a dizzying array of stringed instruments with a long list of confusing names. However murky, virtually all represent some type of lyre or harp. Ancient Mesopotamia had its own story of how the lyre came to be. The Sumerian Hymn "Enki's Journey to Nibru" says that the god of water and wisdom, Enki, made the lyre. Sumerian lyres appear in the archaeological record starting around 3000 BC. Sumerian lyres were long at first, over a hundred centimeters in length. Musicians played them from a standing-up position, the lyre held vertically. Later lyres, however, were shorter and played in the more traditional style, cradled in one arm of the player while the other arm reached across the body to pluck the strings.[15] Carvings of lyres found on the walls of the British Museum's Assyrian Palace Reliefs feature rectangular shapes. Many scholars have theorized the rectangular shapes to represent the hollow spaces of sound holes for acoustical amplification.[16]

Lyres or harps also appeared early in Egypt. Something like the Arab oud also appears in ancient Egypt. Its headstock bends back practically at a right angle to produce that distinct nasal sound.[17] Egyptian musicians also enjoyed another instrument called the *nofre*, forerunner of today's mandolins. In general, the Egyptians honored lyre and harp players. They featured them prominently in their art. Wall paintings and statues often depict lute and harp players, usually larger than other members of the servant class. Sometimes their statues are almost life-size.[18] In the famous paintings at the Tomb of Nnkht, topless women playing stringed instruments and dancing appear, an image also found in famous ring-bezels from the El-Armana site in excavations from 1926 to 1932.

Excavations of the tomb of the royal official named Rekhmire (c. 1450 BC) also contained many artifacts of musical interest. Rekhmire's tomb contained harps and lyres, including a long-necked, three-stringed instrument resembling the lute.[19] We sometimes call this "long-neck" lute a *pandura*.[20] Paintings on the walls of Rekhmire's tomb, celebrated for their well-preserved slices of everyday life, also depict music. One painting shows two female musicians, scantily clad. They seem professional.[21] One woman plays a large harp while seated. The other, standing, plays a lute-type instrument. Of particular note is the position of the female harpist. Her hands seem to show delicate fingering of the harp. By the posture of the harpist, as well as the positioning of the hands, one can tell that the woman had acquired the finely honed muscle-memory motor skills required to play a more sophisticated instrument like a harp.[22]

THE MATERIALS USED IN STRINGED INSTRUMENTS

As with other instruments, early harps and lyres often were made of animal parts. The Roman poet Horace (65 BC–AD 8) references an ivory lyre.[23] With stringed instruments, the most prevalent animal part commonly used was the intestinal guts of animals used for strings, an essential material in the days before the existence of nylon or wire. In Asia, where stringed instruments appear as early as the Han Dynasty (220 BC–AD 220), early stringed instruments used silk for strings, another animal product. The Chinese *erhu*, one of the most famous stringed instruments of Asia, used silk strings for many centuries, though today other materials are far more common.[24] The ancient Hebrew instrument called the *nebel*, not that well understood, got its name from the ancient Hebrew term for gut or stomach, perhaps like a pouch, or strings. *I Chronicles* 13:8 features the *nebel*, though nobody can really say what it exactly looked like.

Along with guts for strings, the earliest lyres frequently made use of the tortoise shell. Hollow tortoise shells provided the proper acoustic qualities, shape, and size for a stringed instrument sound chamber. Indeed, in the Greek language, the word for tortoise, *chelys*, served as a synonym for lyre. In similar fashion, we still today use the term "bullhorn" as a synonym for a loudspeaker.[25] Tortoise-shell lyres appear in tombs in both Italy and Greece. Tortoise-shell lyres also have appeared far away from Greece as the Persian Empire. Excavations discovered several tortoise-shell lyres in tombs in Gordion, Phrygia (modern-day Turkey), found in 1951, 1994, 1995, and 1997, respectively. Little holes for drills left in the shells provide evidence of their use as well-crafted musical instruments made from animal parts.[26]

HERMES AND THE SEVEN-STRINGED LYRE

An ancient poem, the Homeric Hymn to Hermes, recounts how Hermes invented the lyre from a tortoise shell.[27] Apollo was so charmed upon hearing Hermes play that he traded some of his cattle for the lyre. Apollo thereupon became the deity most closely associated with the lyre, as well as music and the arts overall.[28] The myth juxtaposes how the Olympian deities of Hermes and Apollo reflected an interplay of competing but ultimately complementary human dynamics—the intellectual brilliance of Apollo versus the energetic inventiveness of Hermes.[29] Still another hymn, The Hymn to Zeus, by the third-century Greek writer Callimachus, also praises Hermes as the lyre's inventor.[30] According to the story, upon his birth in a cave, Hermes found a tortoise. Killing the tortoise, he pulled strings over its shell, thereby inventing the lyre. The same hymn also states that Hermes made the tortoise-lyre with seven strings. This myth gives the origin of the famous seven-string lyre.[31]

The myth of Hermes inventing the lyre shows that by 600 BC (around the time that somebody wrote the Homeric Hymn to Hermes), the "seven-string lyre" had become almost as standard a fixture as today's "six-string guitar." Going forward, most lyres seem to have had seven strings. The seven-string lyre also corresponded to the seven-tone scale popular in ancient music. There were alternative versions of the lyre, however. By the fourth century BC, scholars believe some Greek lyres sometimes had more than seven strings. A fragment of a poem by Ion of Chios (490 BC–420 BC) references an eleven-string lyre.[32] Such instruments seem to have been relatively rare.

FANCY LYRES

Lyres and harps became high-value items in the culture and economy of ancient peoples. Along with fine woods, they often used precious metals and jewels for more exquisite ornamentation. The *Aeneid* depicts a lyre-player named Iopas entertaining guests at the royal place of Dido, Queen of Carthage. Iopas plays a gilded lyre (*cithara aurata*). It might have been painted gold or even had actual gold.[33] Though he might have wrote metaphorically about the beauty of Iopas's music, Vergil might also have been referring to the exquisite and precious nature of Iopas's lyre itself—the way today we might speak of a fine piano or violin. We know that ancient artisans made lyres with charming aesthetics and fine details. Some Minoan lyres featured swan-shaped necks, a mark of the elegant sophistication of the late Bronze Age world of Minoan Crete. Archaeology has also found swan-neck lyres on the Greek mainland dating from the same Bronze Age period.[34] Aside from the graceful beauty of swans, it also seems like swans have a natural association with music and songs.

The large lap lyres called the *phorminx* are probably one of the most substantial and well-constructed lyres from the instrument's formative period. The *phorminx* appears prevalently in the culture of songs and stories around the Aegean world. Specimens of the *phorminx*-style of lyre also found in Knossos from Minoan Crete and in stone friezes from Akhenaten's Egypt, the famous Egyptian pharaoh who ruled around 1350 BC.[35] This is the beautiful instrument played by the bards in Homer's *Iliad* and *Odyssey*.[36] A type of lyre called the *cithara* was also popular, a word related to the modern word "guitar." Compared to *phorominx*, historians usually consider the *"cithara"* as the heavier and more substantial of the two instruments. The *cithara* appears in Homer's *Iliad* where it is called *cytheris*.[37] In Cicero's oration *For Murena* (*Pro Murena*), the Roman lawyer implies that the *cithara* involved more skill than playing the flute.[38] Both the *phorminx* and the *cithara* contrasted with the simpler folk lyres equated with earlier rustic settings, like the old tortoise-shell lyres.

Stringed instruments became closely associated with fine woods. Scientists and technicians studying woods tell us that wood is one of nature's best conductors for sound and vibrations, making it an obvious choice for musical instruments. Because a stringed instrument, in particular, involved finding woods that vibrated sympathetically with the plucking of the strings, luthiers have preferred low-density woods for the soundboards and resonant parts of stringed instruments since ancient times. Piney woods like spruce and cedar have long been associated with stringed instruments, especially soundboard woods that need to resonate.[39]

It can be hard to tell exactly what woods ancient artisans used in making lyres and harps, but they were usually soft, light ones. Traces of the original wood that remained on the famous "Silver Lyre of Ur" is unidentifiable with certitude. Scholars usually see it as a light, conifer wood.[40] Instruments were lightly finished, if at all. Ancient artisans knew of shellac, for example, as early as the Bronze Age. The lacquer of shellac came from the amber excretions of the bug called, in Latin, *laccifer laca*. With this insect being native to India, Indian furniture and other wood items are among the first examples of shellacking woods known to history.[41] One problem is that to analyze these precious existing musical instruments from so long ago would probably require destroying some or all of the original materials. It is clear, though, the artisans lovingly smoothed and polished the wood. They fashioned it to the best of their abilities so that it suited the instrument just right, both functionally and aesthetically.

THE CITHARA AND THE CHELYS

The *cithara* was an instrument ostensibly reserved for virtuosos, compared to the simpler lyres of earlier times, like the tortoise-shell *chelys* lyre. Because Apollo had acquired the lyre from its inventor Hermes, ancient myth closely associated the *cithara* with Apollo. Unlike the impatient Hermes, Apollo had mastered the instrument. In subsequent centuries, the ancient arts frequently depicted the *cithara*, especially on vases and statuary. An ancient

Greek amphora, today housed in the Hearst Collection in New York, depicts a mortal youth playing the *cithara*. The vessel shows that lyre players had entered the upper echelons of Greek cultural life, like wrestlers, or learned philosophers. A notable detail on the amphora is that the youth plays the lyre with a plectrum, visible because it has tassels hanging from it. The tassels dancing along with the time of the music no doubt created a striking decorative effect to watching the *cithara player* at work on his craft.[42]

Artemis also played the lyre, which seems appropriate, given her close association with the bow. Artemis is often more associated with the tortoise *chelys* lyre. The Spartans called Artemis *Chelitis*, usually thought to derive from the word for tortoise.[43] Apollo was also a master of the lyre, in his case the *cithara*. The Greeks developed a special term for those with expertise at playing the lyre, *citharoedus*. The term was especially associated with Apollo. Hesiod also used the word.[44] Pindar (c. 518–438 BC) calls Apollo *Citharoedus*.[45]

TUNING ANCIENT LYRES

How did ancient musicians tune their lyres and harps? An Egyptian girl playing lute in the El-Armana ring-bezel has tassels hanging from the strings of her lute. The tassels probably decorated tuning pegs, a seemingly common feature of the instruments' tuning mechanisms in ancient times.[46] The lyres of Ur evidence tuning levers.[47] Aside from levers or pegs, musicians also probably tuned some ancient stringed instruments with tuning keys. In 1959, excavations of the Dardanos tombs, found in the Dardanelles and containing the royal Dardanos tombs (dating from the sixth century BC to the third century BC) found fragments of a lyre. The end of the lyre holding the strings in place leaves no room for fingers. Musicians could not simply tune such an instrument "by hand." Scholars have surmised that musicians playing these instruments must have used a tuning-key, similar to the devices used today for tuning a piano.[48]

Ancient lyres and harps probably used tuning systems crude by today's standards. Players probably tuned lyres to some sort of an open tuning or a given scale. In the absence of a neck for their instrument, ancient lyre players may have achieved note changes by stopping the strings, creating an artificial fret with their hands.[49] Blocking some strings with the non-picking hand, letting the others ring free, also could affect chordal and interval changes. There was no "standard tuning" familiar to many stringed instrumentalists today. Many players probably developed their own different tunings and ways of playing. Ancient musicians probably most closely resembled the "singer-songwriter" style of player familiar to today's popular music than the formally trained, conservatory musicians coming out of formal music academies and universities. Standard musical forms and approaches were a work in progress.

LYRES AND HARPS IN THE BIBLE

The lyre is perhaps most famous because of its prominent role in the Bible, especially the stories surrounding the ancient King of Israel David. The Bible introduces readers to David in *I Samuel*. One of King Saul's servants recommends that David, at that time an obscure shepherd boy, come to Saul's camp to play soothing nighttime music. David played the lyre called the *kinnor*. *Kinnor*-like instruments appear widely in the art of the Mesopotamian world, as early as 2500 BC. There has been some confusion over the ancient Hebrew term over the centuries. Many translations over the centuries have translated *kinnor* as "harp," like the Spanish *Reina Valera* (*harpa*). The Latin Vulgate uses the term *cithara*, the term related to the modern word guitar. The English-language Catholic Douay Bible translates the passage with the word "harp." David's *kinnor* was probably a relatively portable size, as opposed to the large harps and lyres found in more established domestic settings like royal palaces.[50] Another ancient stringed instrument closely associated with the Bible was the *nebel*, popular throughout the Ancient Near East. As is so often the case, exact descriptions of the *nebel* leave much to the imagination. The Bible references the *nebel* in *I Chronicles* 13: 8 when David celebrates the bringing of the Ark of the Covenant to Jerusalem.[51]

In general, harps and lyres seemed highly valued in the economic or cultural sensibilities of the Bible. *I Chronicles* reports that David hired lyre players, harpists, and cymbalists to accompany the army.[52] King Solomon (c. 950 BC) had 40,000 harps built, part of the imagery of wealth and cultural sophistication that marked his reign. These harps were made of electrum, an alloy of gold and silver.[53] Electrum seems to have enjoyed a special status in music, appearing as a material sometimes in instruments of the highest status. One of the trumpets found in Tutankhamen's tomb also seems made with electrum.[54]

AMPHION AND LINUS

Along with gods who played music, ancient mythology told of numerous wonderful musicians in early ages. Amphion was one of Greek mythology's most famous lyre players. The myth of Amphion relates how the musician played his lyre, the sheer force of his originality creating the fabled walls of

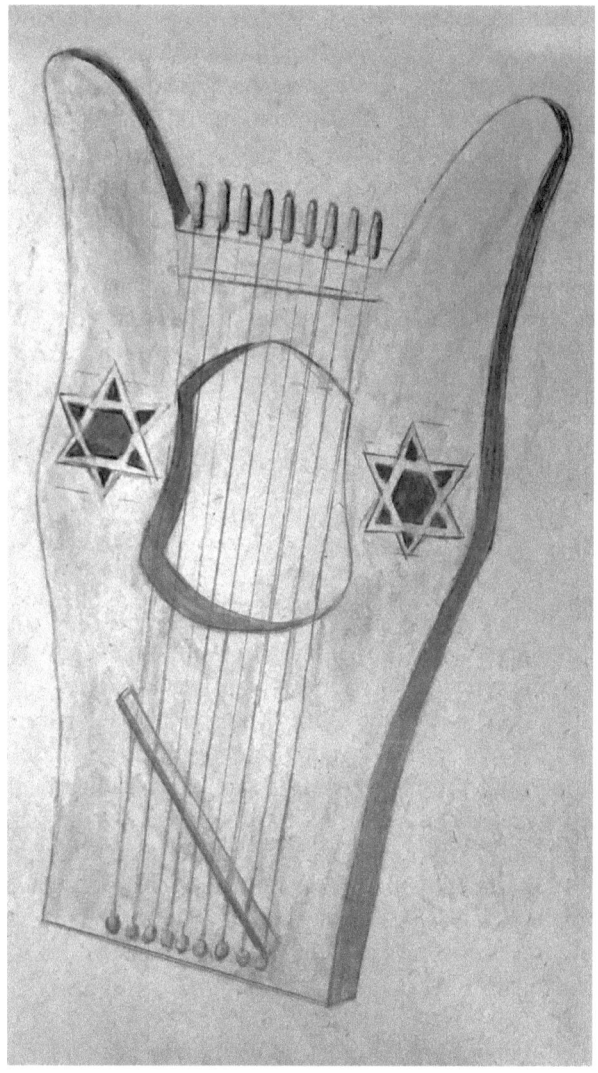

Figure 3.2 Artistic representation of King David's lyre. Note the angle of the bridge in this example. Also, note the tuning pins at the top of the instrument.

Thebes. Amphion was the son of Zeus and Antiope. Supposedly, Amphion and his brother built the walls of Thebes. Following behind his brother, Amphion played the lyre and sang. He made such beautiful music that the rocks followed him, falling into place to build the city's famed fortifications.[55] The second-century AD Greek geographer Pausanias, in his *Description of Greece*, says that Amphion played in the Lydian mode.[56]

Greece's other "founding" musician lyre-player was Linus of Thrace. Ancient writers likened Linus to Orpheus, a figure that united the role of musician, poet, and philosopher. Linus was one of the seminal figures in music, the original language by which all the other forms of expression had evolved.[57] While Linus of Thrace is himself a mythic figure, his name seems to have become almost a synonym for a type of song. In Homer's *Iliad*, the bard depicts the shield of Achilles as depicting a youth singing a "Linus song." Achilles's shield, crafted by none other than Hephaestus himself, depicted two cities— one at war and one at peace. One city reflected bounty and harmonious music, the antitheses of violence and hatred depicted in the other city.[58] Interestingly, Achilles himself played the lyre, somewhat playing against stereotypes of both brutish warriors and softie singers. Homer says that Achilles would serenade his companion Patroclus on the harp.[59] A whole person, Achilles could sing songs about the heroes of old as well as hack away in battle. He was a historian, a singer, and a storyteller, as well as a great fighter.

SAPPHO AND ALCAEUS

Sappho was another of the ancient world's most important musicians, closely associated with the lyre and poetry. Scholars know relatively little about her actual life. She lived on the Greek isle of Lesbos and died around 570 BC. Because of the nature of her love poetry, and where she lived, people equate Sappho with the origin of the term "Lesbian." Plato called her "beautiful," supporting a widespread tradition that depicts Sappho as a woman of exceptional physical beauty.[60] By the time of the Romans, writers already frequently depicted as one of Antiquity's most famous lyre players. Sappho's homeland of Lesbos was especially associated with the instrument. In a debated passage, the Roman poet Horace lauds the muses Euterpe and Polyhymnia with a reference to the "Lesbian Lyre," an apparent tribute to Sappho's legendary skill with the instrument.[61]

Along with Sappho, the poet Alcaeus was another important lyric writer from Lesbos (b. c. 625). Scholars sometimes see a fifth-century vase painting depicting two figures playing the lyre as showing Sappho and Alcaeus.[62] Alcaeus had an influence on Latin poets, especially Horace.[63] Horace admired the ability of Alcaeus to combine warlike prowess and political acumen with an artistic flare for verse. Alcaeus also had a deep knowledge of the ancient myths and a heart for love, physical and spiritual. Both Sappho and Alcaeus employed the style of verse known as "monodic." Monodic means "sung solo."[64] A soloist sang lines of verse, followed by a choral response. This pattern of solo verse and choral response seems prevalent in many settings and styles in the ancient world, including the Bible.

POLYGNOTA OF THEBES

Sappho reflects a reality, sometimes overlooked, that Antiquity featured many fine female musicians and poets. In 1977, Sarah Pomeroy published a groundbreaking article, "*Technikai kai Mousikai*: The Education of Women in the Fourth Century and in the Hellenistic Period." Pomeroy looked at, among other things, women in the ancient arts.[65] One of the most notable details in the essay focused on an inscription lauding a certain woman, Polygnota of Thebes. Polygnota received the sum of 500 drachmas for her lyrical recitations at Delphi. Pomeroy noted that this Polygnota—about whom we wish we knew so much more—indicates that women could achieve respect for their musicianship and artistry.[66]

Polygnota's musical skills contrast with the "flute girls"—*auletrides*—who performed at banquets like those described in Plato's *Symposium*. Flute-girls were diverting entertainers at best, and perhaps even strippers or prostitutes. They apparently played music for feting males, but not as serious musicians. The partying men sent them away before settling into their loftier philosophical discussions.[67] The term "flute girls" even seems to have been a crude double-entendre for a sex act, presumably performed by the servant flautists on the male celebrants.[68] By contrast, women like Polygnota, or Sappho, seem to have attained a more respected level of artistry and excellence.

NERO AND THE LYRE

The Greek musical tradition of the lyre seems to echo in the heritage of Rome, Greece's neighbors to the West. While many of Rome's deities mirrored those of Greece, native Rome itself seemed to have less in the way of lyre-playing mythic heroes and deities like Apollo, Artemis, Sappho, Alcaeus, Orpheus, or others. Still, the tradition of epic versification—a tradition closely associated with the lyre—translated well into Latin. The poet Horace (65 BC–8 BC) wrote verse in the ancient Greek style, a genre closely associated with the lyre. Vergil also wrote epic verse in the lyric tradition and heralded music in his narrations. Of historical lyre players in Rome history, probably the most famous is none other than the emperor Nero. Nero played the lyre, presumably quite well. The instrument commonly associated with Nero was the *cithara*. Virtually all the ancient writers who describe Nero's lyre playing use the term *cithara*.

In AD 66, Nero made a trip to Greece that highlighted his love of the lyre. Nero's entourage included several lyre players. Nero's trip to Greece was a conquest of sorts, except that its weapons were the lyre, the plectra, and the tragedian's mask of the theater.[69] Nero often performed himself when visiting Greek cities. The emperor performed at the city competition in Cassope, which had one of the ancient world's most important theaters.[70] History does not remember favorably all of Nero's dalliances with the lyre, however. When Rome caught fire, Nero supposedly played his lyre and sang about the sacking of Troy while he watched his city burn. He did this, by tradition, from the Tower of Macenas. The image of Nero playing the lyre as he watched Rome burning gave rise to the popular image of "fiddling while Rome burns," though the fiddle would not be invented for another thousand years.[71]

By the time of Nero, lyre playing seemed to have enjoyed something of a status as a viable profession. Rome at the very least there seems to have had good musicians around, able to perform at a high level. Ancient sources depict a class of musicians who feel remarkably modern—practicing, teaching, and performing. Lyre players earned money by giving lessons. Nero himself took lessons from a lyre-player named Terpnus. Terpnus's instruction to Nero involved traditional lyre exercises to train the fingers.[72] Nero also learned exercises and practices designed to strengthen singing skills. Some of these involved various instructions like lying on one's back with weights on the chest to strengthen the lungs, and avoiding certain foods, including fruits. Traditional Roman folk medicine viewed certain foods as bad for the voice, notably the fig.[73] Lyre players received ample rewards. Emperor Vespasian (r. 69–79) paid the lyre players Terpnus and Diodorus 200,000 *secestres* each for their performances, probably a good amount of money.[74] The Roman emperor Titus (r. AD 79–81) also played the lyre, quite skillfully according to ancient accounts. Titus was admirable—not only a superb physical specimen of sound mind and body but also a man known for his verbal eloquence, overall appreciation of music, and his fine singing voice.[75]

STRINGED INSTRUMENTS BEYOND THE WESTERN WORLD

Lyres or other early forms of stringed instruments seem less a "worldwide" phenomenon than some other ancient musical instruments like drums or flutes, which truly do seem to have a global presence across time. The developed tribes of pre-Columbian America mostly seem to have had no stringed instruments, though they did nurture a rich love of music and musical instruments, notably a ceramic flute widely admired for its artistic and musical properties, both.[76] Though its use was limited, some pre-Columbian American societies apparently did understand the properties of making music with strings pulled tight, with a bow-like stringed instrument known as the *quijongo* being the most prevalent example of a stringed instrument in the Americas before the arrival of Columbus in 1492.[77] The use of this instrument, and its scarce prevalence in geographic terms, has been the subject of debate among scholars. Upon contact with Europeans, many indigenous peoples in South America or Central America adopted the harp. The Yoreme tribe in Mexico, for example, adopted the harp so extensively that it virtually became part of their indigenous culture.[78]

Lyres also appeared early in Asia. Ancient China understood the principles of making music with stringed instruments. Their folk instrument called the *guzheng* appeared in many areas of Western China as early as the Han Dynasty period (206 BC–AD 220). Some ancient Chinese writers seem to disparage the *guzheng*, making it seem like an instrument more associated with the lower-classes, despite the long record of literature, poetry, and tune-making associated with the instrument.[79] Another ancient Chinese stringed instrument called the *Se* was plucked like a zither. Chinese poetry going back to as early as the seventh century BC makes many references to the *Se*. As was the case in the West, stringed instrument in Asia became closely associated with literature and poetry, no doubt, again, because of their unique ability to harmonize the music of the voice with the music of the hands. The wide variety of topics raised in conjunction with references to the *se* includes love, politics, and nature.[80]

Japan probably borrowed its traditional type of lute called the *biwa* from China by the eighth century. The *biwa* is closely associated with Buddhist prayers as well as a tradition of blind musicians.[81] Scholars think the *biwa* a variant of the *pipa*, another lyre-type stringed instrument imported into east Asian lands like Korea from Western China during the Han Dynasty period, still more testimony to the important cultural heyday that the Han Emperors represented in the history of China. Though it evolved considerably over the centuries, the *pipa* seems to have usually consisted of silk strings, as well as, notably, a neck with a fretted fingerboard.[82] The aesthetic, ethereal charms of the stringed instruments of Asia became closely associated with the cultures of the east, something like the way that haunting flutes became associated with Native American cultures or the nasal, hypnotic beauty of Arab and Persian oud stringed instruments became associated with the cultures of the Islamic World. Like gongs, the singular, jangling string sounds of Asian stringed instruments became a common feature of the "orientalism" that prevailed in some of the Western arts, and Hollywood. Such images owed much to the imperialism of the nineteenth century. The distinctions between the different musical traditions of places like Thailand, Japan, Korea, or China were often lost on Western ears, who simply seemed to hear the music as an exotic affectation. Actually, one of the places that became closely associated with Asian music in the Western mind was the Chinese Restaurant, where people gained exposure to Asian music with stringed instruments as a background to their multicultural dining experience.[83]

THE BOW OF MUSIC: FINAL REFLECTIONS ON STRINGED INSTRUMENTS IN HISTORY

However unlikely the pairing might seem, stringed instruments closely relate to the technology of the bow and arrow. The "bow of music" borrowed from archery the principle of pulling a string to just the right tension, creating the bowing effect that could either spring an arrow into flight or sound a note when plucked. Like archery, stringed instruments come somewhat later to history, and in a smaller range of geographical areas. Stringed instruments involved more working parts and subtler principles of craftwork, usually the by-products of more complex societies. Some of the most precious artifacts remaining from Antiquity are stringed instruments. Their presence in any given culture invariably reflects a people who had excellent artisanal skills, and who placed a high value on creative expression.

Antiquity's two main stringed instruments—the harp and the lyre—so closely relate to each other as to seem almost indistinguishable. The critical difference was that the lyre featured a "bridge" to support the strings over the main body of the instrument. The bridge would later pave the way for all sorts of sophisticated stringed instruments—everything from guitars and violins, to pianos. Just as today, many people would find confusing the plethora of different labels we assign to guitars—parlor guitars, classical guitars, dreadnaught guitars, and everything else in-between—the ancient world's stringed instruments featured a dizzying array of idiosyncratic variations. All shared the basic mechanism of strings pulled to just the right tension. Along with lyres and harps, some ancient stringed instruments also seem to have resembled present-day auto-harps or dulcimers.

There is no one single "most important" musical instrument. All have made enormous contributions, each distinct and wonderful in its own way. That said, it seems like stringed instruments occupy a special place in history. Because they could accompany the voice, stringed instruments played a formative role in religious expression, as well as the development of literature and poetry. By modern standards, ancient musicians faced limitations because their instruments lacked the fuller tonal possibilities ours usually have. But they made do. Stringed instruments make sounds with a haunting beauty, something that still speaks to us today, all these centuries later. The beauty and balance they represented inspired everyone from poets, to philosophers, to seekers of divine revelation. Even now, lyres and harps are associated with elegance and decorum. They feature prominently in everything from formal weddings and orchestras to fine décor.

NOTES

1. Percival R. Kirby, *The Musical Instruments of the Indigenous People of South Africa* (Johannesburg: Wits University Press, 2013), pg. 260.

2. *Homeric Hymns*, Hymn to Apollo, 135, translated by Jules Cashford (New York, NY: Penguin Books, 2003), pg. 34.

3. James B. Harrod, "The Bow: A Techno-Mythic Hermeneutic: Ancient Greece and the Mesolithic," *Journal of the American Academy of Religion*, Vol. 49, No. 3 (September 1981), pp. 425–46, pg. 432.

4. Seth Benardete, *The Bow and the Lyre: A Platonic Reading of the Odyssey* (Lanham, MD: Rowman and Littlefield, 1997), pg. 126.

5. Homer, *The Odyssey*, translated by Emily Wilson (New York, NY: W.W. Norton and Company, 2017), XXI. 404–12. See also Harrod, "The Bow," 425–46, pg. 431.

6. Horace, *Odes*, XV.

7. Plato, *Symposium*, 187.

8. Plutarch, *On the Contentedness of Mind*, XV.

9. Steve A. Tomka, "The Adoption of the Bow and Arrow: A Model Based on Experimental Performance Characteristics," *American Antiquity*, Vol. 78, No. 3 (July, 2013), pp. 553–69, pg. 553.

10. Charles E. Grayson, Mary French, and Michael J. O'Brien, *Traditional Archery from Six Continents: The Charles E. Grayson Collection* (Columbia, MO: The University of Missouri Press, 2007), 2.

11. Bo Lawergren, "Distinctions among Canaanite, Philistine, and Israelite Lyres, and Their Global Lyrical Contexts," *Bulletin of the American Schools of Oriental Research*, Vol. 309 (February 1998), pp. 41–68, pg. 41.

12. Harold Steafel, "Jew's Harp," *The Galpin Society Journal*, Vol. 29 (May 1976), pp. 122–23, pg. 122.

13. Desiderius Erasmus, Adages, in *Collected Works of Erasmus*, Vols. 31–36 (Toronto, Buffalo, and London: University of Toronto Press, 1982–2006), Vol. 31, pgs. 288–89, as referenced in Walter S. Gibson, "Asinus Ad Lyram: From Boethius to Bruegel and Beyond," *Simiolus: Netherlands Quarterly for the History of Art*, Vol. 33, No. 1/2, *Nine Offerings for Jan Piet Filedt Kok* (2007/2008), pp. 33–42, pg. 35–36, especially ff. #14.

14. Robert L. Alexander, "Neoclassical Wrought Iron in Baltimore," *Winterthur Portfolio*, Vol. 18, No. 2/3 (Summer–Autumn, 1983), pp. 147–86, pgs. 167–68.

15. Sachs, *The History of Musical Instruments*, 78.

16. Bo Laweregren and O. R. Gurney, "Sound Holes and Geometrical Figures: Clues to the Terminology of Ancient Mesopotamian Harps," *Iraq*, Vol. 49 (1987), pgs. 37–52, pg. 37.

17. Sarah S. Frishmuth, "Stringed Instruments," *Bulletin of the Pennsylvania Museum*, Vol. 3, No. 11 (July 1905), pp. 45–48, pg. 45.

18. J. Leibovitch, "The Statuette of an Egyptian Harper and String-Instruments in Egyptian Statuary," *The Journal of Egyptian Archaeology*, Vol. 46 (December 1960), pp. 53–59, pg.53.

19. Jeffrey Pulver, "The Music of Ancient Egypt," *Proceedings of the Musical Association 48th Sess.* (1921–1922), pp. 29–55, pg. 31.

20. Ephraim Segerman, "A Short History of the Cittern," *The Galpin Society Journal*, Vol. 52 (April 1999), pp. 77–107, pg. 78.

21. Kathryn A. Bard, editor, *Encyclopedia of the Archaeology of Ancient Egypt* (London: Routledge, 1995), pg. 547.

22. Dorothea Arnold, "Ancient Egyptian Art: Image and Response," in *Amilla: The Quest for Excellence. Studies Presented to Guenter Kopcke in Celebration of His 75th Birthday*, edited by Robert B. Koehl (Philadelphia, PA: INSTAP Academic Press, 2013), pgs. 3–16, pg. 10. See also. Amélineau, "Un Tombeau Égyptien," *Revue de l'histoire des religions*, Vol. 23 (1891), pp. 137–173, pg. 149.

23. Horace, *Odes*, 2. 11.

24. Colin Huehns, "The 'Early Music' Erhu," *The Galpin Society Journal*, Vol. 54 (May 2001), pp. 56–61, pg. 60.

25. E. K. Borthwick, "The Riddle of the Tortoise and the Lyre," *Music & Letters*, Vol. 51, No. 4 (October 1970), pp. 373–87, pg. 373.

26. Samuel Holzman, "Tortoise-Shell Lyres from Phrygian Gordion," *American Journal of Archaeology*, Vol. 120, No. 4 (October 2016), pp. 537–64, pg. 538.

27. *The Homeric Hymns*, "Hymn to Hermes," IV. 17–20.

28. *The Homeric Hymns*, "Hymn to Hermes," IV. 490–95.

29. See also Christopher Bungard, "Reconsidering Zeus' Order: The Reconciliation of Apollo and Hermes," *The Classical World*, Vol. 105, No. 4 (Summer, 2012), pp. 443–69, pg. 443.

30. In "Hymn to Zeus" in *Callimachus: The Poems*, edited with an introduction, translation and commentary by Susan A. Stephens (New York, NY: Oxford University Press, 2015), 49.

31. *The Homeric Hymns*, "Hymn to Hermes," IV. 50.

32. Martha Maas, "Polychordia and the Fourth-Century Greek Lyre," *The Journal of Musicology*, Vol. 10, No. 1 (Winter, 1992), pp. 74–88, pg. 76.

33. Vergil, *The Aeneid*, I. 740–46.

34. Leopold Vorreiter, "The Swan-Neck Lyres of Minoan-Mycenean Culture," *The Galpin Society Journal*, Vol. 28 (April 1975), pp. 93–97, pgs. 97–98.

35. Rodney Castleden, *Myceneans* (New York, NY: Routledge, 2005), 138.

36. Susan Sherratt, "Homeric Epic and Contexts of Bardic Creation," in *Archaeology and Homeric Epic*, edited by Susan Sherratt and John Bennet (Philadelphia, PA: Oxbow Books, 2017), pp. 35–53, pg. 41.

37. Homer, *Iliad*, XV. 432. See also Mary Francis Gyles, "Nero Fiddled while Rome Burned," *The Classical Journal*, Vol. 42, No. 4 (January 1947), pp. 211–17, pg. 212.

38. Cicero, *Pro Murena*, 29. See also John T. Ramsey, "Cicero Pro Murena 29: The Orator as Citharoedus. The Versatile Artist," *Classical Philology*, Vol. 79, No. 3 (July 1984), pp. 220–25, pg. 221.

39. Ulrike G. K. Wegst, "Wood for Sound," *American Journal of Botany*, Vol. 93, No. 10 (October 2006), pp. 1439–48, pg. 1445.

40. R. D. Barnett, "New Facts about Musical Instruments from Ur," *Iraq*, Vol. 31, No. 2 (Autumn, 1969), pp. 96–103, pg. 98.

41. A. J. Gibson, "The Story of Lac," *Journal of the Royal Society of Arts*, Vol. 90, No. 4611 (April 17, 1942), pp. 319–35, pg. 320.

42. J. D. Beazley, "Citharoedus," *The Journal of Hellenic Studies*, Vol. 42, Part 1 (1922), pp. 70–98, pg. 70.

43. Clement of Alexandria, *Protrepticus*, II. 33. See also the discussion of this passage in Elinor Bevan, "Ancient Deities and Tortoise-Representations in Sanctuaries," *The Annual of the British School at Athens*, Vol. 83 (1988), pp. 1–6, pg. 2.

44. Hesiod, *Theogony*, 94.

45. Pindar, IV. 313. See also Matthias Klinghardt, "Prayer Formularies for Public Recitation. Their Use and Function in Ancient Religion," *Numen*, Vol. 46, No. 1 (1999), pp. 1–52, pg. 30.

46. Kate Bosse-Griffiths, "Two Lute-Players of the Amarna Era," *The Journal of Egyptian Archaeology*, Vol. 66 (1980), pp. 70–82, pg. 70.

47. Barnett, "New Facts about Musical Instruments," 96–103, pg. 97.

48. Maurice Byrne, "The Dardanos Fragments and the 40° Angular Lyre," *The Galpin Society Journal*, Vol. 46 (March 1993), pp. 3–25, pg. 6.

49. R. P. Winnington-Ingram, *The Classical Quarterly*, Vol. 6, No. 3/4 (July–October 1956), pp. 169–186, pg. 169.

50. Nahman Avigad, "The King's Daughter and the Lyre," *Israel Exploration Journal*, Vol. 28, No. 3 (1978), pp. 146–51, pg. 149.

51. *I Chronicles* 13:8.

52. *I Chronicles* 25:1.

53. Josephus, *Antiquities*, VIII. 1. 8.

54. Jeremy Montagu, "One of Tut'ankhamūn's Trumpets," *The Journal of Egyptian Archaeology*, Vol. 64 (1978), pp. 133–34, pg. 133.

55. Apollonius of Rhodes, *Argonautica*, as cited in Alexander H. Krappe, "The Legend of Amphion," *The Classical Journal*, Vol. 21, No. 1 (October 1925), pp. 21–28, pg. 28.

56. Pausanias, *Description of Greece*, translated by W. H. S. Jones (Delphi Classics, OnLine edition, 2014), IX. 5. 7.

57. Quintilian, *The Orator's Education*, translated by Donald A. Russell (Cambridge, MA: Harvard University Press, 2002), 1. 10.

58. Homer, *The Iliad*, XVIII. 569–71. See also Susan A. Stephens, "Linus Song," *Hermathena*, Vol. 173/174, *Studies in Hellenistic Poetry* (Winter 2002 and Summer 2003), pp. 13–28, pg. 13.

59. Homer, *The Iliad*, IX. 182–86. See also Andrew Ford, *Homer: The Poetry of the Past* (Ithaca, NY: Cornell University Press, 1992), pg. 16.

60. Plato, *Phaedrus*, 235a. See also Maarit Kivilo, *Early Greek Poets' Lives: The Shaping of the Tradition* (Boston, MA: EJ Brill, 2010), pg. 173.

61. Horace, *Odes* I. 1, translated by David West (New York, NY: Oxford University Press, 1997). See also R. O. A. M. Lyne, "Horace Odes Book 1 and the Alexandrian Edition of Alcaeus," *The Classical Quarterly, New Series*, Vol. 55, No. 2 (December 2005), pp. 542–58, pg. 542–43.

62. John Boardman, *Athenian Black Figure Vases: The Archaic Period* (London: Thames and Hudson, 1975), 136.

63. Horace, *Odes*, I. 32.5.

64. John G. Landels, *Music in Ancient Greece and Rome* (New York, NY: Routledge, 1999), 11.

65. Sarah Pomeroy, "Technikai kai Mousikai: The Education of Women in the Fourth Century and in the Hellenistic Period," as referenced in Roger Harmon, "Plato, Aristotle, and Women Musicians," *Music & Letters*, Vol. 86, No. 3 (August 2005), pp. 351–56, pg. 351.

66. Plato, *The Republic*, 455.e, as referenced in Sarah Pomeroy, "Plato and the Female Physician (Republic 454d2)," *The American Journal of Philology*, Vol. 99, No. 4 (Winter, 1978), pp. 496–500, pg. 500.

67. Plato, *The Symposium*, translated by Christopher Gill (New York, NY: Penguin Books, 1999), 176e.

68. Plato, *Symposium*, 176; see also Plato, *Symposium*, 215, and Aristophanes, *The Wasps*, 1346 and *The Frogs*, line 503. See also John R. Porter, "Aristophanes," *Acharnians*. 1118–21 151, in Greece & Rome, Vol. 51, No. 1 (April 2004), pp. 21–33, pg. 27 and Marina Fischer, "Ancient Greek Prostitutes and the Textile Industry in Attic Vase-Painting ca. 550–450 B.C.E," *The Classical World*, Vol. 106, No. 2 (Winter, 2013), pp. 219–59, pg. 235.

69. Cassius Dio, 63. 8. 4. See also K. R. Bradley, "Nero's Retinue in Greece, A.D. 66/67," *Illinois Classical Studies*, Vol. 4 (1979), pp. 152–57, pg. 152.

70. Suetonius, *Nero*, 22.

71. Suetonius, *Nero*, 38.

72. Suetonius, *Nero*, 20.

73. Pliny the Elder, *Natural History*, translated by W. H. S. Jones (Cambridge, MA: Harvard University Press, 1951), 23, 120–21. See also Mary Francis Gyles, "Nero: Qualis Artifex?," *The Classical Journal*, Vol. 57, No. 5 (February 1962), pp. 193–200, pg. 194.

74. Suetonius, *Vespasian*, 19. See also G. Kenneth, "Roman Actors," *Studies in Philology*, Vol. 16, No. 4 (October 1919), pp. 334–82, pg. 373.

75. Suetonius, *Titus*, 3. See also E. Beulé, "Études Et Portraits Du Siècle D'auguste: VI. Le Véritable Titus," *Revue des Deux Mondes* (1829–1971), Seconde Période, Vol. 84, No. 3 (1er Décembre 1869), pp. 674–708, pg. 677.

76. Michael E. Smith, *The Aztecs* (Chichester, West Sussex: Wiley and Sons, 2012), 275.

77. M. H. Saville, "The Musical Bow in Ancient Mexico," *American Anthropologist*, Vol. 11, No. 9 (September 1898), pp. 280–84, pg. 280.

78. Helena Simonett, "Envisioned, Ensounded, Enacted: Sacred Ecology and Indigenous Musical Experience in Yoreme Ceremonies of Northwest Mexico," *Ethnomusicology*, Vol. 58, No. 1 (Winter, 2014), pp. 110–32, pg. 112.

79. Cao Zheng and Yohana Knobloch, "A Discussion of the History of the Gu zheng," *Asian Music*, Vol. 14, No. 2, *Chinese Music History* (1983), pp. 1–16, pg. 4.

80. *The Culture of China*, edited by Kathleen Kuiper (New York, NY: Rosen Educational Publishing, 2011), pg. 236.

81. David W. Hughes, "*Japon: L'épopée des Heike (Junko Ueda: satsuma-biwa)*," a review in *British Journal of Ethnomusicology*, Vol. 1 (1992), pp. 161–62, pg. 161.

82. Bang-Song Song, "The Korean Pip'a and Its Notation," *Ethnomusicology*, Vol. 17, No. 3 (September 1973), pp. 460–93, pg. 462.

83. Terry Miller, "Appropriating the Exotic: Thai Music and the Adoption of Chinese Elements," *Asian Music*, Vol. 41, No. 2 (Summer/Fall, 2010), pp. 113–48, pg. 117.

Chapter 4

Music and Storytelling

In this chapter, we will look at how ancient music developed as a vehicle for storytelling and literature. Music has a critical relationship with storytelling. Still today, we use music to enhance stories—whether outright operas and musicals or simply the critical role of musical soundtracks in any given film. Even so, we can too easily overlook music's essential role in storytelling. Storytelling involves much more than simply "Once upon a time." Our memories are stories. History is a story. All humans have their own personal stories. All groups have stories. The impulse to tell our stories—to transmit them from one generation to the next—is a powerful human impulse, almost like the drive for sex or love. We have a compelling drive to express ourselves, to share our stories. When we relate our ideas and experiences, we invariably tell some form of story. Providing context and depth involves storytelling. We use storytelling to express our feelings. In this sense, all literature that expresses human feelings and responses comes from the storytelling impulse.

In the history of storytelling, music played a critical role. To understand this critical relationship between music and storytelling, we must first consider some of the Ancient World's important ideas about speech and language. In earliest human history, there were no books. There was no literature. The word "literature" explicitly refers to a written text, coming from the Latin *legere*, meaning "to read." The word passed into the Romance languages as in the French *lire*, with its conjugated form of *lit*, or the Spanish *leer*. Literature, however, came to history much later than stories, music, or language itself. In a world before literature, both poets and singers expressed themselves orally, without a written text.[1] Above all, an innate desire to communicate expressively helped drive both music and storytelling.

RHETORIC AND POETRY

As it involved speaking, storytelling helped foster the tradition of eloquence, a truly ancient art form. The Ancient Greeks called eloquence "rhetoric." The word "rhetoric" comes from the Greek *rheo*, which means to "flow." We still have this sense of flowing speech, as in our word "fluent." Scholars also sometimes define "rhetoric" as the "art of persuasion." The ability to persuade people is one of the most critical skills any leader can possess. This skill involves language, among other things. To persuade others, leaders learned to beautify their speech. They mastered the art of eloquence—rhetoric, however defined. Just as a sculptor sought to turn a cold stone into something beautiful, so, too, rhetoricians created artistic beauty with raw words. After all, most of the great teachers have been speakers, not necessarily writers—Socrates, Christ, and the Buddha, among many others.[2]

Because rhetoric was the art of pleasing people's ears with the beauty of language, poetry was an especially significant form of rhetoric. After all, unattractive speech is unlikely to persuade many people. The word "poet" comes from the Greek "*poiein*, to make." In Greek, the word "poet"—*poiētēs*—literally meant "a maker." *Merriam Webster's Collegiate Dictionary* defines a poet as a "maker of verse." This idea of a poet as a "maker" contrasted that of a theoretician, from the word "*theoros*," meaning "observer." We get our English word "theater" from this word *theoros/theoroi*. Unlike the observers in the audience, a poet takes the stage. The poet does something. The poet makes something. A *poiētēs* takes the risk of creating something new and tangible, putting it out there. The chorus in a Greek play—the observers that seemed to see everything and know everything—were like *theoroi*. They stood in the wings, watching. During critical moments, they entered the action to make their knowing insights. It seems like the satyrs in Ancient Greek Satyr Plays, with their satiric commentaries and bawdry send-ups, were also like *theoroi*.[3] They were more like meta-narrators.

MUSIC AND POETRY

Music was a sister art of rhetoric. It played a critical role in the disseminating of words and literature. In fact, very early music and poetry were really two sides of the same coin. Upon reflection, poetry has musical qualities like pitch, dynamics, and rhythm. Artists create both music and poetry for listening. Both music and poetry also preceded writing by thousands of years. In those misty early earliest periods, music and poetry were practically the same thing. Today, we are so used to the familiarities of both language and music that we have trouble imagining how ancient people must have experienced music and poetry. Those of us living in the twenty-first century can never un-hear all the pleasing harmonic structures, rhythms, and melodic conventions that surround us daily, the finely honed products of thousands of years of musical evolution. Similarly, we can never unlearn our own languages. Today, when we hear music or poetry, we almost automatically categorize them according to these deeply embedded acculturations. If we could go back in time, however, we would find a much blurrier line separating poetry and music. They truly share a common stock.

Figure 4.1 The poet and his lyre.

Long ago, the ancient people discovered the awesome power of music to enhance language. In English, we commonly call the words set to music "lyrics" because of their ancient association with the lyre. Lyrics, however, are much more than simply words to songs. Lyrics are one of history's most important types of literature. From hymns to classic rock anthems to popular songs, music has provided one of history's most effective vehicles for sharing the awesome power of words. Ideas, feelings, stories, colorful characters, and issues all have found some of their most eloquent and effective forms of expression in words set to music. Music thus played a critical role in the development of literature and writing. The timeless stories that have survived from so long ago owe a great debt to music.

THE EPIC

Along with rhetoric and poetry, the storytelling tradition closely relates to the development of the "epic." Epic is one of the world's most important storytelling traditions. Contrary to the way we sometimes use the term today, the term "epic" does not simply mean a long, written narrative with grandiose themes. In a classic epic, a narrator speaks. The term "epic" comes from the Greek word *epein*, which means "to say." Musical settings played a critical role in the early development of epic. Epic storytellers traditionally accompanied their tales with the lyre. They recited their stories in poetic verse. Epics often chronicled heroic feats, like in Homer, or taught lessons, like the Greek writer Hesiod (c. 700 BC).[4] After long centuries of honing, ancient people thankfully wrote-down some of the most popular epics for posterity and greater dissemination. The act of writing these epics into fixed literary form no doubt changed such works in significant ways, turning them into literature. What had once been amorphous tales—often sung—became canonical texts.

Because it involved poetry, ancient epic verse often functioned as a type of music. Telling an epic tale involved an acquired skill—just as today pianists must develop their talents through countless hours of painstaking practice. In *Listening to Homer: Tradition, Narrative and Audience*, Ruth Scodel says that ancient poets blended memorized verse with improvisation. Such mastery reflected long-hours of preparation. Yet each performance also involved spontaneity. Poets added elements to the plot on the fly.[5] Good poets could thus take an acquired skill to the next level by being in the moment. Like all good performers, they would feed off the energy of their audience. Poet storytellers responded to the setting, just as good musicians do.

THE EPIC OF GILGAMESH

Probably the earliest extant epic is the Mesopotamian *Epic of Gilgamesh*. Our scanty knowledge of how the Gilgamesh text got into its present form reminds us of how complex and diverse the sources for such epic works can be. Like the epic verses told by Greeks centuries later, stories of Gilgamesh originally came from a world of recited tales, meant to be heard, not just read. Unfortunately, the Gilgamesh epic is too old to know many details about its composition.[6] Nonetheless, *Gilgamesh*'s epic qualities and storytelling prowess seem hard to deny, even when read in translation. It is one of history's first important works of poetry.

Gilgamesh first appeared in writing around 2100 BC. Scribes wrote this early Gilgamesh in the Sumerian language, the tongue of the southernmost (and most ancient) part of Mesopotamia. Around 1600 BC a second iteration of the epic appeared, this time in Akkadian, the language of the "Old Babylonians." A third version of Gilgamesh appeared around 600 BC. Scholars often call this third version of Gilgamesh "SB," for the "Standard Babylonian" version of the tale. (We sometimes call the Old Babylonian version "OB.") Scholars would naturally look to the OB as an invaluable resource, just because of the fact that it is older, if nothing else. Scholars usually consider the SB version a more developed poem. It has longer poetic passages, including repeated phrasings. The SB version of Gilgamesh seems to reflect a very self-conscious attempt at the use of poetic language, the hallmark of an advanced literary culture, and a sense of musicality.[7]

THE EPIC HERO

Because of the huge influence of Homer's war-centered stories, the epic came to be almost exclusively associated with heroic valor. Such valor typically offered a model of manhood that valued action over reflection. For the famous English Classical scholar C. M. Bowra, a heroic poem—that is, an "epic"—concerns "any action on which a man stakes his life on his ideal of what ought to be."[8] In the sixth and seventh centuries BC, writers like Hesiod viewed the epic heroes as superior beings. Honor supposedly motivated such figures, not base priorities like money or position. They were also people of action. Bowra also distinguished between "authentic epics," performed orally, and "literary epics," offered in written form. He argued that "authentic epic" reflected the storytelling modes of nomadic or tribal societies with little writing, if any.[9]

Without a doubt, the most important epic-writer in Western literature was Homer. Homer's writing is so important that scholars also often credit him with singlehandedly creating the seminal dramatic categories of tragedy and comedy. *The Iliad*, with its emphasis on the consequences of human wrath, is a terrible tragedy. The *Odyssey*, with its overall happy ending and homecoming story, is a comedy.[10] Heroic epics also played an important role in the Germanic and Celtic epics of northern Europe. There is also a strong heroic epic tradition in India that roughly dates to around the time of the Greek epic writers.[11]

MIMETIC POETRY

How did ancient people preserve their epic narratives over the long centuries in which little writing existed, if any? In a world with little writing, memorization would obviously play a key role. Preserving stories in such a world required heavy memorization. Music thus played a vital role in how ancient people handed-down such tales. For one thing, music provided a powerful aid to memory. In Plato's *Republic*, stories sung to music played an important role in the childhood education received by the "guardians," the elite class bred to rule Plato's ideal state.[12] This type of education often emphasized "mimetic poetry." The word "mimetic" comes from the same root as the word "mime," meaning to imitate or repeat.

With a mimetic pedagogical approach, children would recite poems taught to them by their elders. Mimetic poetry drilled its cadences and lessons into the minds of young children. They learned to spout back the pleasing tunes and rhymes taught to them by their elders. In this way, children learned more than specific things like grammar rules or math principles. Such rhymes naturally involved rhythm, one of music's most basic attributes. Children learning such verses absorbed the values contained in the stories.[13] As anybody who can remember television commercial jingles from their childhood will attest, few things work their way into your permanent memory better than catchy tunes. Perhaps one of the most important features of such musical memorization is that we often effortlessly memorize such tunes, even in spite of ourselves.[14]

The use of rhythm as a memory-aid is well known. The famous psychology experiments of the nineteenth and early twentieth centuries by G. E. Müller and Frederich Schumann in 1887 showed the connection between rhythm and memory by attaching syllables to a machine that showed them at regular time intervals.[15] In their own way, the ancients seem to have understood these principles. In *The Art of Memory*, Frances Yates highlighted how the Greeks developed complex systems of memorization, a vital necessity in the world lacking much in the way of written record-keeping. One of the most important techniques was "mnemotechnics." Mnemotechnies trained people to associate memorized details with landmarks on a given route, a kind of guided-imagery approach to memory using travel-based settings.[16] The Romans similarly used such mnemonic devices. Indeed, they would continue to play an important role in medieval education, and on down to the present.

Learned people in Antiquity memorized vast amounts of information. They were like walking, talking libraries. Perhaps this is why so many ancient cultures seemed to value old people, the "wisdom of the elders." When an older person of such learning died, the cultural loss was huge. Ancient cultures valued the treasure-troves represented by the information old people knew. Along with the normal act of living life, most copious amounts of memorization probably involved some intentional form of rhythmic or musical component to aid in learning. In the Bible, *Psalm* 78, attributed to the biblical musician Asaph, seems like a "mnemohistory," with its highlighting the saga of the Children of Israel, especially their epic Exodus.[17] This blend of learning and rote memorization seems common in many of the ancient world's educational settings. In AD 79, the Roman writer Pliny lauded L Scipio, consul in 190 BC, because he ostensibly knew the names of all Romans.[18] The Roman writer Seneca the Elder wrote that as a boy he had memorized over 2000 names drilled into him by instructors, along with over 200 poems.[19]

Like today, rote learning ("kill and drill") had its critics. In his famous *Confessions*, written in the late fourth century AD, Saint Augustine of Hippo writes of his distaste for the odious singsong rhymes (*odiosa cantio*) of his youth, particularly those by which he learned to count.[20] Augustine also uses the Latin word for "song" (*cantatem*) as a synonymy for the Greek and Latin stories he learned as a child.[21] Augustine's insights in this regard are telling. He notes that as a young person he preferred reading daring tales of heroes like Aeneas to counting and grammar rhymes—something of a criticism of rote memorization, probably not unlike the familiar criticisms of rote memorization and drill that often dominate debates about pedagogy and childhood education approaches still today. However, looking back later in life, Augustine realized the little singsong rhymes and drills he endured as a child had a lasting value. Meanwhile, as he matured, Augustine grew to disdain the dubious morals and fictitious stories of ancient epic literature.[22]

POETRY AND MUSIC AS A DISCIPLINE

In general, ancient learning saw poetry and music as critical components of a fine education. In similar fashion, we still today refer to people as being "well-read" or "well-versed." Plato believed music one of the best types of training for the future "Guardians" of a republic to receive. Popular vernacular often labels such figures "Philosopher Kings." Plato reasoned that music learned at a young age enters into the deeper parts of the human psyche. Music therefore provided aptitudes that would last a lifetime.[23] Musical training also fostered a sense of harmony and beauty, so important to the Greek sensibility of balance and moderation. Such moderation would aid leaders in having the reasoned judgment that make for the best governance. Knowledge of music and poetry would also have inherently involved learning the ancient stories, critical to the identity of the group.

Plato saw training the soul and training the body as two sides of the same coin. A training that focused only on the body would produce savagery and brutality. Conversely, training that focused solely on the soul would produce cowardice and inactivity.[24] For similar reasons, Plato espoused gymnastics. The discipline and decorum of the training Plato envisioned counted for nearly as much as whatever it was that students actually learned.[25] Platonic educators understood that the gymnasium was good for the body, while music and poetry were good for the soul.[26] The second-century AD "Neo-Platonist" thinker Plotinus echoed this idea of music as a vehicle for divine balance.[27] Plotinus viewed music as helping humans achieve their Higher Selves.[28] The idea of balance and symmetry in such thinking also linked to ancient ideas of beauty, the study of Aesthetics.[29]

BLIND POETS

Then, as now, some noted ancient storytelling musicians seem to have been blind. This makes some sense. Since ancient music had little in the way of musical notation, blindness was less of a hindrance to the would-be musician.[30] Indeed, still today, music can be a powerful outlet for the blind. Blind people can develop their four remaining senses to heightened levels, especially hearing. Even today, blindness has failed to stop some of our most beloved musicians from excelling at their instruments. Excluded from much of life's other possibilities, they develop other talents. The voices and instruments of blind musicians often seem to combine in an especially powerful way.

The blind often develop amazing memories, making them great storytellers. By tradition, Homer was blind, the proverbial "Blind Bard." This moniker of Homer as the "Blind Bard" highlights Homer's role as a musician and a reciter of verse—not a writer. Long tradition has depicted Homer as blind, especially the ancient mysterious author commonly called Pseudo-Herodotus, to whom was credited a biography, the *Life of Homer*. An ancient hymn to Apollo includes a reference to the "blind bard, often thought to mean Homer."[31] Of course, we do not know who the actual Homer was—or even if Homer was a man or a woman. Whoever Homer actually was, however, the person who wrote the *Iliad* and *Odyssey*, by hand, certainly could see. Yes, some more recent authors have been blind—John Milton, James Joyce, and Jorge Luis Borges, to name a few. The relatively modern amenities of their respective times compared to the ancient world, however, mean that their examples have little relevance to Antiquity, with its far greater limitations.[32]

Blind musicians appear in other places in the ancient world, outside of Greece. A painting in an Egyptian from around 1400 BC seemingly depicts a blind harpist.[33] This tradition of the blind musician seems strong in other cultures, too. In Japan, the Japanese lute known as the *Biwa* is closely associated with the narrative tradition of reciting tales or poetry. The *Biwa* tradition traditionally emphasizes blind players, frequently of lower-class background.[34] Japan even featured guilds of blind men and women—cooperative units of sorts. The guilds of the blind provided the material and emotional support blind people needed. Among the guilds' major livelihoods was music and entertainment, which makes some sense.[35] Musicians probably received tips or gifts for their performances, playing everywhere from streets to private homes to parties. Blind people, sadly, have sometimes had to resort to begging, whether in the streets or on the fringes of social gatherings, places we also often seem to find musicians.

THE BALLAD

In English, one type of story song that particularly harkens somewhat to the ancient storytellers is the ballad. Today, we usually consider the ballad as a type of song that recounts a tale. Along with having a musical connotation, a ballad also usually tells a story or, more broadly, treats a subject. The word "ballad" comes from the Latin *ballare*, to dance, like the Spanish *bailar*.[36] The suffix "ad" when attached to the word means "Song of," as in *The Iliad*, that is, *A Song of Troy (Ilium)* or *The Aeneid*, that is, *A Song of Aeneas*. This "ad" suffix reminds us of the important sense in which these ancient epics were a form a music. Instead of "The Song of Troy" or "The Song of Aeneas," we could just as easily label The *Aeneid* or the *Iliad* "The Ballad of Troy," or "The Ballad of Aeneas."

The first ballads of Western literature reflected centuries of development prior to having emerged in their written terms. They had a music to them, a quality they retain, even in translation. Some of the most famous phrases in Homer frequently recur in a way that seems to evoke a familiar device as one might find in a refrain—a well-worn turn of phrase, or a particularly evocative figure-of-speech. Many of these works have recurring phrases that passed into the English language as famous Homeric lines like "rosy-fingered dawn," "owl-eyed" Athena, "sea girt Ithaca," and Achilles, the "sacker of cities."[37] Probably bards like Homer sang their stories with an element of memorized key phrases or passages, even as they also improvised new stylistic elements, phrases, and even details.[38] In this way, the stories kept getting better and better as the years went by.

THE BALLAD IN THE ROMAN WORLD

In the Roman world, the storytelling tradition survived, strongly influenced by Rome's Greek neighbors. Nobody really knows the extent to which there was an "autochthonous" Roman music of old folk songs or cultic religion, as opposed to the Greek-influenced writings of later Latin poets like Vergil, Horace, and Ovid.[39] A paucity of sources providing samples of native Latin music in the earlier periods of Roman history raises many questions. The scanty to nonexistent evidence of native Roman music might indicate that that the gruff early Romans had little in the way of such niceties—or simply that little has survived. One thing that is clear, however: Greek influence heavily shaped Rome's tradition of epic poetry.

By the first century, Latin culture had developed a strong tradition of the storytelling poet. Scholars usually translate the Latin word *vates* into English as "bard," defined by *Merriam Webster's Collegiate Dictionary* as "a tribal poet-singer skilled in composing and reciting verses on heroes." Vergil referred to himself as *vates* in Book VII of *The Aeneid*. Vergil asks the goddess muse to breathe into him, her bard, inspiring him to tell the tales of the people in epic fashion.[40] The other important Latin writer most closely associated with being a *vates* is Lucan. Lucan lived during the reign of the emperor Nero (AD 54–68). He saw *vates*/bards as singers of epic tales, entrusted to keep alive the memories of valorous deeds from ancient times.[41]

Probably more than any other Latin writer, Vergil reflected Rome's imitation of the Greek, Homeric ballad. Vergil's *Aeneid* begins with a reference to music, "*arma virumque cano*—I sing of arms and the man."[42] The reference to singing is important. It reminds us that Vergil meant his *Aeneid* for recitation aloud. In his *Life of Vergil*—a work often argued to have been effectively plagiarized from an earlier biographer of the great Latin writer Suetonius—the fourth-century Latin writer Aelius Donatus provides some descriptions of the way Vergil's writings like *The Aeneid* and his *Eclogues* were read aloud for entertainment and inspiration.[43] In one telling detail, Vergil read sections from the *Aeneid* to the emperor Augustus, a command performance of books II, IV, and VI.[44] Vergil also did a number of other public recitations of *The Aeneid*.[45] Other poets similarly performed Vergil's poetry in public, sometimes apparently with Vergil in attendance. Singers also frequently sang from Vergil's other important work, the *Eclogues*.[46] The emperor Nero used to perform Vergilian verses in the theater as a musical dance.[47]

STORYTELLERS AS CHARACTERS IN THE STORIES

Both Homer and Vergil included singer-reciters as characters in their stories. Homer's *Odyssey* depicts a bard named Phemius as singing with his lyre. Phemius tells the tale of the "Hero's Homeward Journey from Troy."[48] When Odysseus's long suffering wife Penelope hears Phemius singing, it breaks her heart.[49] Another important bard found in Homer is Demodocus, the minstrel who sings in the court of King Alcinous that Odysseus visits during his travails.[50] Demodocus sang tales of heroes and the gods, including the quarrel between Agamemnon and Achilles. Odysseus wept as he listened. While in some ways the poets of Homer's world were skilled artisans like metalworkers or carpenters, Homer seems averse to including singers in the ranks of servants.[51]

Vergil also included singer-poets as characters in his tales. In the *Aeneid*, Vergil depicts a musician named Iopas singing stories in the palace of the Carthaginian Queen Dido. Celebrated for his long hair, Iopas plays for the guests on his "golden lyre—*cithara aurata*." Iopas's music had an educational function as well as an entertaining one. Vergil describes Iopas as teaching (*docuit*) the guests with his song. He sings of the heavens and creation. Iopas's verses seem to have focused on long ago or far away topics—the origins of the earth and human beings, or explanations for things like the constellations, ocean tides, or the reasons for night and day.[52] In this way, Iopas taught natural philosophy to his audiences, a professor of sorts.[53] Another important warrior-bard in the *Aeneid* is Cretheus, master of song and lyre. Vergil describes the singer as a "comrade of the muses (*musarem comitem*)," a master of the *cithara*.[54] Unfortunately, Cretheus is killed in battle.[55] In eulogizing the poet, Vergil says that Cretheus sang of "steeds and weapons, of men and battles." Vergil also says that Cretheus was no part-timer. The source of his joy was "always (*semper*)" the lyre and song.[56]

ORPHEUS

Of all Antiquity's poet-singers, Orpheus may have been the most iconic. Orpheus was a master of the lyre and a poet of the first rank. The various versions of Orpheus's story recount different details. The most famous says that he was born in Thrace, a child of the muse Calliope and Apollo. Thrace was a place associated with the mythic musician Linus and even the birth of music itself.[57] The most famous story about Orpheus involves the death of his lover, Eurydice, killed by a snakebite.[58] Grief-stricken, Orpheus trekked to the underworld. Upon arrival, Orpheus played his lyre for Hades, pleading for his lover's return. Orpheus's sang so beautifully that Hades agreed to let Eurydice return to the upper world of the living. Unfortunately, in classic mythological fashion, Hades accompanied this affirmative decision with a single "Don't Do It" mandate—so simple to understand, yet so hard to do: Hades stipulated that Orpheus was not to turn around and look at his lover during the trek out of Hell. If Orpheus looked back, Eurydice would return to the realm of the dead. Of course, Orpheus failed to obey Hades's simple rule. When he turned, Eurydice disappeared back into the Underworld.

Orpheus's sacred story of death and resurrection became closely associated with a kind of musical mysticism, "Orphism."[59] Scholars often view Orphism as one of the "Mystery Cults" popular in later ancient religion. Such groups typically emphasized a life after death, a belief inherent in the myth of Orpheus and Eurydice.[60] In Orphism, people can reach the sacred and eternal world inside us all through the music. Music takes people to the realm of the soul—a world beyond life and death. The sacred stories told by musicians and poets gave a glimpse into this other realm, otherwise beyond human comprehension. Orphism also has close associations with Neo-Platonism, the notion of a Real World beyond this imperfect one. Such ideas might have influenced the Apostle Paul, seemingly proto-Christian.[61]

Greek history taught that the Orphic musical traditions came from Egypt, along with those of Dionysus.[62] Many scholars have also noted an affinity between the mystic ideas of Orphism and those of India.[63] Orphism vaguely harkens to ideas popularly associated with India, including reincarnation. In Orphism, musical sounds are a kind of metaphor for reincarnation. After all, the sounds of music never really die. While ever fainter, they still evolve. Fading musical sounds transform into newer forms—like celestial vibrations. Music was thus a connection to the infinite and the eternal. In this, Orphism believed in the immortality of the soul. Along these lines, some Mystery Cults involved trance-like states, a window into the subconscious.[64] Orphism's belief in reincarnation also hinted at vegetarianism, another idea closely associated with the East. In the Latin storyteller Ovid's *Metamorphoses*, the story of Orpheus and Eurydice features a beautiful vignette on plants. Vegetation absorbs the echoes of Orpheus's music in an eternal cycle, providing woods and fibers for human usage.[65]

THE MUSES

Music and storytelling in Antiquity also closely related to the nine "muses." The word "music" come from the muses, as does the term "museum." The muses were daughters of Zeus.[66] They represented personifications of the arts and learning, the way popular imagery still personifies many abstract qualities—Lady Luck, Lady Liberty, Uncle Sam, Father Time, the Grim Reaper, and Mother Nature, among many other such examples. Euterpe was the muse of music. Her music gives pleasure.[67] Murky figures, the muses played a critical role in how ancient people approached the arts and learning. The poet Hesiod says that muses bestowed upon him his knowledge of the gods and heroes.[68] The muses hosted a contest of singing and the arts every four years, not unlike the Olympics.[69] The muses often used a musical-style of banter featuring a pattern of question and response, something like the Antiphon style of hymn that later influenced Christian hymnody. They told stories and recounted history.[70] They were beautiful, elegant, and graceful, perhaps throwbacks to a time when the Fine Arts were closely associated with femininity, leaving the glories of war more exclusively to men.

The muses also seem to have had a metonymic aspect.[71] *Merriam Webster's Collegiate Dictionary* defines "metonymy" as substituting a name for an attribute with which that thing is associated. We employ metonymic speech when use terms like "the Vatican" to refer to the Papacy, "Washington" to refer to the U.S. government, or "the Pentagon" to refer to military brass. In similar fashion, the Greek muses were metonymic, virtually figures of speech. Greek muses became synonyms for their respective spheres. Clio, for example, was the Muse of History. Still today, we might say we "contemplate Clio" as a metonymic way to describe thinking about history.

INSPIRATION AND THE MUSES

Along with other gods like Dionysus or Apollo, the muses inspired poets, singers, and storytellers. The word "inspiration" literally means "to breath into." When we say that artists are "inspired," we mean that their music almost seems to come from some otherworldly, divine source. In Antiquity, music was closely associated with divine inspiration, as was theater. The famous masks worn by performers in ancient performances enabled divine inspiration. The god would inspire the mask-wearing performer, just as spirits might similarly possess an oracle or seer. Wearing the mask of a god would literally fill that person with the god, a direct form of divine inspiration.

Ancient authors and musicians looked to the muses for inspiration. They would speak of "summoning the muse" as they began their creative efforts. Still today, we often describe singers as "evoking the muse" when they begin to compose. In ancient literature, the "introit" at the beginning of an epic typically evoked the muse.[72] Today, the term "introit" usually references the musical opening of a worship service. Conversely, in Antiquity, the "introit" is closely related to the Greek word *proem*. Meaning something like *preface*, a *proem* is a brief hymn-like introduction presented prior to a poetic epic. By offering an introit, the poet would summon the muse.[73] Both the *Iliad* and the *Odyssey* feature classic introits where Homer seeks divine inspiration. The opening lines of the *Odyssey* specifically ask for divine guidance from Mousa, the Muse. The *Iliad* seeks inspiration from the goddess Thea.[74] The introit in the *Iliad* sings of the anger of Achilles, with its tragic consequences of death and despair. The introit encapsulates the epic's entire meaning in but a few inspired lines. In the *Odyssey*, the muses inspire the "songs of return (*nostoi*)." *Nostoi* were a collection of stories that related the returning voyages of the Greek heroes after the wars.[75]

POPULAR SONGS

Since music seemed such a popular presence in ancient life, one wonders if the mass culture of the Greeks or the Roman Empire featured anything like "hit songs." Did common-knowledge tunes such as "Happy Birthday" or "Twinkle-Twinkle Little Star" even exist, let alone a market for songs, per se? Did popular songs work deep into the collective consciousness of ancient society, the way today tens of thousands can sing along to a Beatles song at a Paul McCartney concert, or join-in on something like White Christmas, with little or no prompting? While it is hard to imagine that the ancient world had anything like the mass-media saturation we have today, there do seem to have been relatively familiar tunes and even lyrics. Numerous studies have shown that allusions to Classical writings and sayings were a hallmark of a fine education in the heyday of the Greco-Roman world, which seems common-sensical.[76] This means that common sayings had entered into the discourse, perhaps the way today educated people might quote Shakespeare (in English), the *Bible*, *Poor Richard's Almanac*, or Yogi Berra.

Some "songs" apparently entered into the popular culture by the time of the Roman Empire. A political song mocked the emperor Nero during the build-up to his fall from power.[77] Nero wrote a song about his rival Galba, the man who ultimately succeeded him in power. Nero performed his Galba-mocking tunes in public, along with corresponding gestures and expressions. Nero's Galba-mocking song remained popular even after Nero's suicide death in AD 68.[78] A year later, musicians still performed Nero's songs as part of an apparent official policy of rehabilitation of Nero's public image.[79] At least some people must have remembered them.

GERMANIC AND CELTIC POETS

Along with the famous singing poets of Greece and Rome, the cultures of the north produced a comparably rich tradition of storytelling and verse. The

Germanic storytelling cultures of northern Europe blended music and singing almost seamlessly into an oral culture. With no writing to speak of, the Germans presumably had no other way of remembering the past than by singing about it.[80] This was how they remembered their stories of the gods and heroes, and their founding myths, like that of Mannus, the first man. These songs were presumably very old. They reflected an indigenous culture rooted in time and place—not the sensibilities of immigrants or nomads.[81]

The German word for song is *"lied,"* as in the *Niebelungenlied* (*Song of the Niebelungen*), source of the famous corpus of German mythology that would later inspire the operas of Richard Wagner. The word *"edda"* is yet another ancient Germanic term for song, albeit with unknown origins. Some see the term *"edda"* as a Germanic variant of the Greco-Roman word "ode," like a song or a poem.[82] Researchers have often equated the old *edda* with folk music, surviving medieval texts preserving truly ancient songs.[83] Ancient Germanic peoples probably memorized many of these poems/songs, as poets did in Greece and Rome. The *edda* often had a familiar, formulaic "refrain" serving as something like a chorus in a more conventional modern song.[84]

The Anglo-Saxon epic *Beowulf* provides probably one of the best examples of how ancient Germanic peoples valued music and poetry. Warriors in *Beowulf* possessed a high command of language. They could also sing and perform. At one point in *Beowulf*, one of the hero's comrades even improvises a song.[85] Beowulf himself is similarly verbal. Though not exactly prone to flowery speech, which might connote deceit, Beowulf nonetheless communicates with forthright clarity and power. Even today, many view Germanic languages as capable of precise and nuanced expression, while also remaining curt and down-to-earth. Such a linguistic quality seems present in the earliest Germanic cultures.

The musical traditions of the Germans seem closely related to warfare. The Germans recited poetic verses in unison to inspire courage and group cohesion prior to battles. This male singing before battle seems to confuse a Roman practice of *barritus*, which also had the troops chorusing in unison during the final moments before battle—a no-doubt ominous sound meant to inspire the army and terrify the enemy. The tradition seems akin to the Roman practice of the *"clamor,"* a general din created by soldiers crashing their swords (*pila*) against their shields (*scuta*).[86] A *barritus* began as a low, barely audible hum before becoming a full-throated roar. Soldiers would presumably perform a *barritus* in the final moments of calm before a battle ensued, providing an important rousing effect.[87] Such full-throated battle vocalizations were no doubt primitive. In general, both the Romans and the Germans seemed to have used full-throated singing during battles as a way to inspire their own, and instill fear in the enemy. Prior to battles, the Germanic warriors would sing prayers, recalling the glories of their warlike ancestors, now in Valhalla.

Chapter 4

THE SCOP

In the Germanic cultures of the north, bard-like figures played a prominent role. *Beowulf* depicts musicians singing to warriors with an almost uncanny similarity to the epic lyric versifiers of the Classical Mediterranean world like those found in Homer, or Vergil. A term worth noting in this regard is "*scop*." *Scop* (usually pronounced "shop") is an Old English term that seems to mean something like "Bard" or "Minstrel." In *Beowulf*, the *scop* provides both background music and featured selections while people socialize in their Great Hall. The *scop* would recite entire epics. Like the poets in Vergil or Homer, the *scop* possessed genuine learning. He knew a great body of songs that contained a storehouse of cultural information. Beowulf's *scop* is "mindful of songs." He remembers the great deeds of the past. Michael Alexander's translation of *Beowulf* says that the *scop* "gave gold to the language," and the "treasured repository," the people's anthology of music, and tales that formed his repertoire.[88]

Like bards or Druids, the *scops* in *Beowulf* had memorized a great deal. The main subjects of their songs were heroes and dead kings. They thus blurred the function of poet, storyteller, historian, and even classroom teachers. In *Beowulf*, the *scop* at one point sings a tale of the creation of the world.[89] The *scop* also sang upon the occasion of mighty victories.[90] One tale the *scop* sang in *Beowulf* was that of a dragon-slaying hero named Sigemund, probably a version of the story that later became so famous in the Icelandic Sagas.[91] Community members would sit and listen to these tales, almost the way today people enjoy films. In her commentaries on *Beowulf*, Ruth Johnson Staver notes that the function of the poet in *Beowulf* was to praise the warriors—to tell their colorful stories in epic fashion. The Germanic poets flattered their leaders, building their posterity for the long term.[92]

The *scop* in *Beowulf* composes music contemporaneously, creating verse to suit the occasion. This reflects the way that Anglo-Saxon musicians probably composed, often spontaneously, in the presence of listeners. From this, we can guess that memory played an important role in verse in the ancient Germanic dialects.[93] Key passages or stock poetic lines were part of a memorized repertoire, just as musicians, past and present, tend to memorize certain clichés or riffs, combing rote memory with spontaneity.[94] The writer of *Beowulf* used many recurring phrases. Just as Homer had stock phrases like "rosy-fingered dawn" and "owl-eyed Athena," *Beowulf* contains an arsenal of stock phrases. Such lines would have included terms like "ring-giver" and "all fell quiet." Since the authorship of *Beowulf* remains unknown, produced later during a period when Anglo-Saxon scholars primarily wrote and read in Latin, some have even alleged stylistics borrowings from the classic epics, especially Vergil.[95] Some scholars have also argued that the author of *Beowulf* imitated Vergil, just as intentionally as Vergil himself once imitated Homer.[96]

BARDS

The musical traditions of the Germanic and Celtic tribes closely intertwined with the tradition of the "bard," a term sometimes confused with the Latin "*barritus*."[97] The word "bard" has a complex meaning and murky etymology. An Old English word probably coming by way of the Celtic languages, "bard" means something like "singer of stories." In English, the term "bard" has acquired a romance that frequently makes it a confusing word. Over the years, bards acquired a lot of the cultural baggage of popular imagination, especially with the Celtic Romanticism that emerged in the nineteenth century. Such antiquarianism often highlighted non-English aspects of Irish, Scottish, or Welsh culture. Gypsy musicians who came to the British Isles also often borrowed from the bard repertoire and tradition.[98]

Bards share a confusing association with Druids, another strange but highly popular term. When Caesar conquered Gaul (the land that would become France) during the first century BC, he wrote about a class of leaders among the Gauls called Druids. The Druids blurred at least some of their functions with what people often call "bards." According to Caesar, the Druids did not train for war, unlike most upper-class Gallic men. Instead, they focused on learning of the intellectual variety. The Druids memorized copiously. Such memorization provided the knowledge base required for leadership.[99] Their education involved memorization of history, along with laws, religious ideas, and practical or scientific knowledge.[100] As it did in Greece and Rome, music and poetry helped would-be Druids to learn details by rote.

Ancient writers sometimes distinguished between Bards and Druids. Bards sang heroic epics to the lyre, much in the tradition of the Latin *vates*. The Druids, on the other hand, were a formal organization, probably something like a guild or a fraternity.[101] A Greek writer named Diodorus Siculus, living in the first century BC, spoke of a class of learned Druid figures whose aptitudes included music. They sang their wisdom to the tones of the lyre. They performed a wide range of genres, including eulogies and satire. Their verses provided social and political commentaries, much in the way folk-singers have long done since time immemorial.[102]

The word "*parasite*" also appears as a reference to ancient singers and poets among the tribes facing Rome, especially the Celts. *Parasites* publicly praised prominent leaders for their great deeds. Parasites also gave eulogies to fallen warriors. This reflected the ancient belief that praise is supportive while satire is destructive. Parasites sang their praises with harps or lyres. They sang tales of war and heroism to encourage the warriors.[103] In the Greek language, *"parasite"* means something like "alongside the food." This may mean that singers or eulogizers were camp followers. They would have performed various menial tasks, but also served roles we equate today with people like chaplains. To the cultivated Greeks and Romans who wrote these sorts of descriptions, with their fragmented details, the function of bards, Druids, or parasites may have seemed something like that of a "barbarian philosopher," for lack of a better term.[104]

In Ireland, the Druidic bards also recited verse. Indeed, Irish poets are among the most famous examples of such figures. The "Irish Bard" became something of an iconic figure. The heyday of the "Irish Bard" started around 600 and went to around 1100, when stronger influences of Latin education, or Anglo-Saxon conquest, came to affect traditional Celtic culture more dramatically. In Ireland, tradition often views bards as the heirs of the pre-Christian Druids. The Norse and Anglo-Saxon poets follow a similar timeline and pattern. Though many questions remain, such musical recitations are no doubt very ancient. The persistent image of the harp in Irish lore and identity sometimes seems to offer an alternative of refinement and sophistication, contrasting an otherwise harsh world that had long existed on the fringes of Europe.[105]

FINAL REFLECTIONS ON THE MUSIC'S RELATIONSHIP TO STORYTELLING IN HISTORY

Because they enabled musicians to sing and play at the same time, stringed instruments became an enormously powerful tool to combine the expressive powers of language with the enhancing flavors of musical sounds. For this reason, stringed instruments became enormously influential tools in the history of poetry and literature. Upon reflection, stories are the heart of human consciousness. Our memories are stories. History is a story, as is the way we relate to ideas and beliefs. Stories are much more than just "Once upon a time." When we share our experiences and thoughts with one another, we invariably engage in forms of storytelling. Sacred stories also form the heart of religion, as well as cultural, ethnic, and political identities—founding myths that help define both groups and individuals.

Music—especially stringed instruments—played a critical role in the development of storytelling. Ancient people typically lacked even books—not to mention movies, television, or the computer. Instead, they recounted their stories to one another in powerful but simpler ways. In particular, storytellers helped create the tradition of poetry—a high form of language that combines words with musical elements like rhythm, rhyming sounds, tonality, and dynamics. Storytellers often accompanied themselves to the

Figure 4.2 A traditional harp. Note how it lacks a "bridge," the key distinguishing feature of a lyre.

music of the harp or lyre, adding ambiance and feeling to their poetic tales. This tradition of adding musical beauty and fluid speech to language closely relates to the ancient emphasis on "rhetoric," the old Greek term for "eloquence." Rhetoric lies at the heart of both poetry and music—the idea that spoken words should have beauty and persuasive elegance, just as music does. The eloquent speech of oratory and the beauty of music share this common stock—a tradition predating written history itself. Both poetry and music stimulate our sense of hearing, one of the five human senses. Both poetry and music delight the ears.

In the hands of a skillful storytelling poet, the meaning of words and the evocative sounds of music combined to add imaginative power to the tale. The rhythmic cadences of speech and the rhyming power of words worked in tandem with the sounds of the lyre to package stories in attractive ways that made them more memorable to the listener. Music thus aided poetry in the critical sense that it provided emotive sounds and patterns to the plain beauty of human speech. Poetry's musical rhythms and rhyming patterns also made stories easier to memorize, a critical consideration in a world that mostly had no books. When they finally appeared in written literature, ancient myths had already been around for many centuries. In this way, music and poetry helped shape both the formation of core stories, and the literary traditions they would ultimately spawn. We still use the term "lyric" today, reminding us of how ancient people once composed verse to the sounds of stringed music, the lyre in particular.

NOTES

1. Andrew Ford, *Homer: The Poetry of the Past* (Ithaca, NY: Cornell University Press, 2013), pg. 14.

2. Jorge Louis Borges, *This Craft of Verse*, edited by Calin-Andrei Mihailescu (Cambridge, MA: Harvard University Press, 2000), 7.

3. Clemente Marconi, "Early Greek Architectural Decoration in Function," in *KOINE: Mediterranean Studies in Honor of R. Ross Holloway*, edited by Derek B. Counts and Anthony S. Tuck (Oxford, United Kingdom: Oxbow Books, 2009), pgs. 4–17, pg. 12.

4. E. D. Perry, "Greek Literature," *The Classical Weekly*, Vol. 5, No. 23 (April 20, 1912), pp. 178–82, pg. 180.

5. Ruth Scodel, *Listening to Homer: Tradition, Narrative and Audience* (Ann Abor, MI: The University of Michigan Press, 2009), 1–2.

6. Michael Schmidt, *Gilgamesh: The Life of a Poem* (Princeton, NJ: Princeton University Press, 2019), pg. 110.

7. Thomas Van Nortwick, *Somewhere I have Never Travelled: The Hero's Journey* (New York, NY: Oxford University Press, 1996), 9–10.

8. C. M. Bowra, *Heroic Poetry* (London: McMillan and Co., 1952), 48.

9. C. M. Bowra, *From Vergil to Milton* (London: McMillan and Co., 1945), pg. vii, as referenced in H. L. Tracy, "The Epic Tradition," *The Classical Journal*, Vol. 42, No. 2 (November 1946), pp. 78–81, pg. 78.

10. John Kevin Newman, *The Classical Epic Tradition* (Madison, WI: The University of Wisconsin Press, 1986), pg. 15.

11. Samuel Noah Kramer, "Heroes of Sumer: A New Heroic Age in World History and Literature," *Proceedings of the American Philosophical Society*, Vol. 90, No. 2 (May 1946), pp. 120–30, pg. 120.

12. Plato, *The Republic*, II. 376–92.

13. Philip H. Hwang, "Poetry in Plato's Republic," *Apeiron: A Journal for Ancient Philosophy and Science*, Vol. 15, No. 1 (June 1981), pp. 29–37, pgs. 31–32.

14. Carolina Araújo, "Plato's Republic on Mimetic Poetry and Empathy," in *The Many Faces of Mimesis: Selected Essays from the 2017 Symposium on the Hellenic Heritage of Western Greece*, edited by Heather L. Reid and Jeremy C. DeLong (Parnassos Press—Fonte Artusa, 2018), pgs. 75–85, pg. 80.

15. Edward J. Haupt, "The First Memory Drum," *The American Journal of Psychology*, Vol. 114, No. 4 (Winter, 2001), pp. 601–22.

16. Frances Yates, *The Art of Memory* (London: Routledge, 1966), xi.

17. Karl N. Jacobson, *Memories of Asaph: Mnemohistory and the Psalms of Asaph* (Minneapolis, MN: Augsburg Fortress Press, 2017), pg. 142.

18. Pliny, *Natural History*, VII. 24.

19. Seneca the Elder, *Controversiae*, I. 2, as referenced in William Harris, *Ancient Literacy* (Cambridge, MA: Harvard University Press, 1989), 31–33.

20. Augustine, *The Confessions*, translated by William Watts (Boston, MA: Harvard University Press, 1950), I. 13.

21. Augustine, *The Confessions*, I. 14.

22. Hildegund Müller, "Challenges to Classical Education in Late Antiquity: The Case of Augustine of Hippo," in *A Companion to Ancient Education*, edited by W. Martin Bloomer (Chichester, West Sussex: Wiley Blackwell and Sons, 2015), pgs. 358–73, pg. 362.

23. Plato, *The Republic*, III. 376e.

24. Plato, *The Republic*, 376a. See also Laura Liliana Gómez Espíndola, "Plato on the Political Role of Poetry," in *Politics and Performance in Western Greece: Essays on the Hellenic Heritage of Sicily and Southern Italy*, edited by Heather L. Reid, Davide Tanasi, and Susi Kimbell (Parnassos Press—Fonte Aretusa, 2017), 237.

25. Peter J. Steinberger, "Ruling: Guardians and Philosopher-Kings," *The American Political Science Review*, Vol. 83, No. 4 (December 1989), pp. 1207–25, pg. 1217.

26. Plato, *The Republic*, II. 376e. See also Espíndola, "Plato on the Political Role of Poetry," 237.

27. Plotinus, *First Ennead, On Dialectic*, 1.

28. Plotinus, *First Ennead, On Dialectic*, 6.

29. Christos C. Evangeliou, "Portraits of Plotinus and the Symmetry Theory of Beauty," in *Looking at Beauty to Kalon in Western Greece: Selected Essays from the 2018 Symposium on the Heritage of Western Greece*, edited by Heather L. Reid and Tony Leyh (Parnassos Press—Fonte Aretusa, 2019), pp. 256–68, pg. 263.

30. Louis T. Shepherd, Jr. and Gene M. Simons, "Music Training for the Visually Handicapped," *Music Educators Journal*, Vol. 56, No. 6 (February 1970), pp. 80–81, pg. 80.

31. "Homeric Hymn to Apollo," 172–76, as referenced in Robert Dyer, "The Blind Bard of Chios (Hymn. Hom. AP. 171–76)," *Classical Philology*, Vol. 70, No. 2 (April 1975), pp. 119–21, pg. 119.

32. Alexander Beecroft, "Blindness and Literacy in the 'Lives' of Homer," *The Classical Quarterly*, New Series, Vol. 61, No. 1 (May 2011), pp. 1–18, pg. 1.

33. Anna Ruiz, *Spirit of Ancient Egypt* (New York, NY: Algora Publishing, 2001), pg. 61.

34. Hugh de Ferranti, "Transmission and Textuality in the Narrative Traditions of Blind Biwa Players," *Yearbook for Traditional Music*, Vol. 35 (2003), pp. 131–52, pg. 133.

35. Maren A. Ehlers, *Give and Take: Poverty and the Status Order in Early Modern Japan* (Cambridge, MA: Harvard University Press, 2018), pg. 162.

36. Louise Pound, "The Ballad and the Dance," *PMLA*, Vol. 34, No. 3 (1919), pp. 360–400, pgs. 361–62.

37. Moses Finley, *The World of Odysseus* (New York, NY: New York Review of Books, 1982), 21–22.

38. Ian Morris, "The Use and Abuse of Homer," *Classical Antiquity*, Vol. 5, No. 1 (April 1986), pp. 81–138, pg. 83.

39. See the review of Günther Wille's *Musica Romana, die Bedeutung der Musik im Leben der Römer* by Flora R. Levin, in *The Classical Journal*, Vol. 65, No. 5 (February 1970), pp. 226–28, pg. 227.

40. Vergil, *The Aeneid*, VII. 41; see also Dolores O'Higgins, "Lucan as 'Vates,'" *Classical Antiquity*, Vol. 7, No. 2 (October 1988), pp. 208–26, pg. 208.

41. Lucan, *Pharsalia*, I. 63; *Poetry and Drama: Literary Terms and Concepts*, edited by Katherine Kuiper (New York, NY: Britannica Educational Publishing, 2012), pg. 17. See also O'Higgins, "Lucan as 'Vates,'" 208–26, pg. 210.

42. Vergil, *Aeneid*, I. 1.

43. Scott McGill, "The Plagiarized Vergil in Donatus Servius, and the 'Anthologia Latina,'" *Harvard Studies in Classical Philology*, Vol. 107 (2013), pp. 365–83, pg. 365.

44. Aelius Donatus, *The Life of Vergil*, 31–32.

45. Aelius Donatus, *The Life of Vergil*, 33.

46. Aelius Donatus, *The Life of Vergil*, 26. See also Thomas D. Kohn, "An Early Stage in Vergil's Career," *The Classical World*, Vol. 93, No. 3 (January–February 2000), pp. 267–74, pg. 267.

47. Suetonius, *The Twelve Caesars: Nero*, 56.

48. Homer, *The Odyssey*, I. 325–27.

49. Pura Nieto Hernández, "Penelope's Absent Song," *Phoenix*, Vol. 62, No. 1/2 (Spring–Summer/*printemps-été*, 2008), pp. 39–62, pgs. 43–44.

50. Homer, *The Odyssey*, VIII. 44–65.

51. Graham Wheeler, "Sing, Muse . . . : The Introit from Homer to Apollonius," *The Classical Quarterly*, Vol. 52, No. 1 (2002), pp. 33–49, pg. 22.

52. Vergil, *The Aeneid*, I. 740–46.

53. Paul Carranza, "Philosophical Songs: The 'Song of Iopas' in the 'Aeneid' and the Francesca Episode in Inferno 5," *Dante Studies*, with the *Annual Report of the Dante Society*, Vol. 120 (2002), pp. 35–51, pg. 5.

54. Vergil, *The Aeneid*, translated by H. Rushton Faircloth (Cambridge, MA: Harvard University Press, 1986), IX. 774–76.

55. Lauren Curtis, "War Music: Soundscale and Song in Vergil, *Aeneid* 9," *Vergilius* (1959), Vol. 63 (2017), pp. 37–62, pg. 56.

56. Timothy Power, "Vergil's Citharodes: Cretheus and Iopas Reconsidered," *Vergilius* (1959) Vol. 63 (2017), pp. 93–124, pg. 97.

57. A. N. Marlow, "Orpheus in Ancient Literature," *Music & Letters*, Vol. 35, No. 4 (October 1954), pp. 361–69, pg. 362.

58. Ovid, *Metamorphoses*, X. 1–85.

59. Cicero, *On the Nature of the Gods*, I. 34.

60. Miguel Herrero de Jáuregui, *Orphism and Christianity in Late Antiquity*, translated by Agestrad (New York, NY: Walter de Gruyter, 2010), pg. 2.

61. Vittorio Macchioro, "Orphism and Paulinism," *The Journal of Religion*, Vol. 8, No. 3 (July 1928), pp. 337–70, pg. 338.

62. Herodotus, II. 81. See also Christopher Moore, *Calling Philosophers Names: On the Origins of a Discipline* (Princeton, NJ: Princeton University Press, 2020), 113.

63. A. Berriedale Keith, "Pythagoras and the Doctrine of Transmigration," *The Journal of the Royal Asiatic Society of Great Britain and Ireland* (July 1909), pp. 569–606, pg. 585.

64. Euripides, *Hippolytus*, 948–50.

65. Ovid, *Metamorphoses*, X. 75–85. See also Wade C. Stephens, "Descent to the Underworld in Ovid's Metamorphoses," *The Classical Journal*, Vol. 53, No. 4 (January 1958), pp. 177–83, pg. 178.

66. Hesiod, *Theogony*, 75–85.

67. Alex Hardie, "Etymologising the Muse," *Materiali e discussioni per l'analisi dei testi classici*, Vol. 62 (2009), pp. 9–57, pg. 12.

68. Hesiod, *Theogony*, 1–15.

69. *Greek Gods and Goddesses*, edited by Michael Taft and Michael Croce (New York, NY: Rosen Publishing Group, 2013), pg. 59.

70. Hesiod, *Theogony*, 27–29. See also James E. Miller, "Ancient Greek Demythologizing," in *Myth and Scripture: Contemporary Perspectives on Religion, Language, and Imagination*, edited by Dexter E. Callender (Atlanta, GA: Society for Biblical Literature Press, 2014), pgs. 213–29, pgs. 214–15.

71. Hardie, "Etymologising the Muse," 9–57, pg. 36.

72. Wheeler, "Sing, Muse . . . ," 33–49, pg. 33.

73. James Redfield, "The *Proem* of the Iliad: Homer's Art," *Classical Philology*, Vol. 74, No. 2 (April 1979), pp. 95–110, pg. 95.

74. Carol G. Thomas and Edward Kent Webb, *Persuasion: Greek Rhetoric in Action*, edited by Ian Worthington (New York, NY: Routledge, 1994), pgs. 3–26, pg. 8.

75. Zachary Biles, "Perils of Song in Homer's *Odyssey*," *Phoenix*, Vol. 57, No. 3/4 (Autumn–Winter, 2003), pp. 191–208, pg. 194. See also Hugh G. Evelyn-White, "The Myth of the Nostoi," *The Classical Review*, Vol. 24, No. 7 (November 1910), pp. 201–5, pg. 201.

76. Jack Mitchell, "Literary Quotation as Literary Performance in Suetonius," *The Classical Journal*, Vol. 110, No. 3 (February–March 2015), pp. 333–55, pg. 333–34.

77. Suetonius, *Nero*, 39. See also Guy de la Bédoyère, *Domina: The Women Who Made Imperial Rome* (New Haven, CT: Yale University Press, 2018), pg. 257.
78. Suetonius, *Nero*, 42.
79. Suetonius, *Vitellius*, 11. See also C. E. Manning, "Acting and Nero's Conception of the Principate," *Greece & Rome*, Vol. 22, No. 2 (October 1975), pp. 164–75, pg. 170.
80. Tacitus, *Germania*, 2, translated by Harold Mattingly (New York, NY: Penguin Books, 2010).
81. W. Beare, "Tacitus on the Germans," *Greece & Rome*, Vol. 11, No. 1 (March, 1964), pp. 64–76, pg. 65.
82. Sivert N. Hagen, "On the Origin of the Term Edda," *Modern Language Notes*, Vol. 19, No. 5 (May 1904), pp. 127–34, pg. 127.
83. Julius Goebel, "On the Original Form of the Legend of Sigfrid," *PMLA* (i.e., *Publications of the Modern Language Association*), Vol. 12, No. 4 (1897), pp. 461–74, pg. 470.
84. Lars Lönnroth, "Hjálmar's Death-Song and the Delivery of Eddic Poetry," *Speculum*, Vol. 46, No. 1 (January 1971), pp. 1–20, pg. 3.
85. *Beowulf*, 867–74. See also Robin Waugh, "Literacy, Royal Power, and King-Poet Relations in Old English and Old Norse Compositions," *Comparative Literature*, Vol. 49, No. 4 (Autumn, 1997), pp. 289–315, pg. 298.
86. Polybius 15. 12.8 and Plutarch, *Mark Antony*, 39. 4, as referenced in Ross H. Cowan, "The Clashing of Weapons and Silent Advances in Roman Battles," *Historia: Zeitschrift für Alte Geschichte*, Bd. 56, H. 1 (2007), pp. 114–17, pg. 114.
87. Ammianus Marcellinus, *The Later Roman Empire (AD 354–78)*, translated by Walter Hamilton (New York, NY: Penguin Books, 1986), XVI. 42. See also Bo Lawergren, "The Origin of Musical Instruments and Sounds," *Anthropos*, Bd. 83, H. 1./3. (1988), pp. 31–45, pg. 33.
88. *Beowulf*, translated by Michael Alexander (New York, NY: Penguin Books, 2001), 870–80. See also Robert E. Bjork, *Old English Verse Saints Lives* (Toronto: University of Toronto Press, 1985), pg. 8.
89. *Beowulf*, 35.
90. *Beowulf*, 837–990.
91. Kemp Malone, "Coming Back from the Mere," *PMLA* (i.e., *Publications of the Modern Language Association*), Vol. 69, No. 5 (December 1954), pp. 1292–99, pg. 1294.
92. Ruth Johnson Staver, *A Companion to Beowulf* (Westport, CT: Greenwood Press, 2005), 56–57. See also Scott Gwara, *Heroic Identity in the World of Beowulf* (Boston, MA: EJ Brill, 2008), 59.
93. *Beowulf*, 863–73.
94. Alan Jabbour, "Memorial Transmission in Old English Poetry," *The Chaucer Review*, Vol. 3, No. 3 (Winter, 1969), pp. 174–90, pgs. 179–80.
95. John Nist, "Beowulf and the Classical Epics," *College English*, Vol. 24, No. 4 (January 1963), pp. 257–62, pg. 257.
96. Richard North, *The Origins of Beowulf: From Vergil to Wiglaf* (New York, NY: Oxford University Press, 2006), 2.

97. Hermann Fischer, "Barditus," *Zeitschrift für deutsches Altertum und deutsche Literatur*, Bd. 50, H. 1./2. (1908), pp. 145–48, pg. 146.

98. Roslyn Blyn-Ladrew, "Ancient Bards, Welsh Gipsies, and Celtic Folklore in the Cauldron of Regeneration," *Western Folklore*, Vol. 57, No. 4, *Locating Celtic Music (and Song)* (Autumn, 1998), pp. 225–43, pg. 227–28.

99. Caesar, *The Gallic Wars*, VI. 14.

100. Caesar, *The Gallic Wars*, VI. 14.

101. Marcellinus, *The Later Roman Empire*, XV. 9. 8. See also "Bardism. General Principles of the Institutions," *The Cambro-Briton*, Vol. 1, No. 12 (August 1820), pp. 445–52, pgs. 447–48.

102. Diodorus Siculus, *The Library of History*, V. 31, as cited in Miranda Aldhouse-Green, *Caesar's Druids: Story of an Ancient Priesthood* (New Haven, CT: Yale University Press, 2010), pg. 183, ff# 59.

103. Athenaeus, VI.246C-D. Daith Hogain, *Celtic Warriors* (New York, NY: Saint Martin's Press, 1993), 23.

104. James B. Rives, "Aristotle, Antisthenes of Rhodes, and the Magikos," *Rheinisches Museum für Philologie, Neue Folge*, Bd. 147, H. 1 (2004), pp. 35–54, pg. 46.

105. Mary Helen Theunte, *Memory Ireland: History and Modernity*, Vol. 1 (Syracuse, NY: Syracuse University Press, 2011), pg. 56.

Chapter 5

Festivals and Parties

Some of the most important features of ancient music emerged from ancient public festivals. The Latin word for holidays was *fasti*, related to the Modern English world "festival" or the Spanish word "*fiesta*," which means "party." In Modern English, too, the word "festival" has a party connotation. The word *fasti* more literally, however, really refers to the ancient calendar. These ancient festivals were important for simple time-keeping purposes. Often pegged to agricultural cycles or astronomical markers like the solstices, festivals marked times of harvest, sowing, plowing, and so forth. Festivals provided a powerful way to reflect on the passage of days, months, and years. As societies grew more complex, such calendrical markers helped fix dates, so important for coordinating business or public events. The ancient festivals also tied-in with religion. They provided powerful cosmologies that explained life, from the most grandiose beliefs of human existence down to everyday little pleasures like mating, eating, or dancing.

Beyond serious associations like myth and religion, the festivals provided some fun. Work stopped at festival time. The normal strictures of everyday life were relaxed. Behaviors normally deemed inappropriate gained approval, as with parties or festivals today. Communities gathered in a time of sharing. Like our holidays today, such festivals became traditions celebrated for century upon century, a critical feature of ancient life. Because of this important public function, ancient festivals played an important role in the history of the music and the Fine Arts. This chapter will discuss how ancient festivals helped drive creativity and development in music. Festivals also helped drive the evolution of related endeavors like theater and sports.

THE DYING AND REVIVING GOD

Many ancient festivals of prehistory centered on the theme of fertility. Fertility is the essence of life itself—the way the earth revives each spring and dies each fall, or newborn babies represent collective deliverance from aging and death. In his monumental work *The Golden Bough*, Victorian scholar Sir James George Frazer highlighted the vast influence of fertility beliefs on ancient religion and myth.[1] A key feature of such beliefs was the myth of the "dying and reviving god." Such myths usually featured some young god, tragically killed in the prime of life. After the untimely violent death, the deity's partner would enter into a period of intense mourning. The partner's lamentations would succeed in bringing the god back to life, affirming the regenerative powers of nature.

There were scores of dying and reviving gods, scattered across many regions and cultures. They often told similar stories with different names and details. Some of the more prominent myths of dying and reviving gods included the myth of Adonis and his lover Venus, Osiris and his lover Isis, Persephone and her mother Demeter, among many others. Frazer recounted how myths of a dying god tied into the life cycles of the earth. When the god died, so, too, did the earth. This would be tantamount to fall and winter. When the deity revived, along came the beauties of springtime. The myth of the "dying and reviving god" closely related to the calendar, especially seasonal patterns like spring, summer, fall, and winter, as well as agricultural markers like sowing, growing, and harvesting. Long before temples or even established priesthoods, ancient peoples marked their calendars' sacred moments with these popular festivals that celebrated life and death.

The nature of the various festivals usually corresponded to the time of year, which itself related to the life cycle of the god. Happy customs that celebrated renewal characterized spring festivals, when the god came back to life. Alternatively, the death of the deity in the fall inspired great grieving rituals. Wailing and other forms of lamentation often characterized such festivals of death.[2] Festivals also provided a time for people to reflect on the mysteries of mythology. Worshippers staged dramatic reenactments of the divine myths that told the stories of their gods, especially the core myth of death and resurrection. The reenactments became early versions of the theater. They also played an important role in the history of music. During the reenactments, worshippers sang, danced, and chanted. Beyond music and theater, the ancient festivals played a formative role in many other cultural traditions, including sports.

FESTIVALS IN ANCIENT EGYPT

Some of the earliest festivals came from Egypt. We can tell that these festivals, distant as they might seem, made early use of music, dancing, and reenactments. The Egyptians introduced the use of music as a prelude to formal assemblies. They also introduced the practice of "litanies," which is formal chanting used in royal or sacred assemblies. Many of these festivals were local or regional. The festival held in honor of the Egyptian Diana in the city of Bubastis was one of the most prominent. It featured men and women singing, as well as professional pipers.[3]

The Egyptian festival tradition also seems to have provided some early examples of theatrical reenactments, far predating those of Greece. One of the earliest such functions was the Abydos Passion Play in Egypt. The Abydos Play annually depicted the story of the death of Osiris, killed by his brother Set. The lamentations of Isis brought the great Nile deity back to life. Scholars surmise that these depictions of the story of Osiris probably date back to the earliest days of Bronze Age Egypt, c. 3100–2200. The plays had an amazing run, considering that the Egyptians continued performing their annual dramatization for thousands of years. The annual play continued unabated until it succumbed to the suppression of Christianity in AD 400.[4] As in other rituals, dancing and processions played a key role. A divine retinue of dancers and worshippers paraded to the tomb of Osiris, which in Abydos was associated with an early pharaoh named King Zer (c. 3000 BC).[5] Another festival that reenacted the sacred myth of Osiris was the Egyptian Opet Festival at Thebes, extant as early as 1600 BC.[6] The Opet Festival highlighted the Nile's season of flooding, roughly comparable to spring.[7] The Opet Festival featured chanted prayers. The extremely ancient tradition of chanting, dancing, and reenactment of sacred myths heavily influenced Egypt's later neighbors.[8]

FESTIVAL ELEMENTS IN THE BIBLE

Festivals also played an important role in the public life of the ancient Hebrews. Biblical festivals typically featured both singing and dancing. In the *Bible*, the biblical prophet Miriam, sister of Aaron, led a retinue of timbrel-playing women in a procession to celebrate the drowning of pharaoh's army after crossing the Red Sea, an allusion later vaguely remembered in the famous spiritual "Oh Mary, Don't You Weep."[9] Many scholars regard this tune, "The Song of Miriam" as the oldest specimen of song found in the

Bible. The Dead Sea Scrolls also contain an alternative version of the tune, perhaps an entire song.[10] Another of the Bible's most famous examples of ritual dancing featured King David. In *2 Samuel* 6, David performs a sacred ritual dance after having captured Jerusalem from the Jebusites.[11]

Though ostensibly monotheistic, Hebrew festivals often resembled those of their polytheistic neighbors. In the Bible, God commands the Israelites to maintain three major annual festivals, all tied to the agricultural cycle and the most important of the Mediterranean staple crops—grain, grapes, and olives. One of the festivals was the Feast of Unleavened Bread, usually associated with barley. Another was the Feast of the Harvest. Another festival was the Feast of Booths, when olives and grapes ripened.[12] Like other ancient fertility-based festivals, these biblical celebrations usually involved pilgrimages to the festival site. The wearying journey enhanced the excitement of arrival to the festival-goers.[13] In some ways, we can even consider the Sabbath a kind of festival. It was a regular pause for communities to recuperate, celebrate and worship, except on a weekly basis instead of an annual one.

However scanty, the Bible does provide some tantalizing descriptions of the size of some of these festivals. Crowds were large. This meant that festivals required larger musical ensembles to carry over the noise of the assembly. In *II Chronicles*, a large ensemble with hundreds of players accompanied the bringing of the Ark of the Covenant into the Temple. The sounds produced by such "orchestras" must have been quite a concoction. Rhythms provided a dominant component, along with blaring noises. The Bible tells of 120 trumpeters. Instruments included timbrels, cymbals, and other percussion devices joining in what must have been a cacophony.[14] Rhythm instruments seem to be what the Psalmist refers to in *Psalm 150*—"Praise him upon the loud cymbals" in the famous King James Version.[15] The passage seems evocative of David's final instructions to future king Solomon regarding the temple administration. David's orders included the appointment of no less than twenty-four separate divisions of musicians, especially cymbal instruments and lyres.[16] This sort of a potpourri of sounds made by a large orchestra also seems implied in *Daniel* 3, the famous story of Shadrack, Meshack, and Abednigo and the fiery furnace. Babylonian instruments played in the story included lyres, pipes, a stringed instrument called the *trigon*, and rhythm instruments.[17] This passage in Daniel may also reflect a later Greek influence, perhaps even the way Greeks used musical devices in the theater.[18]

FESTIVAL DANCING

The use of rhythm instruments for festival events dovetailed along with the development of dancing. Upon reflection, dancing played an integral role in the history of music. Dancing is also one of the oldest of all human art forms. Festival dancing in ancient times often happened as part of what we would call a parade. Along with rhythmic swaying, such dancing also included elaborate acrobatics. There was also "kinetic dancing," which featured simply moving the body, or even playing ball according to some pulsing rhythm.[19] In *Ecclesiastes*, ritual dancing is included with the various times of life, like mourning and rejoicing.[20] Praising god through choreography or physical posturing all related to the larger practice of ritual religious dances. *Psalms* 149:3 talks about praising god with dancing, among other musical tributes.[21] In *I Samuel* 10:5, Samuel tells Saul to go to Gibeah of God, where he will encounter a retinue of ritual dancers accompanied by musical instruments. Samuel says that dancing will prompt prophecy.[22] In *I Kings* 18, the priests of Baal perform ritual dances as part of their miracle contest with Elijah on Mount Carmel.[23]

In the Bible, the ritual dancing in ancient fertility religions often seems gendered. Women dominated the dancing processions. Military victory songs are almost always associated with women—perhaps because war itself was so associated with men.[24] In Greece, the ancient dancers of the Dionysus cult at the beginning seem to have featured rites that were all but exclusively female. In the worship of Dionysus, women dancers were *"maenads."* They often carried rhythm instruments like the *sistrum*. Dionysian rites existed, which featured dancing and rituals exclusive to women—notably in the Greek sites of Miletus and Lesbos. By the first century AD, however, mixing of the sexes seems more common.[25]

THE *BACCHAE*: ONE OF THE MOST FAMOUS STORIES INVOLVING THE MAENADS

One of the most famous glimpses of women dancing to Dionysian rites come from the Greek play the *Bacchae*. The *Bacchae* was written in the fifth century BC by the playwright named Euripides. The title *Bacchae* means "women of Bacchus," the Latin name for Dionysus. The *Bacchae* takes place in the wild mountain haunts of Mount Kithaeron, nearby to Thebes. Kithaeron has obvious etymological connections to the word *cithara*, that is, lyre. In the story, Dionysus's seductive music lured the women of Thebes to nearby Mount Kithaeron.[26] There, they ran in ecstasy, with unkempt hair and freely lactating breasts.[27] Alas, the story also ended with brutal violence. In the end of the tale, the ecstatic women celebrating the rites of Dionysus tear-apart the King of Thebes, Pentheus, after they caught him peeping at their freewheeling antics. The tale demonstrated the excessive mania with which some ancient critics associated the rites.

Figure 5.1 Woman dancing and holding a *"sistrum."*

Because Euripides's story about Dionysian ecstasy ended with violent social disruption, the *Bacchae* seems a cautionary tale. To those who think music should be refined, stately and composed, the festival sounds of Dionysus worship apparently provided a stark contrast, perhaps not so different than wild rock or rap music today. The noise and revelry associated with the cult of Dionysus gave rise to the deity's pejorative nickname *Bromius*. The term *"Bromius"* seems to have meant something like "King of Clamor," Lord *Bromius*.[28] It seems almost like the kind of nickname we would give to a rock-star or an athlete. The reckless music associated with the rites of Dionysus seemed juxtaposed to the notion that music should be the servant of language—in the Greek mind closely associated with the lyre and its relationship to poetic verse.[29] Of course, there are stately hymns to Dionysus, like the prayer that begins Euripides's play the *Bacchae*, which summons the audience to reverence.[30] After the attention-getting verbiage of the introductory prayer, however, the theme of the play seems more along the lines of wild natural music and even reckless abandon.

THE CHORUS

The festival tradition also helped prompt the tradition of the "chorus," one of music's most important developments. In Greek, the word "chorus" is *khoros*. The word "chorus" originally referred to a group of participants who danced in a circle, often singing or reciting as they did so. The reenactments of myths that the festivals popularized came to feature a chorus of actors intoning commentaries. The chorus acted as meta-narrators of sorts. The rise of the chorus also shows how festival performances increasingly featured preparation and direction. They were so much more than mere spontaneous outpourings. Unfortunately, we are unable to say exactly what this early choral music sounded like. We also know that the music of the *aulos*—a reed—typically accompanied the chorus.[31]

Choruses had the benefit of being large, tending to produce a better audience. It facilitated a great focus on the action on the stage and on the subtleties of dramatic dialogue. A larger chorus of participants naturally attracted more onlookers. Friends and family would have enjoyed watching their loved ones perform, building a critical mass of people. Thus, the crowds of earlier times became to develop into a formal audience.[32] In this way, festival reenactments began to evolve into something like early versions of theater.

By the heyday of Classical Greece, theater had become an important part of public life. In Athens, would-be poets/playwrights would approach city magistrates and ask them to sponsor a chorus. Wealthy citizens provided this support, something like Modern-day "patronage" of the Fine Arts. Greek vocabulary called the one receiving such support a *choregos*—a choir leader. Armed with this important credential, the *choregos* began training his retinue for performances. The Athenians took choral participation so seriously that members assigned to a choral production even gained exemption from military service.[33]

THE DITHYRAMB

The choral component of ancient festival performances spawned numerous distinct traditions in Greek music. Of these, few are as influential as the "dithyramb." This special ritual dance is especially associated with the rites of Dionysus. The *dithyramb* probably came to Greece from Asia Minor, Modern-day Turkey. Based on the etymology of the word, it seems like the term "*dithyramb*" meant something like a "grave-song" or, as we might say in English, a "dirge."[34]

The *dithyramb* originally functioned as a lamentation, part of the annual funeral rites based on the myths of death and resurrection. Such "laments" featured prominently in fertility religions because ancient peoples believed that sincere grief spurred resurrection. Given its associations with Dionysus, the *dithyramb* usually emphasized wild, grief-stricken emotion. Because of its unrestrained approach, scholars often contrast the *dithyramb* with the refined, stately Apollonian "*paeans*."[35] Aristotle argued that the *dithyramb* was like epic poetry or tragic theater in that it sought to imitate—to recreate feelings and responses presumably experienced by other characters, including mythological or historical figures.[36] Choral vocalists performing *dithyrambs* took on another persona, the way a singer or actor today might do in telling a story.

While many of the dances and chanting associated with fertility festivals emphasized the sounds of the reed (*aulos*), the *dithyramb* came to be more closely associated with the lyre. The greater use of the lyre in choral music was a breakthrough. It accommodated more complex poetry being sung on the stage. Scholars often credit a verse-reciting musician named Lasus of Hermoine with having translated the music of the reed to the lyre.[37] Lasus's contributions in this regard might be analogous to how the nineteenth-century Romantics succeeded in translating the lyrical folksong melodies of lutes and guitars to the newfangled piano. It seems like the *dithyramb*'s capacity to take the emotional and sensual power of the reed and transfer it to the lyre represented a major innovation in music.[38]

AGONISTIC FESTIVALS

As time passed, festivals came to host competitions in things like athletics, drama, music, or literature. Such festivals are usually called "*agonistic* festivals," after the Greek word for contest, *agon*. The Olympics, which began in 776 BC and continued for the next 1,200 years until AD 393 are the most famous of the many such *agonistic* festivals—one of the most amazing traditions of the ancient world.[39] *Agonistic* competitions lent a formal element of judgment and merit to activities like dancing, drama, sports, and music. Such events encouraged intense preparation on the part of participants—just as today students prepare for a race in track, a finely honed argument on debate team, or a piano solo in music festivals. Festival competitions also brought together people from different towns and regions. Festival competitions provided a chance to have one's efforts judged, not only by the public but also by experienced experts. As competition always does, festival contests drove participants to new heights of excellence.[40]

Today, we still remember how the Greek word *arete* roughly translates as "excellence." *Arete* was closely associated with athletics, but also applied more broadly to the larger ancient Greek admiration for outstanding human achievement in all its forms—in music, sports, oratory, the Fine Arts, and in admirable human characters such as virtue, courage, and eloquence.[41] The fame and fortune offered to outstanding performances at ancient *agonistic* festivals were as desirable to ancient artists and athletes as comparable rewards in Modern society today. The word athletics comes from the old Greek word for *athlos*, a contest in which the winner won a prize. The most famous prize given by the Greeks as such festivals was the wreath of laurels. We still speak today of people "resting on their laurels." Today, "laurels" tend to be associated with elite academics. Indeed, the word *baccalaureate* comes from the old Latin *bacca lauri*—laurel berries, as in the term "bachelor's degree." These baccalaureate festivals were a hallmark of ancient Greek culture, but they spread into southern Italy and Sicily through colonization. There was a "Sebasta Festival" in Naples, a "Capitoliz Festival" at Rome, and a "Eusebia Festival" at Puteoli.[42]

THE MYTH OF ARION—ANCIENT CONTEST WINNER IN MUSIC

Greek mythology features a number of stories involving musical competitions at the agonistic festivals. One of the most famous is the Myth of Arion. The fifth-century BC Greek historian Herodotus tells that Arion played the lyre exquisitely. He invented the *dithyramb* and also directed a Corinthian Chorus. Arion traveled from his native isle of Lesbos to Sicily to compete in a lyre competition. There, he won great prizes with his skillful playing. Unfortunately, during his return voyage home, the sailors on the ship decided to steal Arion's fortune. Arion, however, convinced the thieving sailors to let him play one final song, a request the pirates granted. Arion sang an *orthios nomos*, a kind of hymn to the gods featuring a shrill, plaintive style of singing.[43] One imagines that perhaps Arion seemed to be singing his death song. Upon finishing, Arion shocked the pirates by suddenly jumping into the sea.

Fortunately, for the musician, his gorgeous music had attracted dolphins to the waters around the ship. A benevolent dolphin then carried him through the ocean waters to safety.[44]

As with so many other myths, Arion's colorful story probably contains kernels of truth. As well as highlighting the dangers of ancient sea travel, the Myth of Arion reflects the fame and fortune that winning one of the ancient Greek world's competitions could bring to the victor. A major contest victory was like winning a gold medal. The story says that Arion also convinced the pirates into letting him change into his performance attire, showing the element of well-dressed formality, and theatrical costume, with which professional music in the ancient world was associated.[45] Finally, the pirates listened respectfully to Arion's music, even though they planned to rob and kill him as soon as he finished playing. The pirate's respect for Arion shows the respect ancient people had for good musicianship, even in the unlikeliest of circumstances or among the most dubious of audiences.

THE SWAN SONG OF THE *ORTHIOS NOMOS*

Another interesting detail found in the Myth of Arion has to do with the type of song he chose to sing, the *orthios nomos*. The *orthios nomos* was a funeral hymn. To the ancients, music about death was just as important as music about life. As we saw with festival celebrations in general, mournful music highlighting death and winter was just as important as music about springtime renewal. Life and death were two sides of the same coin, a balance that ultimately affirmed eternal hope and renewal. Given its importance, ancient music had specific idioms for bereavement and death-related theologies, perhaps something like the Requiem of Catholic cultures. The *orthios nomos* seems like a specimen of this distinctive lamentation, a song reflecting on death and, by extrapolation, the fleeting brevity of human life. Such funeral hymns would have featured prominently in the music associated with fertility-related festivals.

Like the Homeric hymns, or the biblical Psalms, *orthios nomos* hymns were almost inseparable from the lyre or *cithara*. They were usually long and complicated—blends of recitation, wailing, ambient emo music, and personal reflection. (Perhaps Arion was stalling for time before the pirates killed him.) These funeral hymns were also closely associated with Apollo, deity of the arts and music, patron of all *citharodes*.[46] The word "*nomos*" has many connotations besides simply hymn. *Nomos* is also closely associated with the Greek world of law and philosophy and written statutes, so perhaps Arion sang a religious treatise of sorts.[47] A text written around the time of Christ describes a hymn to Apollo, as a "*Nome*." It is a five-part musical rendition featuring flutes and reeds, along with the lyre. The text celebrated Apollo's famous victory over the dragon named Python.[48]

It seems like the *orthios nomos* may have also reflected the powerful familiar musical tradition of the death song, in English sometimes called a "swan song." In Aeschylus famous tragedy play *Agamemnon*, "Cassandra's Lament," the *nome is* compared to a swan song. In fact, the high-pitch singing associated with the *nome* presumably recalled the actual singing of a swan.[49] Plato once wrote that the swan's final song was the most beautiful song a swan sang in its lifetime, since it could see into the happy afterlife.[50] Interestingly, earlier ancient writers seemed to see swan songs as joyful. Like other birds, swans' singing originally made their music part of the joyous sounds of nature.[51] With Aeschylus, however, the notion of the swan's song seems to have settled into its more familiar connotation, as a lamentation bewailing an impending death.[52] The linkage of a swan's song with a final tune expressing an impending death seems to have stuck. In the fourth century BC, Plato also talked about the final song sung by dying swans.[53] These images of a "swan song" as reflecting sorrow and impending death have endured ever since.

THE PLAYWRIGHTS: THEATER AS LITERATURE

By the Classical period, beginning around 500 BC, the old traditions of reenacting stories at the festivals had evolved into outright theater. With the increasing sophistication of writing, Greece even had actual playwrights. The most famous Greek dramatists are probably Sophocles (496–406 BC), Euripides (480–406 BC), Aeschylus (525–456 BC), and Aristophanes (446–386 BC). In Latin, the most famous playwright is probably the first-century playwright Seneca (died AD 65). Translated into scores of languages and lovingly preserved over the centuries, we still read these surviving playwrights' works today. While today we might compartmentalize their works as "theater," they also played an important role in the development of music.

In ancient theater, music played a critical role. Choral recitations associated with the Classical plays actually functioned as a type of music. These performances also involved choreography and plot—natural outgrowths of the dancing and mythic reenactments that had characterized festival rituals from the earliest days. Plays not only included the traditional choral singing, but "monody," usually associated with a lone singer reciting solo. Plays also involved duets, as in the exchange found between two characters in the play *Alcestis* by Euripides (438 BC).[54] In their ancient settings, such dialogues probably probably blended spoken-word and musical, tonal inflections. In preparing such a performance, directors would have worked with the actors on such elements as pacing, dynamics, phrasing, and pronunciation, just like any choral director today.

THEATER CONSTRUCTION

As the festival traditions evolved in sophistication, physical theater spaces emerged. Theater spaces played an important role in both drama and music. Both musical concerts and theatrical plays benefited enormously from the advent of theaters as important centers of municipal life. Upon reflection, the construction and maintenance of designated theater spaces is a very telling detail about any society. Theaters reflect intentional support for the arts and music. When societies build and maintain theater spaces, it shows that they honor and respect a cultural legacy. Theaters indicate a desire to nurture the arts, transmitting them to the broader public. At their best, theaters are much more than mere multipurpose facilities. Theaters create an ideal space for both performing the arts, and enjoying them. Theaters are just as important to performers as to the audience in the seats, enhancing the experience for both.

The advent of theaters, per se, into world architecture evolved slowly over time.[55] Owing to the limitations of their engineering capabilities, Greeks usually built their theaters on the sides of hillsides, outside of the city. Planners found a suitable location in the countryside, a natural theater. Still today, some of the most attractive concert venues use some sort of natural surroundings like hills or sloping mountainsides to create a naturally beautiful concert setting. This was the approach used in Antiquity. Upon identifying a site, the ancients could build seating into the hillside. Stone flooring or walls further defined the stage area. By the heyday of Classical Greece, such theater spaces had emerged as a vital aspect of cultural life. Situated adjacent to bustling city centers, Greek theaters combined the cultural amenities of urban life with the rustic charms of the city's beautiful outskirts. Among the most famous of all Classical Greek theaters was that of Epidaurus. Syracuse, in Sicily, provides another classic Greek theater.

The word "theater" actually comes from the Greek verb "*theastai*," meaning "to view." Today, we say a "theorizer" or "theoretician" is someone who gains knowledge and insight by viewing, by observation. The term "*theoria*"—theory—also involved reverence and wonder, to look upon something with amazement.[56] "Orchestra" is another common term involving theaters. Taken from the Greek verb *orcheisthai*, to dance, the word "orchestra" means "place of dance."[57] In ancient theater, dancing took place in the orchestra, almost like today's use of an orchestra pit, or a chorus placed strategically to the rear or side of the stage. The traditional theater shape is a circular or semicircular space. Theater's circular dimensions harken back to the origins of the ancient orchestra area, where once dancers danced in a circle around an altar to Dionysus.[58] As theater structures developed, builders constructed a *skene*, a solid back behind the stage. This helped define the theater space. It also promoted better acoustics and seeing.[59] It is from the term "*skene*" that we get our word "scene."

PARTIES

Along with festivals, parties and banquets played a comparable role in promoting music and the arts. Festive music was associated with relaxation and sensuality. Relaxation is one of life's most important needs, no mere frill. Festive music offered an opportunity for fun and relaxation. In the *Iliad*, Homer writes that Apollo struck his lyre after driving his chariot of the sun across the sky, signaling the beginning of the nighttime hours, the time for rest, pleasure, and socializing. As Apollo played, the muses took turns singing and reciting.[60] Music was often associated with such nighttime and leisure activities. Music was almost like a drug, in and of itself. Indeed, the story of the Sirens in Homer's Odyssey—with their awesome power to hypnotize and bewitch the minds of sailors—reflected some elemental version of the idea that music is an intoxicant.[61]

One of the most famous types of feasting in the Greek world was the Symposium, made especially famous because of its use by Plato as a setting for one of his most important dialogues, *The Symposium*. The scintillating conversation and debate that accompanied the Symposium helped make the term "Symposium" a word that means a gathering that usually includes food, beverages, and a higher level of conversation. In Antiquity, as now, a symposium usually had some theme. In Plato's *Symposium* dialogue, the guests conversed about love and Eros. Speeches and discussion usually followed dinner. The wine bowl in ancient Greece, known as the *krater* for its distinctive, saucer-like shape, featured prominently.[62]

Sometimes the frivolous music associated with partying evoked criticism, just as today. Such criticism might stem from simple social snobbery or genuine good taste in music. Frivolous party music seems to stand in such stark contrast to the timeless, epic versifications of a Pindar or a Homer. In the Euripides play *Medea* (431 BC), a nurse character criticizes those who use the lyre at parties to increase desire and wanton behavior. Music, she reasons, should calm the angry and grief-stricken, not to make people crazy and lustful. The nurse further regrets that at feasts and banquets from time immemorial partygoers used the lyre to dull the senses. Music, she implies, offers nothing to heal the plight of humankind. The nurse sees music as impractical and something that induces frivolity.[63] Perhaps the nurse criticized upper-class attitudes and fun-filled events that excluded her—a kind of sour grapes take on festive music's joyful lightheartedness. More poignantly, however, the nurse saw the potential of music and songwriting as so much more than mere entertainment and frivolity. She believed music actually had the power to heal.[64]

ROMAN FESTIVALS

The festival traditions of ancient times echoed in the Roman world. Some scholars have seen in the famous Roman "Triumph" parades a legacy of the festival processions of dancing and singing, comparable to those of their Greek neighbors to the east. The Roman Triumph reportedly got its name from the hymn of praise to Dionysus, the *thriambos*.[65] These Roman victory festivals seemed to have resembled the feel and form of ecstatic Dionysus worship. Often remembered today as a kind of victory-parade, the classic Roman Triumph featured all the ancient elements of festival culture—dancing, music, recitations, and athletic acrobatics.

From the very beginning, triumphs featured music, especially the flute. When he returned home from a glorious victory over the Carthaginian navy in the First Punic War, the Roman Senate awarded the military hero Gaius Duillius the honor of a flute playing entourage to herald his arrivals and departures.[66] This venerable tradition would persist, even until the later ages of the Roman Empire. During the reign of the Roman emperor Valentinian (r. 364–375), a Roman official named Apronian was awarded the honor of being followed around by a train of musicians to sing his praises. Later Roman historians called Apronian a "second Duillius."[67]

EMPEROR NERO AND THE GREEK TRADITION OF MUSIC AND SPORTS

Rome's musician emperor Nero (r. AD 54–68) was one of the most famous Roman enthusiasts regarding the Greek custom of festival, especially their ancient tradition of competition. In AD 66 and 67, Nero took a trip to Greece. Significantly, he never even visited Athens. Instead, Nero seems almost exclusively to have focused on the sites of the old festivals. In a famous speech he gave in Corinth, Nero declared the "liberation of Greece."[68] Nero's declaration may have been something of a symbolic move, though scholars argue it probably involved a reduction of taxes paid to the Italians ruling the Roman Empire, as well as perhaps the removal of direct Roman military or administrative supervision in local affairs.[69]

Nero's visit to Greece, and his promotion of the ancient festivals, seems to connote that the old traditions had faded some by the days when Greece was a Roman province. Yet the festival legacy seems to have left a strong afterglow. At least, some people continued to honor the ancient ways. The old festivals had become venerable, almost like tourist draws. Nero also instituted a new music contest at Olympia.[70] The Greeks even changed the dates of the festival to coincide with the visit of such a distinguished guest as the Roman emperor.[71] Nero famously "won" the contests in which he participated. One account says Nero, competing in a ten-horse chariot race, fell from his chariot, failing to complete the event. Nonetheless, doting contest officials declared him the victor.[72]

ROMAN EMPERORS, PUBLIC WORKS, AND SPONSORSHIP OF MUSIC

Despite its numerous drawbacks, Roman power benefited the musical traditions that derived from the ancient festivals. Many emperors made patronage and public works spending a major part of their programs. Rich, powerful, and some of history's greatest executive administrators, if the Romans decided they liked something, if usually augured well for whatever it was that they liked. Public munificence in all its various guises became a core part of the Roman political identity, as well as a useful tool for assimilation. Rome used lavish public works spending to improve the lives of conquered people. Rome beautified their cities and pumped resources into local economies. A public spirit that supported the arts was part of the legacy of the Rome's contributions to history.[73]

In promoting ancient arts like music and theater, Rome actually furthered the influence of its Greek predecessors. Roman administration helped disseminate Greek culture, then, even as Greece itself became a Roman province. Even in far-off cities like Gadeira—present-day Cadiz, in Spain—Rome spread the traditions of ancient Greek music and theater. One ancient writer during the reign of the emperor Nero noted the presence of Greek music and lyric poetry in the Gadeira. He claimed that Spaniards living away from the presence of Roman checkpoints had virtually no knowledge of theater or recited music. Another writer says that people in Cadiz understood the significance of Greek drama and raised their children with a Greek-style education—*paideia*. Meanwhile, in the city's hinterlands, people had never ever heard a lyre.[74] In general, it seems like the areas that respected the ancient Greek traditions of *arete*—excellence—featured an education promoting the Classical balance of music, poetry, geometry, and athletics.[75]

ROMAN SUPPORT FOR BANQUETS AND FEASTING

Along with supporting the festival tradition, Rome also encouraged music with a tradition of lavish banquets. Here, ancient traditions of music long associated with festivals reached a more targeted audience. Access to lavish feasts represented wealth and privilege in ancient Rome, a world where large segments of the population had so little.[76] Emperors and other prominent personages would play a prominent social role in these lugubrious affairs. They would introduce actors and singers, playing the role of host and talent agent.[77] The banquets offered a chance for the emperor to feature select artists and musicians, presumably as something like the after-dinner entertainment.[78] It seems like the emperors' role in such banquets was to preside over the entertainment as a kind of master of ceremonies. Emperors also hosted competitions. Prizes awarded to actors and musicians in such events were lucrative, including a prize of 168 silver drachmas awarded to the best *aulos* (flute) player in a festival at the Greek town of Tanagra honoring the Hellenistic deity Serapis.[79] Attempts at assigning value to ancient coins like the silver drachma have been inconclusive, but this seems a substantial sum.[80]

Some emperors were more associated with the Fine Arts than others. The Flavian Dynasty of Roman emperors (AD 69–96) spent especially lavishly on entertainment, including festivals and banquets. Their efforts in this regard further enhanced the infrastructure and rewards available for musicians, poets, actors, and athletes, a trend already begun under their predecessors.[81] Emperor Vespasian (r. AD 69–79) heavily sponsored the tradition of musical-themed banquets.[82] His son Domitian (r. AD 81–96) was even more lavish. Lucrative prizes in competitions included events in chorus, lyre, and *a cappella* singing.[83]

The audiences musicians enjoyed playing for at these lavish banquets were sometimes fake. Nero so hated playing to an empty house that he hired an audience. Nero once hired a bevy of professional applauders from Alexandria.[84] The professional audience dressed for the occasion as part of their job. Then, as now, musicians wanted to play to a full house. Upon reflection, musicians have often used various artificial means to fill seats, from free promotions to outright pay-to-play scenarios. In some cultures, dating back to ancient Egypt, funeral directors would hire professional mourners to add vocal and visual heft to the sense of lamentation and bereavement, often in quite dramatic fashion. We call such professional mourners "moirologists."[85]

ROMAN THEATERS

Rome also borrowed heavily from Greek traditions in architecture, including theaters. Roman provincial administrators frequently promoted theaters as a tool of Romanization. By the time of the Roman Empire, theaters had evolved from their rustic origins on the hillsides of Greece. They became more urban, part of a city's infrastructure. Emperors usually promoted Classical culture in Roman cities, in Italy, and in the conquered provinces. Along with providing genuine improvements in social life, public works projects like theaters provided the provinces with a sugarcoating on the bitter pill of Roman imperialism. During the days of the Roman Empire, Roman engineers frequently built their own theaters using updated building techniques, but often on the sites of the older Greek theaters. Theaters like the famous Roman theater at Taormina, Sicily offer a fine example of a Roman theater, built on the site—and probably even outlay—of an earlier Greek one.

Augustus built a number of important theaters suitable for music, including the famous Theater of Marcellus and the Theater of Balbus in downtown Rome.[86] These two important theaters were built sometime around 17 BC and 13 BC, the heyday of the Augustan building program.[87] The construction of these two important theaters in Rome featured as part of a larger attention the early Roman emperors gave to the personal comforts of the city, which also included the construction of baths, and two new aqueducts—the Aqua Virgo and the Aqua Alsietina.[88] These Greco-Roman theaters of the later period were often huge. The Roman theater of Sepphoris in ancient Israel/Roman Judaea held 5000 guests. Even more impressive was the theater at Ephesus, which could serve an audience of 24,000 people.[89]

The Odeon provides still another charming specimen of Roman theater construction. Still today, an "Odeon" typically features elements of classic theater design, but on a more intimate scale. The Odeon was originally a Greek theater—a "Place of Song." As with many buildings originating in the Greek East, the Odeon passed over into the Roman world of the Western Mediterranean from the Greek East. It became yet another lovely specimen of Classical architecture. In Roman times, such buildings usually featured a roof. We call a "roofed musical hall" a *theatrum tectum* or roofed theater.[90] The Roman emperor Domitian built an Odeon as part of his overall restorations of buildings burnt in a fire.[91] Pompeii offers still another example of the Empire's charming Odeon theaters. These littler "*odea*" provided settings that were more intimate. They allowed the finer arts—musical, dramatic, literary, and theatrical—to flourish in a way that fostered both cultural development and diffusion. Along with the smaller scale in general, the roof allowed for a sense of enclosure and intimacy that aided complex productions requiring longer dedicated attention spans.[92]

During the days of the Roman Empire, Latin terminology describing elements of theater construction also came into popular usage. The theater proper was the auditorium seating, the *cavea*.[93] The "*scaenae frons*"—the "scenic front"—of the theater—became one of the most important features of theater architecture. Writing around the time of the emperor Augustus, the

Roman writer Vitruvius's famous treatise on architecture, *de architectura—Regarding Architecture*—highlighted some of the most famous aspects of the Roman theater, which included not only the *scene* but also the *pulpitum*—the pulpit. Latin called the classic inclined seating of a traditional theater construction the *gradus*, a grade, as in inclined seating.[94] Today, we still speak of "graded seating" in large arenas or stadiums.

THE GREEK ORIGINS OF THEATER?

An interesting question is whether other nearby ancient cultures established formal spaces designated for theater, music, and sports to the same extent as the Greeks. By most accounts, scholars know little of "spectator" events like sports in Etruscan, Egyptian, or Minoan worlds.[95] Such cultures obviously valued music. Their traditions of festivals were undoubtedly as rich as those of Greece and as old or older. They clearly valued physical prowess and excellence in the arts, which played a prominent role in public life. In Minoan Crete, for example, we can identify outdoor clearings that seem to have been designated for performances and audiences. All the same, they seem to have had little in the way of physical constructions designed specifically for viewing the theatrical arts or athletics.

There is virtually no native theater in the Bible, though the Apostle Paul does give a famous sermon in the theater at Ephesus, which is part of the Greek World.[96] Paul also gives some talks at a rented lecture hall, *scole*, in Ephesus, after wearing out his welcome at the local synagogue.[97] These famous details from the *Book of Acts* seem to juxtapose the Greek traditions of freewheeling debate and theater with the learned culture of Judaism in the first century. Upon reflection, then, the advent of the theater, one of the world's most important types of buildings, seems more closely associated with the Greeks.

SOME FINAL REFLECTIONS ON THE ROLE OF FESTIVALS IN HISTORY AND MUSIC

The festivals of ancient times marked the calendar's key dates each year—spring, fall, or the solstice people observed in the heavens. In some more intimate sense, the ancient festivals also provided a time to reflect upon those little marker moments in human life that shape our personal experiences and memories—things like births, deaths, meals, and marriages. While a host of theologies and customs characterized this diverse array of festivals, most seemed to emphasize the importance of fertility—the eternal cycles of nature, and of life itself. During the festivals, people assembled to celebrate the mysteries of human existence. Festivals also gave an opportunity for the community to highlight the season with rich cultural traditions. They reenacted the sacred stories. They sang, danced, and played sporting games. In this way, the festivals of ancient times played a critical role in the formation of not only music, but also theater and athletics.

The festival tradition in many areas came to include intensely competitive events. Communities hosting the festivals offered lucrative prizes to the winners of such contests. Events ranged from singing poetic verse to choral performances to athletics. Prizes seemed to have included large sums of money. The most famous prize was the honor of winning a wreath of laurels, an accolade that brought lifelong glory and fame. We get the word "baccalaureate" from this laurel prize, coming from the old Latin "*bacca lauri*," that is, "laurel berries." Today, the term "baccalaureate" still connotes an academic tradition of "*arete*," the Greek word meaning "excellence." We also remember baccalaureate education in the Modern phrase "bachelor's degree." Baccalaureate education emphasizes broad learning, mentoring, judging, and friendly competition. Still today, the best schools emphasize these pedagogical approaches to help young people achieve their fullest potential.

The old traditions of the festival passed over into the Roman world. This was especially notable in terms of the distinct Greek heritage of the theater, with its playwrights, verse-recitations, choruses, and mask-wearing thespians. Many Roman emperors openly admired the Greek traditions of theater and music, promoting them in both public works and private settings. The Romans built many of the ancient world's most important surviving theaters, albeit sometimes on earlier sites. In this way, the influence of the ancient traditions of festival music, drama, and sports gained a wider following, with substantial public support.

The festival tradition reminds us of how much of a debt Western music and theater owe to ancient religion, especially that of the Greeks. By constructing special spaces to host storytelling and music, the Greeks gave rise to the tradition of the "theater" as not only a tradition of dramatic reenactments, but also a type of architecture. In general, when theater constructions appear in the ancient world, we know that something important has occurred. Theater constructions reflect a vibrant culture that prioritizes drama, music, and literature. In this sense, our rich and ongoing traditions of the Fine Arts owe a great deal to the festivals of ancient times, once celebrated in the open air.

NOTES

1. The persistent influence of Babylonian theologies in this regard is treated in "*L'idéologie religieuse: la théologie de l'Homme*," in Jean Bottéro, *La Religion Babylonienne* (Paris: Presses Universitaires de France, 1952), 82–107.

2. See "Death and the Reintegration of the Group," in Bronislaw Malinowski, *Magic, Science, and Religion and Other Essays* (Prospect Heights, IL: Waveland Press, 1992), 47–53.

3. Herodotus II:67.139–65.

4. Charles Gates, *Ancient Cities: The Archaeology of Urban Life in the Ancient near East and Egypt, Greece and Rome* (Abingdon, United Kingdom: Routledge, 2011), pg. 6.

5. James Henry Breasted, "The Message of the Religion of Egypt," *The Biblical World*, Vol. 29, No. 6 (June 1907), pp. 427–34, pg. 429.

6. Jo Mackellar, *Event Audiences and Expectations* (Abingdon, United Kingdom: Routledge Press, 2018), pg. 57.

7. John C. Darnell, "The Rituals of Love in Ancient Egypt: Festival Songs of the Eighteenth Dynasty and the Ramesside Love Poetry," *Die Welt des Orients*, Bd. 46, H. 1, *The Song of Songs and Ancient Egyptian Love Poetry* (2016), pp. 22–61, pg. 35.

8. Sherif Abouelhadid, "The Sacred Geometry of Music and Harmony," in *Petrie Museum of Egyptian Archaeology: Characters and Collections*, edited by Alice Stevenson (London: UCL Press, 2015), pgs. 62–63.

9. *Exodus* 15:22. See also Ashley Bryan, *I'm Going to Sing, Black American Spirituals*, Vol. 2 (Carrboro, NC: Alazar Press, 2012), pg. 50.

10. Ariel Feldman, "The Song of Miriam (4Q365 6a ii + 6c 1–7) Revisited," *Journal of Biblical Literature*, Vol. 132, No. 4 (2013), pp. 905–11.

11. *2 Samuel* 6.

12. *Exodus* 23:14–17.

13. J. A. Wagenaar, "The Priestly Calendar Festival and the Babylonian New Year Festivals: Origin and Transformation of the Ancient Israelite Festival Year," in *Old Testament in Its World: Papers Read at the Winter Meeting, January 2003, and Joint Meeting, July 2003, The Society for Old Testament Study*, edited by Robert P. Gordon and Johannes C. de Moor (Boston, MA: EJ Brill, 2005), pgs. 218–53, pg. 219.

14. *II Chronicles* 5:12–15.

15. *Psalm* 150:5.

16. *I Chronicles* 25:1–8. See also Otto Mulder, "Worship in a Restored Second Temple in Sirach 50: The Context of the Feast," in *Various Aspects of Worship in Deuterocanonical and Cognate Literature*, edited by Ibolya Balla, Géza G. Xeravits, and József Zsengellér (Boston, MA: Walter de Gruyter, 2017), pgs. 141–67, pg. 144.

17. *Daniel* 3:10.

18. Michael Lesley, "Illusions of Grandeur: The Instruments of *Daniel* 3 Reconsidered," in *Music in Antiquity: The Near East and Mediterranean*, edited by Joan Goodnick Westenholz, Yossi Maurey, Edwin Seroussi, and Joan Goodnick Westenholz (Boston, MA: Walter de Gruyter, 2014), 201–22.

19. Lillian B. Lawler, "The Maenads: A Contribution to the Study of the Dance in Ancient Greece," *Memoirs of the American Academy in Rome*, Vol. 6 (1927), pp. 69–112, pgs. 74–75.

20. *Ecclesiastes* 3:4. See also Amihai Mazar, "Ritual Dancing in the Iron Age," *Near Eastern Archaeology*, Vol. 66, No. 3, *Dance in the Ancient World* (September 2003), pp. 126–27, pg. 126.

21. *Psalms* 149:3.
22. *I Samuel* 10:5. See also Avraham Biran, "The Dancer from Dan," *Near Eastern Archaeology*, Vol. 66, No. 3, *Dance in the Ancient World* (September 2003), pp. 128–32, pg. 130.
23. *I Kings* 18.
24. Mercedes García Bachmann, "Miriam, Primordial Political Figure in the Exodus," in *Torah*, edited by Irmtraud Fischer, Mercedes Navarro Puerto, Andrea Taschl-Erber, and Jorunn Økland (Society for Biblical Literature, 2011), 329–74, pg. 341.
25. Albert Henrichs, "Greek Maenadism from Olympias to Messalina," *Harvard Studies in Classical Philology*, Vol. 82 (1978), pp. 121–60, pg. 159.
26. Euripides, *Bacchae*, 680–700.
27. Richard Schechner, "In Warm Blood: The Bacchae," *Educational Theatre Journal*, Vol. 20, No. 3 (October 1968), pp. 415–24, pg. 415.
28. Richard Schechner, "'The Bacchae': A City Sacrificed to a Jealous God," *The Tulane Drama Review*, Vol. 5, No. 4 (June 1961), pp. 124–34, pg. 132.
29. A. S. C. Barnard, "The Problem of the "Bacchae," *Greece & Rome*, Vol. 2, No. 6 (May 1933), pp. 170–72, pg. 170.
30. Euripides, *Bacchae*, 64–82. See also Mark L. Damen and Rebecca A. Richards, "'Sing the Dionysus': Euripides' 'Bacchae' as Dramatic Hymn," *The American Journal of Philology*, Vol. 133, No. 3 (Fall, 2012), pp. 343–69, pg. 343.
31. H. D. F. Kitto, "The Greek Chorus," *Educational Theatre Journal*, Vol. 8, No. 1 (March 1956), pp. 1–8, pg. 1.
32. Jesús Carruesco, "Choral Performance and Geometric Patterns in Epic Poetry and Iconographic Representations," in *The Look of Lyric: Greek Song and the Visual: Studies in Archaic and Classical Greek Song*, Vol. 1, edited by Vanessa Cazzato and André Lardinois (Leiden: Brill, 2016), pgs. 69–109, pg. 70.
33. Helen H. Bacon, "The Chorus in Greek Life and Drama," *Arion: A Journal of Humanities and the Classics*, Third Series, Vol. 3, No. 1, *The Chorus in Greek Tragedy and Culture*, One (Fall, 1994—Winter, 1995), pp. 6–24, pg. 6.
34. W. M. Calder, "The Dithyramb: An Anatolian Dirge," *The Classical Review*, Vol. 36, No. 1/2 (February–March 1922), pp. 11–14, pg. 14.
35. A. W. Pickard-Cambridge, *Dithyramb, Tragedy and Comedy*, revised by T. B. L. Webster (Oxford: Clarendon Press, 1962) 24 f., as cited in Richard Hamilton, "The Pindaric Dithyramb," *Harvard Studies in Classical Philology*, Vol. 93 (1990), pp. 211–22, pg. 211.
36. Aristotle, *Poetics*, translated by Anthony Kenny (New York, NY: Oxford University Press, 2013), I. 1. 13–198.
37. *The Odes of Pindar, Including the Principal Fragments*, translated by John Sandys (New York, NY: The MacMillan Company, 1915), 552–53.
38. Plutarch, *De Musica—Regarding Music*, included in A. Barker, *Greek Musical Writings. Volume 1: The Musician and His Art* (Cambridge: Cambridge University Press, 1984), as cited in James Porter, *The Classical Quarterly*, Vol. 57, No. 01 (May 2007), pp. 1–21, pg. 11.
39. *Pausanias, Description of Greece*, translated by W. H. S. Jones, as included in *Pausanias: Complete Works* (Hastings, England: Delphi Classics, 2014), Vol. 10. 1.

See also Jan Reznik, "The Essence of Sport," in *Reflecting on Modern Sport in Ancient Olympia: Proceedings of the 2016 Meeting of the International Association for the Philosophy of Sport at the International Olympic Academy*, edited by Heather L. Reid and Eric Moore (Parnassos Press, Fonte Aretusa, 2017), pgs. 95–104, pg. 95.

40. Stephen M. Stigler, "Competition and the Research Universities," *Daedalus*, Vol. 122, No. 4, *The American Research University* (Fall, 1993), pp. 157–77, pg. 157.

41. Stephen G. Miller and Paul Christesen, *Arete: Greek Sports from Ancient Sources* (Berkeley, CA: The University of California Press, 2012), pg. 15.

42. Irene Ringwood Arnold, "Agonistic Festivals in Italy and Sicily," *American Journal of Archaeology*, Vol. 64, No. 3 (July 1960), pp. 245–51, pg. 246.

43. Vivienne Gray, "Herodotus' Literary and Historical Method: Arion's Story (1.23–24)," *The American Journal of Philology*, Vol. 122, No. 1 (Spring, 2001), pp. 11–28, pg. 12.

44. Herodotus I:23–24.

45. Stewart Flory, "Arion's Leap: Brave Gestures in Herodotus," *The American Journal of Philology*, Vol. 99, No. 4 (Winter, 1978), pp. 411–21, pgs. 413–14.

46. Thomas J. Fleming, "The Musical Nomos in Aeschylus' Oresteia," *The Classical Journal*, Vol. 72, No. 3 (February–March 1977), pp. 222–33, pgs. 224.

47. Martin Ostwald, *Language and History in Ancient Greek Culture* (Philadelphia, PA: The University of Pennsylvania Press, 2009), pg. 109.

48. Strabo, *Geography*, IX. 3. 10, as referenced in Mike Chappell, "Delphi and the Homeric Hymn to Apollo," *The Classical Quarterly*, New Series, Vol. 56, No. 2 (December 2006), pp. 331–48, pg. 339.

49. Aeschylus, *The Oresteia, Agamemnon*, translated by Robert Fagles (New York, NY: Penguin Books, 1977), lines 1444–46. See also J. A. Haldane, "Musical Themes and Imagery in Aeschylus," *The Journal of Hellenic Studies*, Vol. 85 (1965), pp. 33–41, pg. 39.

50. Plato, Plato (Phaedo, 84e–85b). See also Christina Avronidaki, "Swan Riddles in Boeotian Red-Figure Vase-Painting," in *Corpus Vasorum Antiquorum, Österreich, Beiheft 2: ΦΥΤΑ ΚΑΙ ΖΩΙΑ. Pflanzen Und Tiere Auf Griechischen Vasen*, edited by Lang-Auinger Claudia and Trinkl Elisabeth (Wien: Austrian Academy of Sciences Press, 2015), pp. 239–48, pg. 241.

51. See Hesiod, The Shield of Hercules, translated by Hugh Evelyn-White in *Works and Days, Theogony, and the Shield of Hercules* (Mineola, NY: Dover Publications, 2006), pg. 67. See also *Homeric Hymns*, translated by Nicholas Richardson (New York, NY: Penguin Books, 2003), Hymn #21.

52. John Philip Harris, "Cassandra's Swan Song: Aeschylus' Use of Fable in Agamemnon," *Greek, Roman, and Byzantine Studies*, Vol. 52 (2012), pp. 540–58, pg. 540.

53. Plato, *Phaedo*, 615b 2–5. See also W. Geoffrey Arnott, "Swan Songs," *Greece & Rome*, Vol. 24, No. 2 (October 1977), pp. 149–53, pg. 149.

54. Euripides, *Medea*, 244–72. See also Pietro Pucci, *Euripides' Revolution under Cover: An Essay* (Ithaca, NY: Cornell University Press, 2016), pg. 192.

55. Clifford Ashby, *Classical Greek Theatre: New Views of an Old Subject* (Iowa City, IA: The University of Iowa Press, 1999), pgs. 85–86.

56. Andrea Wilson Nightingale, "On Wandering and Wondering: 'Theôria' in Greek Philosophy and Culture," *Arion: A Journal of Humanities and the Classics*, Third Series, Vol. 9, No. 2 (Fall, 2001), pp. 23–58, pg. 24.

57. Lillian B. Lawler, *The Dance in Ancient Greece* (Middletown, CT: Wesleyan University Press, 1964), 11.

58. Elizabeth Gebhard, "The Form of the Orchestra in the Early Greek Theater," *Hesperia: The Journal of the American School of Classical Studies at Athens*, Vol. 43, No. 4 (October–December 1974), pp. 428–40, pg. 428–29.

59. Graham Ley, *The Theatricality of Greek Tragedy: Playing Space and Chorus* (Chicago, IL: The University of Chicago Press, 2007), pg. 8.

60. Homer, *The Iliad*, I. 600.

61. Homer, *The Odyssey*, XII. 39–52; XXIII. 326. See also Marcel Zentner, "Homer's Prophecy: An Essay on Music's Primary Emotions," *Music Analysis*, Vol. 29, No. 1/3, *Special Issue on Music and Emotion* (March–October 2010), pp. 102–25, pg. 102.

62. Euripides, *Bacchae*, 85.

63. Euripides, *Medea*, 198–99.

64. Aristide Tessitore, "Euripides' 'Medea' and the Problem of Spiritedness," *The Review of Politics*, Vol. 53, No. 4 (Autumn, 1991), pp. 587–601, pg. 601.

65. Varro, *On the Latin Language*, VI. 68. See also Mary Beard, *The Roman Triumph* (Cambridge, MA: Harvard University Press, 2007), 245.

66. Livy, *Periochae*, 17.2.

67. Marcellinus, *The Later Roman Empire*, XXVI. 3.

68. Plutarch, *Flaminius*, 12. 8. See also Paul A. Gallivan, "Nero's Liberation of Greece," *Heult'rmes*, Bd. 101, H. 2 (1973), pp. 230–34, pg. 230.

69. George Couvalis, "Alexandrian Identity and the Coinage Commemorating Nero's 'Liberation' of the Greeks," in *Greek Research in Australia: Proceedings of the Sixth Biennial International Conference of Greek Studies, Flinders University June 2005*, edited by E. Close, M. Tsianikas, and G. Couvalis (Adelaide: Flinders University, Department of Languages—Modern Greek), 113–22. Archived at Flinders University: dspace.flinders.edu.au. On-line reference.

70. Suetonius, *Nero*, 23.

71. Jurgen, *Nero* (Oxford, UK: John Wiley and Sons Inc., 2005), pg. 90.

72. Donald G. Kyle, "Winning at Olympia," *Archaeology*, Vol. 49, No. 4 (July/August 1996), pp. 26–29, 31, 33–34, 36–37, pg. 28.

73. Brian Campbell, *The Romans and their World: A Short Introduction* (New Haven, CT: Yale University Press, 2011), pg. 100.

74. Philostratus, *Life of Apollonius of Tyana*, Vol. 8, as referenced in Sebastiana Nervegna, "Staging Scenes or Plays? Theatrical Revivals of 'Old' Greek Drama in Antiquity," *Zeitschrift für Papyrologie und Epigraphik*, Bd. 162 (2007), pp. 14–42, pg. 14.

75. Thomas D. Paxson, Jr., "Art and Paideia," *The Journal of Aesthetic Education*, Vol. 19, No. 1, *Special Issue: Paestum and Classical Culture: Past and Present* (Spring, 1985), pp. 67–78, pg. 67.

76. Christine Richardson-Hay, "Dinner at Seneca's Table: The Philosophy of Food," *Greece & Rome*, Second Series, Vol. 56, No. 1 (April, 2009), pp. 71–96, pg. 71.

77. Suetonius, *Augustus*, 74.
78. Suetonius, *Augustus*, 74.
79. Nervegna, "Staging Scenes or Plays," 14–42, pg. 20.
80. Verne B. Schuman, "The Seven-Obol Drachma of Roman Egypt," *Classical Philology*, Vol. 47, No. 4 (October 1952), pp. 214–18, pg. 218.
81. Perry M. Rogers, "Domitian and the Finances of State," *Historia: Zeitschrift für Alte Geschichte*, Bd. 33, H. 1 (1st Qtr., 1984), pp. 60–78, pg. 69.
82. Suetonius, *Vespasian*, 18–19.
83. Suetonius, *Domitian*, 4.
84. Suetonius, *Nero*, 20.
85. Sandra Helene Straub, *Death 101: A Workbook for Educating and Healing* (Amityville, NY: Baywood Publishing Company, 2002), pg. 16. See also Holly Woodward, "A Moirologist's Notes," *Chicago Review*, Vol. 40, No. 4 (1994), pp. 71–74.
86. Suetonius, *Augustus*, 29.
87. M. K. Thornton and R. L. Thornton, "Manpower Needs for the Public Works Programs of the Julio-Claudian Emperors," *The Journal of Economic History*, Vol. 43, No. 2 (June 1983), pp. 373–78, pg. 377.
88. M. K. Thornton, "Julio-Claudian Building Programs: Eat, Drink, and Be Merry," *Historia: Zeitschrift für Alte Geschichte*, Bd. 35, H. 1 (1st Qtr., 1986), pp. 28–44, pg. 34.
89. Mary T. Boatwright, "Theaters in the Roman Empire," *The Biblical Archaeologist*, Vol. 53, No. 4 (December 1990), pp. 184–92, pg. 185.
90. Roger B. Ulrich and Caroline K. Quenemoen, *A Companion to Roman Architecture* (Hoboken, NJ: John Wiley and Sons, 2013), pg. 492.
91. Suetonius, *Domitian*, 5.
92. George Izenour, "The Ancient Roman Roofed Theater," *Perspecta*, Vol. 26, *Theater, Theatricality, and Architecture* (1990), pp. 69–82, pg. 72.
93. Richard Alan Tomlinson "Theaters (Greek and Roman), Structure," entry in *The Oxford Classical Dictionary*, 4th Edition, edited by Simon Hornblower and Antony Spawforth (New York, NY: Oxford University Press, 2012).
94. Vitruvius, *The Ten Books on Architecture*, translated by Morris Hicky Morgan (Mineola, NY: Dover Books, 1960), Vol. 6. 2–3. See also Steven Cerutti and L. Richardson, Jr., "Vitruvius on Stage Architecture and Some Recently Discovered *Scaenae Frons* Decorations," *Journal of the Society of Architectural Historians*, Vol. 48, No. 2 (June 1989), pp. 172–79, pg. 174.
95. Daniel Menaker, "Watching Sports," *Grand Street*, Vol. 7, No. 1 (Autumn, 1987), pp. 208–13, pg. 209.
96. *Acts* 19:28–34.
97. *Acts* 19:9.

Chapter 6

Church Music as an Heir of Ancient Music

A big part of Western music comes from the Christian Church. Church music itself, however, was highly derivative. Christian music proper, to the extent there is such a thing, developed from the context of the early Church, which has very obscure origins. Despite all the questions that remain, we can say a few things with relative certainty. First, a major part of early Church music borrowed heavily from Judaism, the elder sister faith of Christianity and the birth-religion of most early Christians. Second, along with Judaism, the Church naturally drew on the musical traditions of the Classical world. This means that Church music today, for all its other trappings, traces back to the Ancient Mediterranean world of Judaism and Classical culture. In this sense, Church music served as an important bridge between the rich heritage of Ancient music and that of the Middle Ages. In short, today's traditions of Church music represents one of the oldest living forms of music. Church music offers a tantalizing link to the music of Antiquity, otherwise lost to posterity. This chapter will look at how Church music helped bridge the divide between Ancient and medieval worlds.

MUSIC IN THE NEW TESTAMENT AND EARLY CHURCH

Over time, the Christian Church would create some of the finest music ever made, everything from powerfully simple choruses to Bach and Handel. Yet early on, few could have imagined that the new religion of Christianity would one day inspire such exquisite musical beauty. The early Church usually seems humble and very plain, musically and otherwise. It had no elaborate temples or powerful priesthoods. Early Church music similarly had little in the way of pomp or circumstance. The first Churches seem to have been relatively democratic. This contrasts some with what we know about Temple music in Judaism at the time. In Jewish Temple worship, professional musicians had gained the status of prestigious professionals. Temple singers belonged to the powerful Judaic priesthood. Musicians of the Temple in Jerusalem enjoyed tax-exempt status, along with professional scribes. Preferential treatment in taxes highlighted the privileged favor musicians enjoyed.[1] In Judaism, Temple musicians enjoyed a monopoly on their sacred musical duties, inherited from their tribal status as belonging to the Levite lineage. Conversely, musicians in the early Christian Church seemed to have enjoyed the freedom (and impoverishment) that can go along with amateur status.

The combination of an egalitarian Church service and Hebrew musical traditions helped shape Christian music from its earliest days. In his first epistle to the Church at Corinth (*First Corinthians*), Paul notes that when worshippers came together, one person would sing, another preach, another teach, and so on.[2] The famous tradition of the Lord's Supper, which in those days was an actual meal, accentuated the social nature of early Christian gatherings. Simple songs sung congregationally seem to have been the norm. Unfortunately, we can never know the actual tunes that early Christians sang. Scholars think that *Philippians* 2:6-11, *Colossians* 1:15-20 and *2 Timothy* 3:16 probably have the lyrics of early Christian songs. Others have seen *Hebrews* 1: 3 as containing possible lines from an early Christian hymn.[3]

Outside of the *New Testament*, there are also hymns from in apocryphal texts, that is, sacred texts that, for one reason or the other, did not get included in the final version of the Bible. Such texts usually have a later date or reflect an uneven quality. Some so-called apocryphal texts, however, reflect excellent thinking and writing. The *Odes of Solomon* are among the most important apocryphal Christian hymns from these murky years. Of unknown authorship, the *Odes of Solomon* hymn collection has fine spiritual and expressive qualities. Like many of the Christian texts of this period, it is hard to tell whether the author is of a Jewish or gentile background. The hymns in *Odes of Solomon* often veer into the political realm. *Ode* 4: 1-2 seems to chide the Roman Emperor Titus, who presided over the destruction of the Temple in AD 70.[4] *The Odes of Solomon* also seem to have a flavor of messianic Judaism.[5]

Despite the many questions that remain, one thing is clear: music played an important role in Christian identity from the outset. We know this not only from Christian sources but also, perhaps even more importantly, from the scattered references made by outsiders. Even in the earliest days of the Church, pagan observers came to recognize Christians as singing people. During the persecutions, Christian singing in the face of hungry lions almost became a cliché. Most of the non-Christian sources of these early years say relatively little about Christianity in particular. One consistent detail, however, is the impression outsiders of Christians as singing hymns. One of the most famous Roman, non-Christian sources referencing the early Church comes from the letter of Pliny the Younger, serving as the governor of the Roman province of Bithynia and Pontus in Asia Minor. In AD 112, Pliny wrote to Trajan inquiring about how to handle the growing population of Christians in his province. Along with expressing his overall concerns, Pliny reported that Christians met at dawn to sing hymns, a distinctive behavior that seemed to set them apart.[6]

MUSIC AS PART OF THE CULTURE WARS PITTING CHRISTIANS AGAINST PAGANS

As we know, music can play a powerful role in helping groups to establish identity, something sort of like today's tensions between, say, rebellious hard rock bands and wholesome high-school choruses. In similar fashion, there is some evidence that there was a musical divide between Christians and pagans. Music and worship often factored into the culture wars that seemed to erupt as the Roman Empire Christianized during the late fourth century. In particular, the tradition of Greek/Byzantine Music owes much to these formative years when the Greek culture shifted into a Christian mode.[7] Christians seem to have had a new flavor of music, departing from ancient modes of singing. A late-third-century inscription from the town of Didyma, offered in the voice of Apollo, asks worshippers to sing the "old-fashioned songs." The passage seems to imply that music was undergoing something of a shift as the Church rose in power.[8]

The tension between Christians and pagans like later Antiquity shaped almost all aspects of culture and society, including music. In 381, the eastern part of the Empire outlawed polytheistic incantations in the pagan temples, so long equated with magic and divination. Such incantations descended from what was literally the oldest form of music. Conversely, Christians, for all their associations with hymns, found many kinds of music distasteful on moral grounds, among other problematic associations. The fourth-century Greek Christian theologian John Chrysostom (345–397) cautioned Christians against many kinds of music he deemed inappropriate, especially strange chants that bring about lascivious thoughts and behaviors.[9] He noted that while some of his flock were contemplating holy things and listening to his sermons, others had attended the theater, listening to lewd songs.

The culture-war type quarrels over such things as music went both ways. Pagans criticized Christian musical styles just as must as Christians condemned pagan chanting. A Greek teacher living in the late fourth century named Libanius bemoaned the changes in Greek and Roman traditions. He lamented the increasingly impoverished pagan temples, once the glories of their respective city-centers. Christian groups would apparently loot these temples, robbing them of their history, and their tangible assets. Libanius seemed to identify the Christian vandals and looters by, among other things, their distinctive songs. In one of his letters, a letter on the temples, *Oration* 3, Libanius reports on the state of affairs, including some comments on music. Libanius notes that Julian's successor, the co-Emperors Valens and Valentinian, permitted some residual worship in the pagan temples, including incense.

Prejudices against Christians often blended a distaste for their music with other allegations. Libanius reports that black-clad Christian monks would loot the old pagan sacred spaces. He also commented on the unique style of singing that characterized these monkish figures, a distinctive chant that differed from pagan traditions of singing. This presumably represented the beginnings of the Byzantine style of plainsong that would prove influential in both halves of the Mediterranean.[10] In another *Oration*, Libanius fondly recalls the brief flourishing of paganism enjoyed under the emperor Julian, the last pagan emperor. Under Julian, Libanius notes that the pagans refilled their ancient temples with garlands and singing.[11] Singing, particularly the distinctively Christian variety of chanting, also played a role in taunting the pagans upon the death of Julian. Sources indicate that Christians and pagan crowds clashed in the streets, singing their respective chants to taunt one another, almost like opponents in protests employ political jeers and slogans today.[12]

THE BEGINNING OF LATIN HYMNS

The demise of once brilliant Classical pagan musical traditions seems sad. Yet it did leave a vibrant new musical culture in its wake. As Christianity took root, a distinct musical heritage emerged. From its roots in Greek and Jewish cultures, this new musical culture thrived as it passed into the Latin West. But if Latin Church music owed much to its eastern Mediterranean predecessors, it soon became viable in its own right. As time passed, the Latin Church would develop its own distinct identity. The "Great Schism" between Greek/Byzantine and Roman/Latin Christianity would not formally occur until AD 1054. But we can already see the two halves of the Church growing apart by later Antiquity, two sister faiths, separated by language, culture, and geography. Over time, this brand of Latin Christianity would evolve into the Roman Catholic Church, an institution that has played a critical role in the history of the Western arts, including music.

An important development in the beginnings of Latin hymnody came from the translation of scripture in Latin, a text known as the "Vulgate." A fourth-century effort by Saint Jerome, the *Vulgate* gave a new scriptural corpus for Latin Christians to explore as they developed their own musical variations. It is hard to over-emphasize the significance of Jerome's *Vulgate*. Going forward, Latin became closely associated with Christianity. It was a holy language to Roman Christians, almost as sacred to Catholics as Hebrew is to Jews or Arabic is to Muslims. The love of scripture meant that barbarian tribes usually adopted Latin when they became Christians. Along with religion, then, Latin also became the language of learning and politics. With the spread of Roman Catholic conversions, Latin became the official language of royal courts in Italy, France, and Spain, as early as the late fifth century. This furthered cemented Latin's status as the lingua franca language of Medieval Europe.[13] Musically speaking, this meant that people often heard hymns sung in Latin, whatever the common regional language might have been that they spoke in the street, the kitchen, or the pub. Latin connected otherwise disparate peoples across a wide swath of geography.

The *Vulgate* also reflected important changes in Latin, including pronunciation. Jerome's translation reflected the Church's need to reach a wide variety of peoples, with many languages, backgrounds, and levels of education. Medieval Latin typically is simpler, with fewer subordinate clauses than the wordier Classical Latin of earlier times.[14] For this reason, Jerome's translation of the Bible into Latin played an important role in the development of the romance vernacular languages, especially Italian. Latin hymns became a primary vehicle for educating young people in the sacred language, as well as major tenets of the faith. The *Vulgate* thus became the basis of medieval Church singing. It remains important for choir directors to understand yet today.[15]

Latin hymns would soon become some of the most important writings produced. It was a true living language, borrowing from its predecessors and adding to them. Latin Christianity took the ancient hymn forms and made it its own. For example, the antiphon hymn—with its feature of sung congregational responses to a leader's sung lines—remained a strong tradition in the Roman Church. From Judaism, the antiphon had passed over into the Greek-speaking Churches of the Eastern Mediterranean, and from there to Italy. By the early Middle Ages, the antiphon had become a key element of Western Christendom's distinctive musical heritage. Latin Pope Celestine I (r. 422–432) decreed that congregants sing Latin Psalms in worship in antiphonal fashion. The move had particularly major ramifications for the Book of *Psalms* in the history of Western music, which became especially significant sources of musical inspiration. The antiphon hymn also established patterns for priestly singing and congregational response that would last for centuries to come.[16]

HILARY OF POITIERS

One of the most important of the new breed of Latin hymnists was a man named Hilary of Poitiers (AD 310–368). Historians often cite him as a key figure in the development of Latin hymnody. By combining a precise, powerful usage of Latin with sound theology, Hilary helped usher Latin into a status as one of the world's most cherished sacred languages. His careful phrasing also helped affirm Church doctrines, an especially important consideration in a time rife with heresy. By creating excellent Latin hymns, Hilary also helped shape Latin as a viable sacred language, something that was by no means a given. Already the language of Caesar and Vergil, Latin soon would become a language of Roman Catholic music, liturgy, and theology. Saint Hilary's hymns helped begin this important linguistic blend of doctrine, Latin eloquence, and musicality.

Hilary frequently focused his hymn-writing efforts on the *Psalms*. He especially favored the hymn-type known as the "jubilus," that is, "song of joy." A *jubilus* frequently focused on nature and God's creation. Such hymns featured joyful noises, sometimes not even really having much in the way of an actual text. Some hymns simply repeated words like "alleluia."[17] In fact, hymns like those of Hilary helped the now universally recognized phrase "alleluia" to pass into popular vernacular languages from its more obscure origins in ancient Judaism. "Alleluia" could have remained an arcane foreign word nestled in ancient Hebrew texts that few read outside of Judaism. Instead, it became enormously popular word. Easter services in the North African Church seemed to have borrowed the ancient Hebrew word, in particular. From there, "alleluia" passed into the Churches of both Italy and Greece. Because he especially emphasized the word, the term "alleluia" today owes much to Saint Hilary.

The word "alleluia" served an important purpose in both music and prayer. Some have even likened praying words like alleluia to nonsensical syllables, repeated almost like a mantra.[18] Like any mantra, repeating such sounds clears the mind. Such repetition presumably induces a meditative state, suitable for prayer and worshipful reflection. The use of praise-words like alleluia also helped develop the tradition of "melisma." Melisma occurs when singers sing many notes with one syllable. Melismatic singing would become one of the characteristic features of chanting during the Middle Ages.[19] Another musical tradition of Latin hymnody linked to Saint Hilary is the tradition of *psalmi idiotici*, that is, "personal psalms." In this tradition, hymnists paraphrase the ncient Hebrew Psalms in their own languages. Their words retain idea of the original psalm, with direct allusions to the ancient Hebrew hymns. Such musical phrases were ideal for personal meditation. Musicians still do this today when they adopt popular Psalms in English translation to music. For example, the twenty-third *Psalm* has inspired too much music to recount here, in scores of languages.

Saint Hilary's melismatic hymns also connected to the period when the early Church was honing its major doctrinal pillars like the Virgin Birth or the Trinity. Melisma hymns came to play an important role in promulgating correct theology. During the fourth century, the Church published numerous creeds that affirmed key Christian doctrines. Such pronouncements highly influenced both Greek and Latin hymnody, including that of Hilary.[20] Some subtle doctrines like that of the Trinity or the Virgin Birth defied conventional belief. Mysterious words like "alleluia" thus helped create the aura of majesty and mystery such doctrines required—sacred truths beyond human ken. The Easter Hymn usually attributed to Hilary is one of the most well-known hymns to feature "alleluia" in this context.[21]

LATIN HYMNS AND HOLIDAYS

Along with "alleluia," other still familiar Latin phrases in Western music owe their ubiquity to this formative period of Latin hymnody. The related Latin phrase of *in excelsis deo* also began to appear in hymns around the late fourth century. Today, the phrase is closely associated with the announcement of the birth of Christ to the shepherds in *Luke* 2: 14.[22] As a sacred holiday, Christmas received a boost when Pope Telesphorus (c. 126–137) instituted the midnight mass of Christmas. Christmas music appeared early on as a blend of the old festival style of music, incorporated into the culture, narrative and values of the Christian holiday.[23] Telesphorus took this important step toward making Christmas the major calendar date it would ultimately become by instating the singing of the Latin phrase *in excelsis deo*, still one of the most familiar Christmas Latin expressions found in Christmas music to this day.[24]

Latin hymns helped the Church achieve nominal success in Christianizing many of the old pagan festivities and holidays, as is famously the case with major Christian celebrations like Christmas, Easter, and Halloween (the Eve of All Saints Day), as well as many lesser Saints Days. The Latin Christmas Mass and music emphasized reflected the ancient Latin musical heritage, hymns, and chanting. While the Latin hymns often focused on doctrine and scripture, the Germanic carols that emerged during the Middle Ages often emphasized a tenderness and human warmth—lullabies, fellowship, merrymaking, and charity at the ground level. In the years to come, the Latin sacred heritage would happily, albeit messily, intermingle with the Germanic tradition of the Carol, the medieval style of song most closely associated with the Germanic cultures like the Franks or the Anglo-Saxons.

PRUDENTIUS

Another important Latin hymnist was the Spaniard Prudentius (d. AD 413). Like Hilary, Prudentius's hymns frequently emphasized doctrinal tents. His chant-style late-fourth-century hymn *Corde Natus Ex Parentis*—"Of the Father's Love Begotten"—still appears, in modernized forms, in hymnals around the world. Such hymns reflect Christological theology and a scholarly penchant, important qualities in a time when heresies posed a grave threat.[25] Such hymns emphasized creation, important as a doctrinal point refuting alternative heresies about the nature of God. Prudentius also emphasized the martyrs in numerous poems, highlighting a theme that was still in living memory for many older people during his lifetime.[26] Going forward, themes of martyrdom would become a major element in Christian art, literature, and theology.

Scholars have also seen in Prudentius's hymns a humanistic quality that distinguishes him from his contemporaries. Heavily influenced by the verse of Roman poets like Horace, Prudentius himself was as much poet as hymnist. His hymns made ample use of allegory and symbolism. In one famous example, Prudentius used the image of sleep as a metaphor for death.[27] Such allusive qualities made the hymns of Prudentius an important component in the development of Latin literature and poetry, as well as music. His collection of hymns called *Cathemerinon* is predicated on the concept of a hymn for certain times of the day, or life's little marker moments—the cock crowing at dawn, funerals, holidays, and prayers before meals, among other things. Scholars have noted that Prudentius's work in the *Cathemerinon* follows the ancient poets' pattern of creating a kind of cycle of poems, each one distinct, yet part of a larger thematic whole.[28] He also wrote from within the framework of overarching conceptual structures—like today's "concept albums." These hymns doubled as poetry, some of the earliest literary specimens early Christianity offers.

SAINT AMBROSE

Along with Saints Hilary and Prudentius, Saint Ambrose (late fourth century) is another important figure in the development of Latin hymnody. Had he been born two centuries earlier, a man of Ambrose's intellectual and leadership gifts would probably have become a military general or politician, the highest-status jobs for achieving people in earlier times. By the fourth century, however, times seem to have changed. The elite Ambrose became a priest instead of an outright politician. Among his many other substantial accomplishments, Ambrose was an important writer of Latin hymns. Ambrose probably really wrote a small portion of the many hymns attributed to him. Several surviving Latin specimens, however, do seem to be authentic "Ambrosian" hymns, including *Aeterne Rerum Conditor* ("Eternal Creator of All Things").[29] Like other Christian contemporaries in the West, Ambrose's Latin was not particularly derivative of Classical Latin poets. Ambrose's Latin reflected the new Latin that was evolving—less wordy, and more streamlined.[30]

Ambrose's hymns often countered the more traditional antiphonal style of a congregational response that, in the eyes of some, seemed reminiscent of the old Greek theater traditions, particularly that of the chorus. In times of cultural upheaval like those in which Ambrose lived, the antiphon—for all its beauty—could also sometimes almost seem like an exercise in warlike belligerence.[31] Congregations might cheer back their responses in a way that seemed more provocative than sacred—triumphalism disguised as worship. As an alternative, Ambrose's masterful but concise Latin texts helped establish the Latin hymn as a type of sober theological confession.[32] Like Hilary, Ambrose's hymns frequently stressed creation. A loving, omnipotent Creator God who stood apart from Creation itself was a key doctrine in refuting heresies.[33]

POPE GREGORY THE GREAT AND GREGORIAN CHANTS

As the years passed, Latin hymns and singing became perhaps most closely associated with the early Medieval Pope known as Pope Gregory the Great (r. 590–604), part of the monkish papacy that characterized the early medieval popes. By Gregory's time, the ancient traditions of hymn chanting had come of age. Rightly or wrongly (mostly wrongly), Gregory is often credited with the composition of a host of chants commonly nicknamed "Gregorian." Gregorian Chants also go by another descriptive nickname, "plainsong." Plainsong is a beautiful, descriptive and useful term, if not an entirely precise one. Because it typically featured singing in unison, people sometimes call plainsong chants "monophonic." While he most certainly did not compose all the "Gregorian Chants" commonly labeled as such, Gregory, by all accounts, sang a fine tenor. He also gave an excellent sermon and seems a genuine man of prayer.

Gregory's contributions to music bridged the divide between ancient music and that of the Middle Ages. In this period, figures like Pope Gregory did a lot to spread the evolving brand of Latin music to new geographical areas. They sent rugged missionaries into the forests and mountains of northern Europe, almost a theme of taming the wilderness. Church music became one of the most important ways that the Latin language inculcated itself in areas lying outside of the old Roman Empire or former Roman territories that barbarian tribes now held. Among the most famous missionary voyages of the early Middle Ages was the one Pope Gregory sent to Anglo-Saxon England.[34] Under Gregory's sponsorship, missionaries successfully began a small congregation in Canterbury, capital of a small Anglo-Saxon kingdom named Kent. Going forward, England would become a major center of learning and culture, including music.

THE LAST TRUMPET

As Church music evolved from its ancient settings, it mostly focused on singing. Early Churches often even seemed to eschew musical instruments in the sanctuary. The term "acapella" usually refers to singing performed with no accompaniment of musical instruments. Early on, acapella singing became Christianity's primary musical vehicle. Acapella literally means "in the chapel," a definition that reminds us of the almost exclusive focus of Church musicians on vocal music over instrumentation. Classical Antiquity's rich heritage of musical instruments, however, did come to play an important role in Christian symbolism and iconography. Even if Church music mostly focused on acapella chanting of hymns, certain musical instruments would appear in a wide range of settings, from art to theology. In this way, the Church enshrined important allusions to the music of the pre-Christian past.

One ancient musical instrument that would play an important role in Christian symbolism was the trumpet. While the trumpet's use in actual worship was extremely limited, at best, Christian iconography nonetheless would frequently use the trumpet in some of its most enduring symbols. In particular, popular imagery frequently saw a "last trumpet" as heralding the end of time. These widely recognized images come from a few key biblical passages. *Isiah* speaks of a "last trumpet" that would sound at the end of time.[35] The trumpet blast accompanies the raising of the dead, the resurrection of the flesh, an idea also recounted in the *Gospel of Matthew*.[36] Paul's epistles also contain a number of highly influential references to trumpet's playing at the end of the age, notably *I Corinthians* 15. The Bible also mentions an angelic blast of the last trumpet in Paul's *First Epistle to Thessalonians*.[37] In the Apocalypse of Saint John on the Isle of Patmos, seven angels are given seven trumpets. The blow of each angel's trumpets brings a new pestilence or tribulation to people on earth.[38]

Many African American spirituals have traditionally seen the Archangel Gabriel as sounding the final trumpet, though the New Testament does not specify this. The equation of Gabriel with blowing the trumpet owes much to John Milton's *Paradise Lost*, which helped popularize the image of trumpet-blowing Gabriel in much music in the English-speaking world.[39] An illustration from a Byzantine/Armenian text dated to 1455 depicts Gabriel blowing the last trumpet, two centuries before Milton. Clearly though, such images of Gabriel playing the trump have little if any presence in ancient Christian writings.[40]

LYRES AND HARPS IN EARLY CHRISTIAN ICONOGRAPHY

Along with the trumpet, the lyre also appeared prominently in Christian iconography regarding heaven. In general, the lyre also had a long association in Classical philosophy, equated with balance and perfection. As well as connoting ideal forms and sounds, ancient writers often associated the lyre with serenity and peace. This made it an obvious emphasis for early Church theologians when they talked about music as an extension of the sacred experience, especially in God's perfect heaven.[41] In the Bible, Saint John's *Revelation* described a chorus of harps playing in heaven. Their sound made a noise like rushing water and rolling thunder.[42] John's vision emphasized the use of harp music in heaven as an accompaniment for the voice, an image that would prove highly influential over the centuries. The image of deceased people in heaven, or angels, playing harps gained an almost universal, appearing in a wide range of references from jokes, to Milton's *Paradise Lost*, to the finest art.

As had many Classical philosophers, early "Church Fathers" also sometimes referenced the lyre as an illustrative symbol of Christian perfection and God's eternal beauty. The earliest Christian art was often limited to faint drawings of fish or doves. But such early efforts would establish themes later to flourish in medieval art. The lyre appeared early with the early Christian art that used such symbols. The Christian theologian Clement of Alexandria (d. AD 215) encouraged Christian artists to make use of a few key symbols, including the fish, the dove, and the lyre.[43] Saint John Chrysostom (d. AD 407) was another important early Church Father who helped make the image of the lyre in heaven a popular symbol. In his treatise *On the Incomprehensible Nature of God*, he wrote of voices singing in heaven, accompanied to the music of the lyre.[44] Such thinking helped shape popular ideas about heavenly harps, even if not ever meant in an entirely literal sense. Today, Modern notions of heaven often seem not to include the harp as a literal idea of life in heaven, though it persists as an enduring image in Christian symbolism.[45] As with trumpets, angels playing lyres or harps appear frequently in decorative items, especially around Christmas time.

THE ORGAN

Another musical instrument that would become closely associated with Christian culture was the organ. The organ had its roots in ancient music. Organs had made their appearance during the heyday of the late ancient world, like the famous "hydraulus" organ invention of Ctesibus of Alexandria (second century BC). This instrument made sound by using water-pressure to blow a trumpet. Overall, most ancient organs were an extension of reed instruments. In his extensive writings, Emperor Julian "the Apostate" described an organ of the mid-third century AD as a "strange growth of reeds."[46] This organ appears in ancient art like mosaics, frequently employed in arena settings like fights with animals and gladiator battles. The organist stood behind the device, which sometimes had up to fifteen reeds.[47] Even in ancient times, then, it would seem that the organ's potential as a loud and powerful musical instrument made its use in public settings an obvious choice.

These ancient forerunners of the classic Church organ were nothing like the complex and magnificently versatile pipe organs that appeared later. Such expressive musical power as the organ offered was centuries away. During the early Middle Ages, however, the organ began to make furtive appearances in music. These early organs were still primitive by the standards of later times. Readers should not envision a modern-style organ or piano keyboard. Many of these early organs were handheld folk instruments—almost like push-button concertinas or bagpipes. Such organs were often folk instruments, the way we still categorize figures like "organ grinders" today. Over time, however, ancient forerunners of the organ would evolve, ultimately becoming one of the musical instruments most closely associated with Christian worship.

Though its use was extremely limited at first, the reign of Charlemagne (r. 768–814) saw the organ increasingly play a role as a musical instrument of high-value. Its power and expressive abilities quickly distinguished it from the other more common instruments of folk music or even everyday liturgical music. Historians often cite the gift of an organ from the Greek east to the court of Charlemagne as beginning the organ's major role in Church music. Greek envoys to the Frankish emperor's court brought lavish gifts to Charlemagne from their Greek ruler, including many musical instruments. An

Church Music as an Heir of Ancient Music 131

Figure 6.1   An early style organ.

organ with brass chests and bellows of ox-hide were among the most notable musical instruments cited. It was a fine instrument, yet another example of the often-underappreciated role that musical instruments played as specimens of cultural, technological, and artisanal excellence. The bass notes of the organ were reportedly especially sonorous. The treble notes chimed like bells. The account of the organ, written around 880, seventy years after the death of Charlemagne in 814, notes that this precious organ had already been lost to posterity.[48] This organ had gone into Charlemagne's Palatine Chapel at Aachen, where some of the Frankish Empire's most important religious services occurred.

By the eleventh century, there were organs in some of the most important ecclesiastical centers of the Catholic world, including Canterbury, Cologne, Cluny, and Saint Gall.[49] As worship evolved, the organ played a critical role in the "intersensorial" nature of medieval Christian worship. The word "intersensorial" means that Catholic worship stimulated all five of the senses. The wine and bread, incense, the coolness of the dark church interiors, the dazzling art and architecture—all these powerful stimuli joined with organ music to produce a service that must have thrilled medieval congregants.[50] By the height of the Middle Ages, organs had become an important instrument in European music. The blind organist composer Francesco Landini ranked among the most famous musicians of the fourteenth century. His father was a painter who had studied under Giotto. Because of his blindness, Francesco took to music instead of art, soon becoming one of Europe's finest organ virtuosos.[51]

MARTIANUS CAPELLA AND THE SEVEN LIBERAL ARTS

Another ancient idea that the Church inherited by way of Classical influence was that of the "Seven Liberal Arts." Music was one of the seven liberal arts, usually listed along with logic, grammar, rhetoric, arithmetic, geometry, and astronomy. Though it became especially associated with medieval universities, the idea of the seven liberal arts came from Antiquity. Today, we remember these so-called seven liberal arts almost as a cliché. In their time, however, they represented a powerful vision of learning. Though subjects and foci have developed much over the centuries, we still associate the liberal arts with exposure to all the main areas of knowledge and the arts. Music remains an integral component of the liberal arts today, as it was so many centuries ago. Understanding music and appreciating its mysterious qualities is just as important for students today as it was in ancient times.

Most notions of the "Seven Liberal Arts" as emphasized in the first half of the Middle Ages owed to a few late ancient scholars, especially Martianus Cappella, a Latin North African living in what is now Algeria in the fifth century. Martianus's book *Regarding the Marriage of Philology and Mercury* borrowed heavily from earlier Greco-Roman educational models. Martianus's treatise was largely imitative.[52] Some have called Martianus's work "dull and difficult." It did provide, however, a concise, handy treatment of the seven liberal arts, personified in female form like the ancient muses.[53]

The Marriage of Philology and Mercury presented a view of music as part of the liberal arts. The book imagines pagan wedding nuptials. The happy couple is Mercury and his muse-like fiancé, the maiden Philology. The seven liberal arts are seven wedding presents from the divine guests attending the festivities—the major areas of learning personified as elegant female personas. When it comes time for Mercury to receive his gift of music, Martianus presents her as "Harmony," a beautiful maiden and the daughter of Venus. Harmony carries a shield made of concentric circles, representing the perfect union of shapes and sounds. Harmony wears strange musical instruments as jewelry. Her adornments make heavenly sounds, the likes of which the wedding guests had never heard. When the guests settle, Harmony delivers a long and complicated lecture on the history and theory of music, a summary of existing musical knowledge. Many of the technical and theoretical aspects of music as Harmony presents must have seemed garbled, even to contemporaries. Harmony does deliver, however, some interesting comments on the role of music in medicine. She reminds guests about Herophilus, the famous Alexandrian physician credited with discovering the pulse. Herophilus had used the rhythms of music to measure the pulse-rate.[54]

As one of the seven liberal arts, music would play an important role in medieval learning or, at least what people said about medieval learning. Borrowing from Martianus Capella, medieval schooling placed music into the *Quadrivium*, the four subjects of the liberal arts equated more with knowledge than the arts—geometry, arithmetic, music, and astronomy. In fact, though, music actually played of a driving role in learning during the earlier Middle Ages, when education focused heavily on language, making hymns a critical focus.[55] In much of medieval education, music simply existed as an applied discipline. As the culture of the Middle Ages grew more sophisticated, music arguably became a less important frill compared to major professional studies like medicine or law.[56] Thierry of Chartres, a teacher at Paris around 1130 and the chancellor of Chartres around 1143, produced a work often regarded as representative of the liberal arts education during this period, the *Heptateuchon*. Although admittedly unfinished, the work is notable for its relative de-emphasis on music compared to the other subjects. Thierry has fourteen discussions of dialectic and only one of music.[57]

BOETHIUS

Along with Martianus Capella, another important writer whose ideas bridged the span between Greco-Roman music ideas and those of the Middle Ages was Boethius (b. AD 480). Like Martianus Capella, Boethius's ideas about music showed the influence of Classical philosophy on early Christian music. Sometimes called "the last Classicist," Boethius's work *The Fundamentals of Music* distinguished between a musician (*musicus*) as a student of musical theory, and a singer (*cantor*) as a mere practitioner. For Boethius, a true musician had gained knowledge of music through reflection and study, not merely by working as a chapel singer.[58] Such ideas helped make understanding music theory—as opposed to simply playing music—an influential emphasis in Christian thought that would last for centuries to come.

After Boethius, music became important both in theory and in practice.[59] Like mathematical perfection, music featured an ideal to which students could aspire but never really achieve. This made music a potentially excellent study for contemplating ethics and morality, as well as revealed truth in religion.[60] In his *De Arithmetica*—"Regarding Arithmetic"—Boethius argued that music came from God, a part of creation. As with all things in creation, people discovered music, not invented it. This meant that the principles governing music mirrored the divine creative principles God had also used in creation itself. Music provided a window into the natural world. It could potentially unlock the mysteries of the cosmos—even astronomical movements and the positions of heavenly bodies. Armed with this faith in the sacred nature of music, the musician could train for moral and ethical idealism, while also learning the craft of playing or singing.[61] In another work—*De consolatione philosophiae*—"The Consolation of Philosophy"—Boethius argued that music, like medicine and oratory, represented a pure skill, impervious to greed or ambition. Those who had mastered such things had done so with purer motives and talents than base professionals. Greed or vanity could only take such individuals so far in acquiring musical mastery.[62] To be excellent in music required talent and a love of music—dedication beyond base material incentives.

THE MUSIC OF THE SPHERES

A byproduct of the idea of a musically harmonious universe was the notion of the Music of the Spheres. With its roots in ancient philosophy, the Music of the Spheres would become an important component of medieval cosmology. The Music of the Spheres idea came from the ancient Greek notion that all things vibrate, a theory some might say vaguely foreshadowed the idea of molecules. A famous anecdote related that the Greek musical theoretician Pythagoras had noticed that anvils in blacksmith shops rang at different pitches depending on the strength of the smith, not just the size of the hammer or anvil. It followed that the different velocities of the swinging hammers accounted for the anvils ringing at different pitches. Like many other such influential ideas, Pythagoras's fuzzy observation made just enough sense to prove influential. Aristotle also echoed some of these ideas about the sounds made by vibration. In his treatise *On the Soul*, Aristotle reiterated Pythagoras's view that all matter vibrate. Since vibrations cause sound, the movements of heavenly bodies produced a heavenly music.[63]

These ideas about the musical qualities of vibrations played a major role in much thinking, including about the heavens themselves.[64] It was a simple but powerful concept: all things vibrated. All vibrations made sound.[65] The sounds caused by vibrations would therefore echo in outer space, the results of heavenly bodies in their eternal motions. As they orbited in their vast cycles, the heavenly bodies made a literal, beautiful sound. Far beyond earth, this exquisite heavenly sound, full of ethereal harmonies whizzing and whirring and singing, filled the heavens with unfathomable music. Since the heavens existed beyond the fallen earth, they naturally reflected God's perfect, heavenly nature. The music of heaven was therefore like the proverbial "Lost Chord," or the ethereal sounds Paul spoke of hearing when caught up in the "Third Heaven."[66]

The Music of the Spheres also tied in with the ancient pseudo-science of numerology. Music in both the ancient and the medieval world intertwined with astronomy/astrology, particularly the idea of "Seven Celestial Spheres." These spheres—the planetary orbits—reflected the mystical associations with the number 7 that corresponded to the number of distinct notes in a modal scale. The celestial spheres also vibrated, producing their music. Since the principles of harmony that made music also applied across the board, harmony existed in nature too, including in the heavens. Thus, the "Music of the Spheres" echoed, literally and figuratively, ideas drawn from Plato's *Timaeus*, among other works.[67] Musical harmony was a perfect "platonic ideal." The idea also harkened back to those of Saint Augustine of Hippo, who had argued in his *On Music—de Musica—*that music was a perfect science, based on measuring and movement.[68]

FINAL REFLECTIONS ON CHURCH MUSIC'S LEGACY MOVING INTO THE MIDDLE AGES

Because of the importance of religion in medieval life, the beautiful music of the Church played a huge role in the continuing story of Western music as the Classical world fell into decline. In this, the Church played a critical role in preserving some of the rich musical traditions of the ancient world from which it arose. While it eschewed the pagan gods and their colorful tales, the Church could not but help to maintain some bond to the music of earlier times, especially the rich tradition of ancient hymns and chanting. Along with Classical traditions of singing, the Church also owed a great debt to the Jewish religion, particularly the important role that singing had long played in the synagogues of ancient Israel. At the same time, the Church lacked the hierarchy, resources, and infrastructure of older, more established religions. This helped make early Church music more democratic and plain. In some ways, this egalitarian quality might have helped singing in the early Church to gain popularity as a familiar feature of the Christian religion.

By later Antiquity, the growing cultural divide between the Greek-speaking half of the Roman Empire in the East and Latin speakers in the West had begun to shape Church music. In the fourth century, Jerome's translation of the Bible into Latin—the *Vulgate*—helped legitimize the Latin language as the holy language of Roman Christians. Subsequently, the already important tradition of Christian hymn singing began to develop a Latin flavor for people living in the West. The musical efforts of important figures like Hilary, Ambrose, Prudentius, and many others, provided excellent Latin hymns for future generations. By the sixth century, the Latin hymn had come of age, immortalized in the tradition of "plainsong" monastic chanting commonly associated with Pope Gregory "the Great." It is from Pope Gregory that we get the popular term "Gregorian chant."

Despite its many borrowings, the Church ignored or even outright avoided many aspects of ancient polytheistic culture, including music. Christian hymns often emphasized key doctrinal tenets, hoping to clarify orthodox Church teachings from either paganism or the growing threat of heresies. At least in terms of worship music inside the sanctuary, Church singing was almost exclusively *acapella*—a term meaning "in the chapel." All the same, ancient instruments like the harp or the trumpet came to play an important role in Christian symbolism and iconography. The ancient musical instrument of the organ also began making furtive appearances in worship, especially around the time of the Frankish ruler Charlemagne. Though minimal at first, the organ would become a major feature of Christian worship later in the Middle Ages.

Along with styles of singing, the Church also borrowed heavily from ancient philosophers who had seen music as illustrating divine perfection. As an ideal, music became one of the "seven liberal arts," a core consideration for educated Christians. Learned Christian philosophers like Martianus Capella, Boethius, or Saint Augustine of Hippo popularized the idea that music—with its harmonies and mystical mathematics—provided a glimpse, however imperfect, of God's heavenly perfection. The idea owed a lot to pagan philosophers like Pythagoras, Plato, or Plotinus. God's perfect harmonies had its most colorful illustration in the popular medieval idea of the "music of the spheres." Influenced by the ancient idea that music came from vibration, the music of the spheres envisioned heavenly bodies making ethereal music in their celestial orbits.

Derived from so many ancient philosophers, as well as perhaps a natural human instinct toward the beautiful and perfect, the Church music of medieval times would echo many ancient ideas. Music was part of a perfect, holy realm. Music resonated from God's ethereal sounds in heaven. People could thus experience something of God by contemplating beauty. Christians could approach God in sublime music, just as in fine art, architecture, or deep prayer. These ideas about music would drive medieval culture during a period when it stood at the height of its creative powers.[69] Since God had created humanity in his own image, the arts produced by people inherently reflected divine perfection, however fallen we may otherwise be. In this way, with Christianity's emphasis on sacred beauty and balance, the cultural richness of ancient music lived on after the fall of the Classical world.

NOTES

1. Elias J. Bickerman, *The Jews in the Greek Age* (Cambridge, MA: Harvard University Press, 1988), 146.
2. *I Corinthians* 14:26.
3. These possible New Testament hymns are discussed in Ralph Brucker, "Songs, Hymns and Ecomia in the New Testament," in *Literature or Liturgy? Early Christian Hymns and Prayers in their Literary and Liturgical Context in Antiquity*, edited by Clemens Leonard and Hermut Löhr (Tübingen, Germany: Mohr Siebeck, 2014), pp. 1–14, pgs. 1–2.
4. *The Earliest Christian Hymnbook: The Odes of Solomon*, translated by James H. Charlesworth (Cambridge, United Kingdom: James Clarke and Company, 2009), xiii. See also Larry W. Hurtado, *Destroyer of the Gods: Early Christian Distinctiveness in the Roman World* (Waco, TX: Baylor University Press, 2016), pp. 2–16, pg. 119.
5. Michael Anthony Novak, "The 'Odes of Solomon' as Apocalyptic Literature," *Vigiliae Christianae*, Vol. 66, No. 5 (2012), pp. 527–50, pg. 527.
6. Pliny, *Epistles*, X. 96.
7. Egon Wellesz, "Byzantine Music," *Proceedings of the Musical Association, 59th Sess.* (1932–1933), pp. 1–22, pgs. 4–5.
8. R. Harder, "*Inschriften von Didyma*, No. 217, vers. 4," in *Didyma* 2.217, with R. Harder, in *Navicula Chiloniensis* (Leiden, 1956), 88–97, as cited in Scott Bradbury, "Julian's Pagan Revival and the Decline of Blood Sacrifice," *Phoenix*, Vol. 49, No. 4 (Winter, 1995), pp. 331–56, pg. 336.
9. John Chrysostom, *Homily #3*, "On the Power of Man to Resist the Devil," 1. See also Angela Y. Kim, "Authorizing Interpretation in Poetic Compositions in the Dead Sea Scrolls and Later Jewish and Christian Traditions," *Dead Sea Discoveries*, Vol. 10, No. 1, *Authorizing Texts, Interpretations, and Laws at Qumran* (2003), pp. 26–58, pg. 40.
10. Libanius, *Oration*, 3.

11. Libanius, *Oration*, 2.

12. Sozomen, *Ecclesiastical History*, Vol. 19, as referenced in Maud W. Gleason, "Festive Satire: Julian's *Misopogon* and the New Year at Antioch," *The Journal of Roman Studies*, Vol. 76 (1986), pp. 106–19, especially ff. #38.

13. David Bleich, *The Materiality of Language: Gender, Politics, and the University* (Bloomington, IN: Indiana University Press, 2013), pg. 331.

14. Edwin Ryan, "Medieval Latin in the Secondary School," *The Classical World*, Vol. 52, No. 5 (February 1959), pp. 144–47, pgs. 144–45.

15. Charles Chapman, "How to Avoid Singing in a Vulgar Manner: How The Romans Did It," *The Choral Journal*, Vol. 20, No. 8 (April 1980), pp. 19–22, pg. 19.

16. *The Book of the Popes (Liber Pontificalis). Vol. 1 to the Pontificate of Pope Gregory I*, translated by Louise Ropes Loomis (New York, NY: Columbia University Press, 1916), 92.

17. Robert D. Reynolds, "Textless Choral Music," *The Choral Journal*, Vol. 41, No. 2 (September 2000), pp. 19–34, pgs. 19–20.

18. Augustine, The Expositions on the Psalms, Psalm 148:2, as referenced in Marian Bennett Cochrane, "The Alleluia in Gregorian Chant," *Journal of the American Musicological Society*, Vol. 7, No. 3 (Autumn, 1954), pp. 213–20, pg. 214, ff. #6.

19. William Peter Mahrt, "Gregorian Chant as a *Fundamentum* of Western Musical Culture: An Introduction to the Singing of a Solemn High Mass," *Bulletin of the American Academy of Arts and Sciences*, Vol. 33, No. 3 (December 1979), pp. 22–34, pg. 28.

20. John M. McDermott, "Hilary of Poitiers: The Infinite Nature of God," *Vigiliae Christianae*, Vol. 27, No. 3 (September 1973), pp. 172–202, pg. 189.

21. Ruth Ellis Messenger, "The Descent Theme in Medieval Latin Hymns," *Transactions and Proceedings of the American Philological Association*, Vol. 67 (1936), pp. 126–47, pg. 131.

22. Frank C. Senn, *Embodied Liturgy: Lessons in Christian Ritual* (Minneapolis, MN: Augsburg Fortress Publishers, 2016), pg. 307.

23. Edmondstoune Duncan, "Christmas Carols," *The Musical Times*, Vol. 55, No. 862 (December 1, 1914), pp. 687–91, pg. 687.

24. *The Book of the Popes (Liber Pontificalis)*, 12–13.

25. Clement Miles, *Christmas Customs and Traditions: Their History and Significance* (New York, NY: Dover Publications, 2011), pg. 32.

26. Maurice P. Cunningham, "Contexts of Prudentius' Poems," *Classical Philology*, Vol. 71, No. 1 (January 1976), pp. 56–66, pg. 58.

27. Edward Kennard Rand, "Prudentius and Christian Humanism," *Transactions and Proceedings of the American Philological Association*, Vol. 51 (1920), pp. 71–83, pg. 77.

28. Gerard O'Daly, *Days Linked by Song: Prudentius' "Cathemerinon"* (Oxford, United Kingdom: Oxford University Press, 2012), pg. 17.

29. Maurice P. Cunningham, "The Place of the Hymns of St. Ambrose in the Latin Poetic Tradition," *Studies in Philology*, Vol. 52, No. 4 (October 1955), pp. 509–14, pg. 511.

30. Cornelia C. Coulter, "Latin Hymns of the Middle Ages," *Studies in Philology*, Vol. 21, No. 4 (October 1924), pp. 571–85, pg. 574.

31. Peter Brown, *Through the Eye of a Needle: Wealth, the Fall of Rome, and the Making of Christianity in the West, 350–550 AD* (Princeton, NJ: The Princeton University Press, 2012), pg. 126.

32. Walter N. Myers, "Ancient and Medieval Latin Hymns," *The Classical Weekly*, Vol. 20, No. 20 (March 28, 1927), pp. 155–61, pg. 550.

33. Jan den Boeft, "Delight and Imagination: Ambrose's Hymns," *Vigiliae Christianae*, Vol. 62, No. 5 (2008), pp. 425–40, pg. 426.

34. Venerable Bede, *The Ecclesiastical History of the English People*, translated by Leo Shirley-Price (New York, NY: Penguin Books, 1968), II. 1.

35. *Isaiah* 27:13.

36. *Matthew* 24:31.

37. *1 Thessalonians* 4:16.

38. *Revelation* 8:1–13.

39. John Milton, *Paradise Lost*, ix. 72, as referenced in S. Vernon McCasland, "Gabriel's Trumpet," *Journal of Bible and Religion*, Vol. 9, No. 3 (August, 1941), pp. 159–61, pg. 161.

40. McCasland, "Gabriel's Trumpet."

41. Christian L. Joost-Gaugier, *Measuring Heaven: Pythagoras and His Influence on Thought and Art in Antiquity and the Middle Ages* (Ithaca, NY: Cornell University Press, 2006), pg. 106.

42. *Revelation* 14:2.

43. Clement of Alexandria, *Paedagogus*, 3.59.2–60.1. See also Christine Schenk, *Crispina and Her Sisters: Women and Authority in Early Christianity* (Minneapolis, MN: Augsburg Fortress Press, 2017), pg. 101.

44. Saint John Chrysostom, *On the Incomprehensible Nature of God*, 6. 10. See also *Sayings of the Fathers of the Church: Death, Judgement, Heaven and Hell*, edited by Edward Condon (Washington DC: The Catholic University of America Press, 2019), pg. 71.

45. Colleen McDannell and Bernhard Lang, *Heaven: A History* (New Haven, CT: Yale University Press, 1988), pg. 345.

46. Julian, *Works*, iii. 306, translated by W.C. Wright (Boston, MA: Loeb Classical Library, 1913), as referenced in Helen Robbins Bittermann, "The Organ in the Early Middle Ages," *Speculum*, Vol. 4, No. 4 (October 1929), pp. 390–410, 391–92.

47. David Creese, "Music," in *The Edinburgh Companion to Ancient Greece and Rome* (Edinburgh, United Kingdom: The Edinburgh University Press, 2010), pgs. 413–22, pg. 418.

48. Notker the Stammer, *The Deeds of Emperor Charles the Great*, II. 7.

49. Edmund A. Bowles, "The Organ in the Medieval Liturgical Service," *Revue belge de Musicologie/Belgisch Tijdschrift voor Muziekwetenschap*, Vol. 16, No. 1/4 (1962), pp. 13–29, pg. 13.

50. Jacob M. Baum, *Reformation of the Senses: The Paradox of Religious Belief and Practice in Germany* (Champaign, IL: The University of Illinois Press, 2019), 13–14.

51. Leonard Ellinwood, "Francesco Landini and His Music," *The Musical Quarterly*, Vol. 22, No. 2 (April 1936), pp. 190–216, pg. 190.

52. Edward Gibbon, *The History of the Decline and Fall of the Roman Empire*, edited by J. B. Bury, Vol. 1, 2nd Edition (London: Metheun and Co. Ltd., 1926), 422–23.

53. William Harris Stahl, *Martianus Capella and the Seven Liberal Arts, Vol. 1, The Quadrivium of Martianus Capella* (New York, NY: Columbia University Press, 1971), 21. See also Charles Homer Haskins, *The Rise of Universities* (Ithaca, NY: Cornell University Press, 1957), 28.

54. Stahl, *Martianus Capella*, 205.

55. Willemien Otten, "Nature and Scripture: Demise of a Medieval Analogy," *The Harvard Theological Review*, Vol. 88, No. 2 (April 1995), pp. 257–84, pg. 258.

56. R. W. Southern, *Western Society and the Church in the Middle Ages* (New York, NY: Penguin Boks, 1970), 277.

57. Laura Cleaver, *Education in Twelfth-Century Art and Architecture: Images of Learning in Europe c. 1100–1200* (Woodbridge, United Kingdom: Boydell, 2016), 4.

58. Boethius, *The Fundamentals of Music*, translated by C. M. Bower (New Haven, CT, 1989), p. 50, as referenced in Cleaver, *Education in Twelfth-Century Art*, 130.

59. Willemien Otten, "Christianity's Content: (Neo)Platonism in the Middle Ages, Its Theoretical and Theological Appeal," *Numen*, Vol. 63, No. 2/3, *Special Issue: Divine Word and Divine Work: Late Platonism and Religion* (2016), pp. 245–70, pg. 245.

60. Leo Schrade, "Music in the Philosophy of Boethius," *The Musical Quarterly*, Vol. 33, No. 2 (April 1947), pp. 188–200, pg. 193.

61. David S. Chamberlain, "Philosophy of Music in the *Consolatio* of Boethius," *Speculum*, Vol. 45, No. 1 (January 1970), pp. 80–97, pg. 81.

62. Boethius, *The Consolation of Philosophy*, translated by Victor Watts (New York, NY: Penguin Books, 1999), II. 6.

63. Aristotle, *On the Soul*, I. 2.

64. John Horgan, "Pythagoras's Bells," *Scientific American*, Vol. 263, No. 1 (July 1990), pp. 25–26.

65. Michael Holt, "ABC of Mathematicians," *Mathematics in School*, Vol. 4, No. 2 (March 1975), pp. 8–9, pg. 9.

66. *II Corinthians* 12:2–4.

67. Plato, *Timaeus*, 36C–D, as referenced in István M. Bodnár, "Alexander of Aphrodisias on Celestial Motions," *Phronesis*, Vol. 42, No. 2 (1997), pp. 190–205, pg. 198. See also Otto Kinkeldey, "The Music of the Spheres," *Bulletin of the American Musicological Society*, Vol. 11/12/13 (September, 1948), pp. 30–32, pg. 31.

68. Augustine, *On Music*, 3, as referenced in Otto G. von Simson, "The Gothic Cathedral: Design and Meaning," *Journal of the Society of Architectural Historians*, Vol. 11, No. 3 (October 1952), pp. 6–16, pg. 10.

69. Diane Apostolos-Cappadona, "On the Music of the Spheres: Unifying Religion and the Arts," *Philosophy of Music Education Review*, Vol. 3, No. 2 (Fall, 1995), pp. 63–68, pg. 66.

Epilogue
The Art of Ancient Music

As we have seen, music is an art—something we make or do. As such, music is one of the most important considerations in the long history of human creativity. For one thing, music has helped us make our world more beautiful and meaningful. In that sense, music is an obvious part of the Fine Arts. Music also empowered our communicative abilities, helping us in immeasurable ways. Music has an integral relationship with literature and poetry, in particular. But in a large sense, music also played a critical role in the history of *all* human ingenuity—not just things like painting, architecture, and sculpture. Music played a key role in the development of technology and science. Music is part of the history of tools. It is part of the history of cosmology—the way we understand both our world and the worlds beyond our own. Music is truly an art in the fullest sense of the term. Ancient people gave us this art, the art of ancient music. They did so while lacking so much that we take for granted today. Despite the limitations of their times, ancient people were builders. They made music, and so much more. To them, we owe a great debt.

Music is a perishable item, one of the most ephemeral of all the art forms. Who really knows what happens to music once it has passed into the air? Perhaps in some psychedelic sense, the vibrations of music linger forever. Maybe fading music blends into some cosmic sound vibration that keeps evolving. If so, such fading musical sounds never really die, they just merge into newer sounds, a forever-evolving sound palette. This would make each new sound fading into the ether an inseparable part of all the sound that has ever been or ever will be. Maybe that was what medieval people meant by the music of the spheres—the sum total of all the sounds that the universe has ever made, forever reverberating in harmony with the whirring motions of a lovingly designed creation. It is a beautiful image of music—mytho-poetic and vaguely neo-Pythagorean. What such images mean in real terms, however, is quite another question.

Fortunately for us, music is not just myth. Music is not just philosophy or metaphysical theory. Music is part of history. Indeed, music actually *is* history. Music is the sonic total of the sounds that humans have intentionally created over thousands and thousands and thousands of years. Music exists to delight our hearing, one of our five senses. Moreover, because hearing is a physical sense, music is a physical pleasure. By making music, we therefore offer listeners (and ourselves) some of life's most intense physical pleasures. We share in a very intimate form of communication when we make music. Like all forms of art, music is a language. Music can use words, as in poetry and sung lyrics. Pure music, however, transcends the world of words. This nonverbal quality makes music one of the most important ways we communicate, expressing those things that words cannot. Like poetry, music can use words, even as it elevates them to a level beyond words. Music supplements and enhances words. Music transcends words and goes beyond dictionary definitions. Music exists beyond the realm of established languages and vocabularies.

Perhaps the saddest aspect of this discussion of *The Art of Ancient Music* is the quiet realization of how much music has been forever lost to time. We can never hear the world's first music. Indeed, upon reflection, it seems like of all the Fine Arts from Antiquity, music is the most lost and irretrievable. With the visual arts, we can still see some of the statues and paintings early peoples created. We can admire their beautiful buildings, often still standing. We can read many of their writings. We can even eat some of the things they ate, ancient staple foods like bread, wine, or olives. What we cannot do, however, is hear the music that they left behind. We can never really know what ancient music sounded like, in the way we can see ancient art, or read ancient books. Ancient music is lost forever. Yes, we can get a sense of what it must have sounded like by examining ancient instruments—flutes, reeds, rhythm-making devices, and stringed-instruments like lyres or harps. But beyond merely the sounds these instruments could make, we will never know with specificity what kinds of music they made. We can never know any specific tune, style, or even playing approach, at least for sure. Thus, of all the world's early art forms, music seems the most mysterious, the most lost to posterity.

Despite the limitations we face when discussing early music several important truths emerge. First, while early peoples might not have had complex music, their impulses to make music are the same ones we still share. Music is as old as virtually any other feature of human culture. We find music on the rise almost commensurately with other features of complex human endeavors—religious ideas, symbolic thinking, and expression. We find music when we see early peoples working to beautify or explain their lives. In some of the world's most ancient excavated sites, we find their little flutes, or drums for dancing. Such poignant little artifacts stand among history's earliest examples of tools, an evolving complex culture. From these early clues, we surmise that the drive to make music stems from very basic, seemingly universal impulses. The pleasures of music, and its expressive power, made itself known to tribal peoples, very early on. From there, music continued to evolve, becoming a powerful tool of expression. Second, music has been a vital player in shaping culture, not just reflecting it. Music played an integral role in the development of literature. It was at the heart of the noble human undertakings of religious expression and philosophical inquiry. Early societies interwove music almost seamlessly into the evolution of other human endeavors like theater and sports. Competitions in music featured prizes and judging, core features of a baccalaureate tradition that would one day inform education, at the university level and beyond.

Somewhere, right now, as you are reading this, people all over the world are playing music. Think of this amazing diversity of music! Worldwide, in dozens of styles and languages, in countless settings, people are making music. People are listening to music. Right now, somewhere, musicians are on some beautiful, lavish stage performing before adoring crowds, playing in almost ideal performance conditions. Other musicians, probably many more, might be playing in some small café or living room. Some might be alone, or with others. Some musicians might be playing in an exquisite temple or cathedral. Others might play their simple hymns or songs in some roadside chapel or storefront bar. People might be humming a tune in their cars as they commute to work. Some people are singing silently in their minds, a form of unconscious meditation.

Yes, each day on planet earth, billions of people enjoy music. This music has become a given in today's world, a ubiquitous presence. We hear music in practically every elevator and office. Indeed, we take music for granted, albeit at our peril. We often assume the ability to preserve music. With Modern recording technology, we can playback many fine musical performances, virtually at will. Before recording technology existed, we still have written music, at least going back to the Renaissance. Thanks to musical notation, we can recreate with relative accuracy a composer's vision, even with music written before the invention of the phonograph. But for every "My Girl" or "Ninth Symphony," there are myriads of other compositions that will never even be performed, let alone remembered. Countless concerts, even quite good ones, will fade from memory over time. Indeed, we have already forgotten most shows. This seems the way of all things.

Over the years, the music we take for granted today will probably disappear. Eventually, all of it will be gone. Already, films and books from the 1920s and 1930s are disappearing, along with out-of-print music. Like old toasters, yesteryear's music frequently disappears, re-surfacing in attics, yard sales, and dustbins. Drawers full of old sheet music or flea markets hawking dusty vinyl records remind us how ephemeral music is, how threatened by the passing of the years. It is a bleak and brutal process, this test of time. History apparently destines some songs for oblivion, others for nostalgia or outright obscurity. Meanwhile, as some music disappears, other music grows timeless. Some music fades into nothingness while other music becomes part of a glorious cultural heritage—from classical music to classic rock. Consider how decades after Beatlemania was a crazy teenage fad, the Beatles have become truly important cultural figures. Starting as boyish pop stars, they ultimately became larger than life iconic touchstones, among the twentieth century's most important people. Many of their once famous contemporaries are already obscure, trivial-pursuit at best.

Whether depressingly obscure or immortally famous, all music shares a common stock. All people have derived this musical heritage from the simplest human societies so many centuries ago, our collective ancestors. The rude little flutes and drums of the world's first music would seem ridiculously crude by today's standards. Even the toy musical instruments we give to children today are unfathomably better than practically any early instrument. Who knows? Perhaps someday, centuries from now, people will see our musical efforts as similarly limited. Meanwhile, however, the impulse to please the ear seems destined to continue, an iron law of human tendencies. This musical legacy stands with us, shoulder to shoulder, from the most sublime to the most mundane. All the music that ever was or will be forms a precious part of this shared musical heritage, the music of history. However far music has advanced, we can all still celebrate this legacy of sounds left to us so many centuries ago, the art of ancient music.

A Select Bibliography

Abouelhadid, Sherif, "The Sacred Geometry of Music and Harmony," in *Petrie Museum of Egyptian Archaeology: Characters and Collections*, edited by Alice Stevenson (London: UCL Press, 2015), pp. 62–63.

Ahl, Frederick, "Proemion: Translating a Paean of Praise," in *Tradition, Translation, Trauma: The Classic and the Modern*, edited by Jan Parker and Timothy Mathews (New York, NY: Oxford University Press, 2011), pp. 29–39.

Albright, W. F., "An Archaic Hebrew Proverb in an Armana Letter from Central Palestine," *Journal of Near East Studies*, Vol. 89 (1943), pp. 29–32.

Aldhouse-Green, Miranda, *Caesar's Druids: Story of an Ancient Priesthood* (New Haven, CT: Yale University Press, 2010), pg. 183, ff# 59.

Alexander, Robert L., "Neoclassical Wrought Iron in Baltimore," *Winterthur Portfolio*, Vol. 18, No. 2/3 (Summer–Autumn 1983), pp. 147–186.

Alexandrescu, Cristina-Georgeta, "The Iconography of Wind Instruments in Ancient Rome: Cornu, Bucina, Tuba, and Lituus," *Music in Art*, Vol. 32, No. 1/2, *Music in Art: Iconography as a Source for Music History*, Vol. III (Spring–Fall 2007), pp. 33–46.

Angier, Tom, *'Techne' in Aristotle's Ethics: Crafting the Moral Life* (New York, NY: Continuum International Publishing, 2010).

Apostolos-Cappadona, Diane, "On the Music of the Spheres: Unifying Religion and the Arts," *Philosophy of Music Education Review*, Vol. 3, No. 2 (Fall 1995), pp. 63–68, pg. 66.

Araújo, Carolina, "Plato's Republic on Mimetic Poetry and Empathy," in *The Many Faces of Mimesis: Selected Essays from the 2017 Symposium on the Hellenic Heritage of Western Greece*, edited by Heather L. Reid and Jeremy C. DeLong (Parnassos Press – Fonte Artusa, 2018), pp. 75–85.

Aristoxenus, *The Harmonics of Aristoxenus*, edited and with a translated notes by Henry Macran (Oxford, England: Clarendon Press, 1902), pp. 65–70.

Arnold, Dorothea, "Ancient Egyptian Art: Image and Response," in *Amilla: The Quest for Excellence. Studies Presented to Guenter Kopcke in Celebration of His*

75th Birthday, edited by Robert B. Koehl (Philadelphia, PA: INSTAP Academic Press, 2013), pp. 3–16.

Arnold, Irene Ringwood, "Agonistic Festivals in Italy and Sicily," *American Journal of Archaeology*, Vol. 64, No. 3 (July 1960), pp. 245–251.

Arnott, Geoffrey W., "Swan Songs," *Greece & Rome*, Vol. 24, No. 2 (October 1977), pp. 149–153.

Aroui, Jean Louis, and Arleo, Andy, *Towards a Typology of Poetic Forms: From Language to Metrics and Beyond* (Philadelphia, PA: John Benjamins Company, 2009).

Ashby, Clifford, *Classical Greek Theatre: New Views of an Old Subject* (Iowa City, IA: The University of Iowa Press, 1999).

Assman, Jan, *Moses the Egyptian: The Memory of Egypt in Western Monotheism* (Cambridge, MA: Harvard University Press, 1998).

Avigad, Nahman, "The King's Daughter and the Lyre," *Israel Exploration Journal*, Vol. 28, No. 3 (1978), pp. 146–151.

Avronidaki, Christina, "Swan Riddles in Boeotian Red-Figure Vase-Painting," in *Corpus Vasorum Antiquorum, Österreich, Beiheft 2: ΦΥΤΑ ΚΑΙ ΖΩΙΑ. Pflanzen Und Tiere Auf Griechischen Vasen*, edited by Lang-Auinger Claudia and Trinkl Elisabeth (Wien: Austrian Academy of Sciences Press, 2015), pp. 239–248.

Bachmann, Mercedes García, "Miriam, Primordial Political Figure in the Exodus," in *Torah*, edited by Irmtraud Fischer, Mercedes Navarro Puerto, Andrea Taschl-Erber, and Jorunn Økland (Society for Biblical Literature, 2011), pp. 329–374.

Bacon, Helen H., "The Chorus in Greek Life and Drama," *Arion: A Journal of Humanities and the Classics*, Third Series, Vol. 3, No. 1, *The Chorus in Greek Tragedy and Culture*, One (Fall 1994 – Winter 1995), pp. 6–24.

Baines, Anthony, *Brass Instruments: Their History and Development* (New York, NY: Dover Publications, 1993).

Baines, Anthony, *Woodwind Instruments and their History* (New York, NY: Dover Publications, 1991).

Bamfort, Douglas B., "Flintknapping Skill, Communal Hunting, and Paleoindian Projectile Point Typology," *Plains Anthropologist*, Vol. 36, No. 137 (November 1991), pp. 309–322.

Barker, A., *Greek Musical Writings, Volume 1: The Musician and His Art* (Cambridge: Cambridge University Press, 1984).

Barnes, W. Emery, "Selah—Some Facts and a Suggestion," *The Journal of Theological Studies*, Vol. 18, No. 72 (July 1917), pp. 263–273.

Barnett, R. D., "New Facts about Musical Instruments from Ur," *Iraq*, Vol. 31, No. 2 (Autumn 1969), pp. 96–103.

Barrie, Michael, "Contour Tones and Contrast in Chinese Languages," *Journal of East Asian Linguistics*, Vol. 16, No. 4 (December 2007), pp. 337–362.

Beard, Mary, *The Roman Triumph* (Cambridge, MA: Harvard University Press, 2007).

Beare, W., "Tacitus on the Germans," *Greece & Rome*, Vol. 11, No. 1 (March 1964), pp. 64–76.

Beazley, J. D., "Citharoedus," *The Journal of Hellenic Studies*, Vol. 42, Part 1 (1922), pp. 70–98.

Bedigian, Dorothea, "History and Lore of Sesame in Southwest Asia," *Economic Botany*, Vol. 58, No. 3 (Autumn 2004), pp. 329–353.
Beecroft, Alexander, "Blindness and Literacy in the 'Lives' of Homer," *The Classical Quarterly*, New Series, Vol. 61, No. 1 (May 2011), pp. 1–18.
Benardete, Seth, *The Bow and the Lyre: A Platonic Reading of the Odyssey* (Lanham, MD: Rowman and Littlefield, 1997), pg. 126.
Bennett Cochrane, Marian, "The Alleluia in Gregorian Chant," *Journal of the American Musicological Society*, Vol. 7, No. 3 (Autumn 1954), pp. 213–220.
Bevan, Elinor, "Ancient Deities and Tortoise-Representations in Sanctuaries," *The Annual of the British School at Athens*, Vol. 83 (1988), pp. 1–6.
Bickerman, Elias J., *The Jews in the Greek Age* (Cambridge, MA: Harvard University Press, 1988).
Biles, Zachary, "Perils of Song in Homer's *Odyssey*," *Phoenix*, Vol. 57, No. 3/4 (Autumn–Winter 2003), pp. 191–208, pg. 194.
Biran, Avraham, "The Dancer from Dan," *Near Eastern Archaeology*, Vol. 66, No. 3, *Dance in the Ancient World* (September 2003), pp. 128–132.
Bitterman, Helen Robbins, "The Organ in the Early Middle Ages," *Speculum*, Vol. 4, No. 4 (October 1929), pp. 390–410.
Bjork, Robert E., *Old English Verse Saints Lives* (Toronto: University of Toronto Press, 1985).
Blacking, John, "Problems of Pitch, Pattern and Harmony in the Ocarina Music of the Venda," *African Music*, Vol. 2, No. 2 (1959), pp. 15–23.
Bleich, David, *The Materiality of Language: Gender, Politics, and the University* (Bloomington, IN: Indiana University Press, 2013).
Blyn-Ladrew, Roslyn, "Ancient Bards, Welsh Gipsies, and Celtic Folklore in the Cauldron of Regeneration," *Western Folklore*, Vol. 57, No. 4, *Locating Celtic Music (and Song)* (Autumn 1998), pp. 225–243.
Boardman, John, *Athenian Black Figure Vases: The Archaic Period* (London: Thames and Hudson, 1975).
Boatwright, Mary T., "Theaters in the Roman Empire," *The Biblical Archaeologist*, Vol. 53, No. 4 (December 1990), pp. 184–192.
Bodnár, István M., "Alexander of Aphrodisias on Celestial Motions," *Phronesis*, Vol. 42, No. 2 (1997), pp. 190–205.
Boeft, Jan den, "Delight and Imagination: Ambrose's Hymns," *Vigiliae Christianae*, Vol. 62, No. 5 (2008), pp. 425–440, pg. 426.
Boivin, Nicole, Brumm, Adam, Lewis, Helen, Robinson, Dave, and Korisettar, Ravi, "Sensual, Material, and Technological Understanding: Exploring Prehistoric Soundscapes in South India," *The Journal of the Royal Anthropological Institute*, Vol. 13, No. 2 (June 2007), pp. 267–294.
Borges, Jorge Louis, *This Craft of Verse*, edited by Calin-Andrei Mihailescu (Cambridge, MA: Harvard University Press, 2000).
Borthwick, E. K., "The Riddle of the Tortoise and the Lyre," *Music & Letters*, Vol. 51, No. 4 (October 1970), pp. 373–387.
Bosse-Griffiths, Kate, "Two Lute-Players of the Amarna Era," *The Journal of Egyptian Archaeology*, Vol. 66 (1980), pp. 70–82.

Bowles, Edmund A., "The Organ in the Medieval Liturgical Service," *Revue belge de Musicologie/Belgisch Tijdschrift voor Muziekwetenschap*, Vol. 16, No. 1/4 (1962), pp. 13–29.
Bowra, C. M., *From Vergil to Milton* (London: McMillan and Co., 1945).
Bowra, C.M., *Heroic Poetry* (London: McMillan and Co., 1952).
Bradley, K. R., "Nero's Retinue in Greece, A.D. 66/67," *Illinois Classical Studies*, Vol. 4 (1979), pp. 152–157, pg. 152.
Bradley, Richard, *Architecture, Imagination and the Ancient World*, in *Creativity and Human Evolution and Prehistory*, edited by Steven Mithen (New York, NY: Routledge, 1998), pp. 227–240, pg. 229.
Brand, Manny, "Lullabies That Awaken Musicality in Infants," *Music Educators Journal*, Vol. 71, No. 7 (March 1985), pp. 28–31.
Breasted, James Henry, "The Message of the Religion of Egypt," *The Biblical World*, Vol. 29, No. 6 (June 1907), pp. 427–434.
Brucker, Ralph, "Songs, Hymns and Ecomia in the New Testament," in *Literature or Liturgy? Early Christian Hymns and Prayers in their Literary and Liturgical Context in Antiquity*, edited by Clemens Leonard and Hermut Löhr (Tübingen, Germany: Mohr Siebeck, 2014), pp. 1–14.
Bungard, Christopher, "Reconsidering Zeus' Order: The Reconciliation of Apollo and Hermes," *The Classical World*, Vol. 105, No. 4 (Summer 2012), pp. 443–469.
Byrne, Maurice Byrne, "The Dardanos Fragments and the 40° Angular Lyre," *The Galpin Society Journal*, Vol. 46 (March 1993), pp. 3–25.
Calder, W. M., "The Dithyramb: An Anatolian Dirge," *The Classical Review*, Vol. 36, No. 1/2 (February–March 1922), pp. 11–14.
Carranza, Paul, "Philosophical Songs: The 'Song of Iopas' in the '*Aeneid*' and the Francesca Episode in *Inferno 5*," *Dante Studies*, with the *Annual Report of the Dante Society*, Vol. 120 (2002), pp. 35–51.
Carruesco, Jesús, "Choral Performance and Geometric Patterns in Epic Poetry and Iconographic Representations," in *The Look of Lyric: Greek Song and the Visual: Studies in Archaic and Classical Greek Song*, Vol. 1, edited by Vanessa Cazzato and André Lardinois (Leiden: Brill, 2016), pp. 69–109.
Carthy, J. D., "Animal Language," *Journal of the Royal Society of Arts*, Vol. 115, No. 5128 (March 1967), pp. 296–298.
Cartmill, Erica A., Beilock, Sian, and Goldin-Meadow, Susan, "A Word in the Hand: Action, Gesture and Mental Representation in Humans and Non-Human Primates," *Philosophical Transactions: Biological Sciences*, Vol. 367, No. 1585, *From Action to Language: Comparative Perspectives on Primate Tool Use, Gesture and the Evolution of Human Language* (12 January 2012): 129–143.
Castleden, Rodney, *Myceneans* (New York, NY: Routledge, 2005).
Chamberlain, David S., "Philosophy of Music in the *Consolatio* of Boethius," *Speculum*, Vol. 45, No. 1 (January 1970), pp. 80–97.
Chapman, Charles, "How to Avoid Singing in a Vulgar Manner: How The Romans Did It," *The Choral Journal*, Vol. 20, No. 8 (April 1980), pp. 19–20.
Chappell, Mike, "Delphi and the Homeric Hymn to Apollo," *The Classical Quarterly*, New Series, Vol. 56, No. 2 (December 2006), pp. 331–348.

Clark, Ann, "Is Music a Language?," *The Journal of Aesthetics and Art Criticism*, Vol. 41, No. 2 (Winter 1982), pp. 195–204.

Cloud, Daniel, *The Domestication of Language: Cultural Evolution and the Uniqueness of the Human Animal* (New York, NY: Columbia University Press, 2014).

Collingwood, R. G., *The Principles of Art* (New York, NY: Oxford University Press, 1958).

Cook, Norman D., *Tone of Voice and Mind: The Connections between Intonation, Emotion, Cognition and Consciousness* (Philadelphia, PA: John Benjamins Publishing Company, 2002).

Coulter, Cornelia C., "Latin Hymns of the Middle Ages," *Studies in Philology*, Vol. 21, No. 4 (October 1924), pp. 571–585.

Courlander, Harold, "Notes from an Abyssinian Diary," *The Musical Quarterly*, Vol. 30, No. 3 (July 1944), pp. 345–355.

Cree, Beth A., "Hopewell Panpipes: A Recent Discovery in Indiana," *Midcontinental Journal of Archaeology*, Vol. 17, No. 1 (1992), pp. 3–15.

Creese, David, "Music," in *The Edinburgh Companion to Ancient Greece and Rome* (Edinburgh, United Kingdom: The Edinburgh University Press, 2010), pp. 413–422, pg. 418.

Crocker, Richard L., "Pythagorean Mathematics and Music," *The Journal of Aesthetics and Art Criticism*, Vol. 22, No. 2 (Winter 1963), pp. 189–198.

Cunningham, Maurice P., "Contexts of Prudentius' Poems," *Classical Philology*, Vol. 71, No. 1 (January 1976), pp. 56–66.

Cunningham, Maurice P., "The Place of the Hymns of St. Ambrose in the Latin Poetic Tradition," *Studies in Philology*, Vol. 52, No. 4 (October 1955), pp. 509–514.

Curtis, Lauren, "War Music: Soundscale and Song in Vergil, *Aeneid* 9," *Vergilius* (1959), Vol. 63 (2017), pp. 37–62.

Curtis, Lauren, *Walking through Elysium: Vergil's Underworld and the Poetics of Tradition* (Toronto, Canada: The University of Toronto Press, 2020).

Dahlhaus, Carl, *The Foundations of Music History*, translated by J. B. Robinson (New York, NY: Cambridge University Press, 1982).

Darnell, John C., "The Rituals of Love in Ancient Egypt: Festival Songs of the Eighteenth Dynasty and the Ramesside Love Poetry," *Die Welt des Orients*, Bd. 46, H. 1, *The Song of Songs and Ancient Egyptian Love Poetry* (2016), pp. 22–61.

Dawson, Lawrence E., "Slip Casting: A Ceramic Technique Invented in Ancient Peru," *Ñawpa Pacha: Journal of Andean Archaeology*, Vol. 2 (1964), pp. 107–111.

Dean, Matt, *The Drum: A History* (New York, NY: Scarecrow Press, 2012).

Demand, Nancy, "Pythagoras, Son of Mnesarchos," *Phronesis*, Vol. 18, No. 2 (1973), pp. 91–96.

Doja, Albert Doja, "Socializing Enchantment: A Socio-Anthropological Approach to Infant-Directed Singing, Music Education and Cultural Socialization," *International Review of the Aesthetics and Sociology of Music*, Vol. 45, No. 1 (June 2014), pp. 115–147.

Drew, W. S., "Science and Singing," *The Musical Times*, Vol. 73, No. 1068 (1 February 1932), pp. 115–117.

Duchesne-Guillemin, Marcelle, "Music in Ancient Mesopotamia and Egypt," *World Archaeology*, Vol. 12, No. 3, *Archaeology and Musical Instruments* (February 1981), pp. 287–297.

Duncan, Edmondstoune, "Christmas Carols," *The Musical Times*, Vol. 55, No. 862 (December 1, 1914), pp. 687–691.

Dyer, Robert, "The Blind Bard of Chios (Hymn. Hom. AP. 171–176)," *Classical Philology*, Vol. 70, No. 2 (April 1975), pp. 119–121.

Ehlers, Maren A., *Give and Take: Poverty and the Status Order in Early Modern Japan* (Cambridge, MA: Harvard University Press, 2018).

Elliot, John H., *Beware the Evil Eye; The Evil Eye in the Bible and the Ancient World: Volume One – Introduction, Mesopotamia, and Egypt* (Cambridge, United Kingdom: James Clarke and Co., 2016).

Ellis, George F. R., "Biology and Mechanisms Related to the Dawn of Language," in *Homo Symbolicus: The Dawn of Language, Imagination and Spirituality*, edited by Christopher Henshilwood and Francesco d'Errico (Philadelphia, PA: John Benjamins Publishing Company, 2011, pp. 163–185.

Errico, Francesco d', et al., "Archaeological Evidence for the Emergence of Language, Symbolism, and Music—An Alternative Multidisciplinary Perspective," *Journal of World Prehistory*, Vol. 17, No. 1 (March 2003), pp. 1–70.

Espíndola, Laura Liliana Gómez, "Plato on the Political Role of Poetry," in *Politics and Performance in Western Greece: Essays on the Hellenic Heritage of Sicily and Southern Italy*, edited by Heather L. Reid, Davide Tanasi, and Susi Kimbell (Parnassos Press – Fonte Aretusa, 2017).

Evangeliou, Christos C., "Portraits of Plotinus and the Symmetry Theory of Beauty," in *Looking at Beauty to Kalon in Western Greece: Selected Essays from the 2018 Symposium on the Heritage of Western Greece*, edited by Heather L. Reid and Tony Leyh (Parnassos Press – Fonte Aretusa, 2019), pp. 256–268.

Evelyn-White, Hugh G., "The Myth of the Nostoi," *The Classical Review*, Vol. 24, No. 7 (November 1910), pp. 201–205.

Fagg, Catherine, "What Is a Lithophone – And What Is a Rock Gong?," *The Galpin Society Journal*, Vol. 47 (March 1994), pp. 154–155.

Falk, Dean, *Finding Our Tongues: Mothers, Infants and the Origins of Language* (New York, NY: Perseus Books Group, 2009).

Farber, Walter, "Magic at the Cradle. Babylonian and Assyrian Lullabies," *Anthropos*, Bd. 85, H. 1./3. (1990), pp. 139–148.

Feldman, Ariel, "The Song of Miriam (4Q365 6a ii + 6c 1–7) Revisited," *Journal of Biblical Literature*, Vol. 132, No. 4 (2013), pp. 905–911.

Ferranti, Hugh de, "Transmission and Textuality in the Narrative Traditions of Blind Biwa Players," *Yearbook for Traditional Music*, Vol. 35 (2003), pp. 131–152.

Finley, Moses, *The World of Odysseus* (New York, NY: New York Review of Books, 1982).

Fischer, Hermann, "Barditus," *Zeitschrift für deutsches Altertum und deutsche Literatur*, Bd. 50, H. 1./2. (1908), pp. 145–148.

Fitch, W. Tecumseh, *The Evolution of Language* (New York, NY: Cambridge University Press, 2010).

Fleming, Thomas J., "The Musical Nomos in Aeschylus' Oresteia," *The Classical Journal*, Vol. 72, No. 3 (February–March 1977), pp. 222–233.
Flory, Stewart, "Arion's Leap: Brave Gestures in Herodotus," *The American Journal of Philology*, Vol. 99, No. 4 (Winter 1978), pp. 411–421.
Foote, Theodore C., "The Ephod," *Journal of Biblical Literature*, Vol. 21, No. 1 (1902), pp. 1–47.
Ford, Andrew, *Earth Dances: Music in Search of the Primitive* (Collingwood VIC, Australia: Black Inc., 2015).
Ford, Andrew, *Homer: The Poetry of the Past* (Ithaca, NY: Cornell University Press, 1992).
Foster, Sam, *Hey Diddle Diddle: Our Best-loved Nursery Rhymes and What They Really Mean* (Chichester, West Sussex: Summersdale Publishers, 2008).
Freud, Sigmund, *Jokes and their Relation to the Unconscious* (New York, NY: W.W. Norton and Company, 1960).
Frishmuth, Sarah S., "Stringed Instruments," *Bulletin of the Pennsylvania Museum*, Vol. 3, No. 11 (July 1905), pp. 45–48.
Gaare, Mark, "Alternatives to Traditional Notation," *Music Educators Journal*, Vol. 83, No. 5 (March 1997), pp. 17–23.
Gaddini, Rennata, "Lullabies and Rhymes in the Emotional Life of Children," in *Winnicott Studies*, No. 11, Spring 1996 (London: Karnac Books, 1996), pp. 28–41.
Gann, Kyle, *The Arithmetic of Listening: Tuning Theory and History for the Impractical Musician* (Champaign, IL: The University of Illinois Press, 2019).
Garroway, Kristine Henriksen, *Growing Up in Ancient Israel: Children in Material Culture and Biblical Texts* (Atlanta, GA: The Society of Biblical Literature, 2018).
Gates, Charles, *Ancient Cities: The Archaeology of Urban Life in the Ancient near East and Egypt, Greece and Rome* (Abingdon, United Kingdom: Routledge, 2011).
Gates, Rachael, Forrest, L. Arick, and Obert, Kerrie, *The Owner's Manual to the Voice: A Guide for Singers and Other Professional Voice Users* (New York, NY: Oxford University Press, 2013).
Gebhard, Elizabeth, "The Form of the Orchestra in the Early Greek Theater," *Hesperia: The Journal of the American School of Classical Studies at Athens*, Vol. 43, No. 4 (October–December 1974), pp. 428–440.
Geller, M. J., "Magic and Mesopotamia: How the Magic Works," *Folklore*, Vol. 108 (1997), pp. 1–7.
Gerson-Kiwi, Edith, "Religious Chant: A Pan-Asiatic Conception of Music," *Journal of the International Folk Music Council*, Vol. 13 (1961), pp. 64–67.
Gibson, A. J., "The Story of Lac," *Journal of the Royal Society of Arts*, Vol. 90, No. 4611 (April 17, 1942), pp. 319–335.
Gibson, Walter S., "*Asinus Ad Lyram*: From Boethius to Bruegel and Beyond," *Simiolus: Netherlands Quarterly for the History of Art*, Vol. 33, No. 1/2, Nine Offerings for Jan Piet Filedt Kok (2007/2008), pp. 33–42.
Goebel, Julius, "On the Original Form of the Legend of Sigfrid," *PMLA* (i.e., *Publications of the Modern Language Association*), Vol. 12, No. 4 (1897), pp. 461–474, pg. 470.

Gordon, Edwin E., *Music Learning Theory for Newborn and Young Children* (Chicago, IL: GIA Publications, 2013).

Grayson, Charles E., French, Mary, and O'Brien, Michael J., *Traditional Archery from Six Continents: The Charles E. Grayson Collection* (Columbia, MO: The University of Missouri Press, 2007).

Greek Gods and Goddesses, edited by Michael Taft and Michael Croce (New York, NY: Rosen Publishing Group, 2013), pg. 59.

Gumà, Jesús Salia, *Etnoarqueomusicologia: La producción de sonidos ya la reproducción social en las sociedades cazadoras-recolectoras* (Madrid: Consejo Superior de Investigaciones Científicas, 2015).

Gwara, Scott, *Heroic Identity in the World of Beowulf* (Boston, MA: E. J. Brill, 2008).

Gyles, Mary Francis, "Nero Fiddled while Rome Burned," *The Classical Journal*, Vol. 42, No. 4 (January 1947), pp. 211–217.

Gyles, Mary Francis, "Nero: *Qualis Artifex*?," *The Classical Journal*, Vol. 57, No. 5 (February 1962), pp. 193–200.

Haeberli, Joerg, "Twelve Nasca Panpipes: A Study," *Ethnomusicology*, Vol. 23, No. 1 (January 1979), pp. 57–74.

Hagel, Stefan, "Re-evaluating the Pompeii Auloi," *The Journal of Hellenic Studies*, Vol. 128 (2008), pp. 52–71.

Hagen, Sivert N., "On the Origin of the Term Edda," *Modern Language Notes*, Vol. 19, No. 5 (May 1904), pp. 127–134.

Haldane, J. A., "Musical Themes and Imagery in Aeschylus," *The Journal of Hellenic Studies*, Vol. 85 (1965), pp. 33–41.

Hamilton, Richard, "The Pindaric Dithyramb," *Harvard Studies in Classical Philology*, Vol. 93 (1990), pp. 211–222.

Hardie, Alex, "Etymologising the Muse," *Materiali e discussioni per l'analisi dei testi classici*, Vol. 62 (2009), pp. 9–57.

Harmon, Roger, "Plato, Aristotle, and Women Musicians," *Music & Letters*, Vol. 86, No. 3 (August 2005), pp. 351–356.

Harris, John Philip, "Cassandra's Swan Song: Aeschylus' Use of Fable in Agamemnon," *Greek, Roman, and Byzantine Studies*, Vol. 52 (2012), pp. 540–558.

Harris, William, *Ancient Literacy* (Cambridge, MA: Harvard University Press, 1989).

Harrod, James B., "The Bow: A Techno-Mythic Hermeneutic: Ancient Greece and the Mesolithic," *Journal of the American Academy of Religion*, Vol. 49, No. 3 (September 1981), pp. 425–446.

Haskins, Charles Homer, *The Rise of Universities* (Ithaca, NY: Cornell University Press, 1957).

Haupt, Edward J., "The First Memory Drum," *The American Journal of Psychology*, Vol. 114, No. 4 (Winter 2001), pp. 601–622.

Hay, Harold, *The Organization of the Pyramid Texts* (Boston, MA: E. J. Brill, 2012), pp. 1–2.

Heffron, Yağmur, "Revisiting 'Noise' (rigmu) in Atra-ḫasīs in Light of Baby Incantations," *Journal of Near Eastern Studies*, Vol. 73, No. 1 (April 2014), pp. 83–93.

Henrichs, Albert, "Greek Maenadism from Olympias to Messalina," *Harvard Studies in Classical Philology*, Vol. 82 (1978), pp. 121–160.
Henry, Kenneth G., "Roman Actors," *Studies in Philology*, Vol. 16, No. 4 (October 1919), pp. 334–382.
Hernández, Pura Nieto, "Penelope's Absent Song," *Phoenix*, Vol. 62, No. 1/2 (Spring–Summer/*printemps-été* 2008), pp. 39–62.
Hicks, Michael, "Soothing the Savage Beast: A Note on Animals and Music," *The Journal of Aesthetic Education*, Vol. 18, No. 4 (Winter 1984), pp. 47–55.
Higgins, Dolores O., "Lucan as '*Vates*'," *Classical Antiquity*, Vol. 7, No. 2 (October 1988), pp. 208–226.
Hipsher, Edward Ellsworth, "Do Animals like Music?," *The Musical Quarterly*, Vol. 12, No. 2 (April 1926), pp. 166–174.
Holt, Michael, "ABC of Mathematicians," *Mathematics in School*, Vol. 4, No. 2 (March 1975), pp. 8–9.
Holzman, Samuel, "Tortoise-Shell Lyres from Phrygian Gordion," *American Journal of Archaeology*, Vol. 120, No. 4 (October 2016), pp. 537–564.
Honig, Alice Sterling, "The Language of Lullabies," *YC Young Children*, Vol. 60, No. 5 (September 2005), pp. 30–36.
Honig, Henkjan, Cate, Carel ten, Peretz, Isabelle, and Trehub, Sandra E., "Introduction: Without it No Music: Cognition, Biology and Evolution of Musicality," *Philosophical Transactions: Biological Sciences*, Vol. 370, No. 1664, *Theme Issue: Biology, Cognition and Origins of Musicality* (19 March 2015), pp. 1–8.
Houtman, C., "On the Pomegranates and the Golden Bells of the High Priest's Mantle," *Vetus Testamentum*, Vol. 40, Fasc. 2 (April 1990), pp. 223–229.
Huehns, Colin, "The 'Early Music' Erhu," *The Galpin Society Journal*, Vol. 54 (May 2001), pp. 56–61.
Hume, Lynne, *Portals: Opening Doorways to Other Realities through the Senses* (New York, NY: Berg, 2007).
Hwang, Philip H., "Poetry in Plato's Republic," *Apeiron: A Journal for Ancient Philosophy and Science*, Vol. 15, No. 1 (June 1981), pp. 29–37.
Izenour, George, "The Ancient Roman Roofed Theater," *Perspecta*, Vol. 26, *Theater, Theatricality, and Architecture* (1990), pp. 69–82.
Horgan, John, "Pythagoras's Bells," *Scientific American*, Vol. 263, No. 1 (July 1990), pp. 25–26.
Jabbour, Alan, "Memorial Transmission in Old English Poetry," *The Chaucer Review*, Vol. 3, No. 3 (Winter 1969), pp. 174–190.
Jacobsen, Karl N., *Memories of Asaph: Mnemohistory and the Psalms of Asaph* (Minneapolis, MN: Augsburg Fortress Press, 2017).
Jáuregui, Miguel Herrero de, *Orphism and Christianity in Late Antiquity*, translated by Agestrad (New York, NY: Walter de Gruyter, 2010).
Jones, A. M., "Panpipes and the Equiheptatonic Pitch," *African Music*, Vol. 6, No. 1 (1980), pp. 62–69.
Joseph, Sister Miriam, *The Trivium: The Liberal Arts of Logic, Grammar and Rhetoric: Understanding the Nature and Function of Language* (Philadelphia, PA: Paul Dry Books, 2002).

Joost-Gaugier, Christian L., *Measuring Heaven: Pythagoras and His Influence on Thought and Art in Antiquity and the Middle Ages* (Ithaca, NY: Cornell University Press, 2006).

Keer, Ellen Van, "The Myth of Marsyas in Ancient Greek Art: Musical and Mythological Iconography," *Music in Art*, Vol. 29, No. 1/2, *Music in Art: Iconography as a Source for Music History Volume I* (Spring–Fall 2004), pp. 20–37.

Keith, A. Berriedale, "Pythagoras and the Doctrine of Transmigration," *The Journal of the Royal Asiatic Society of Great Britain and Ireland*, Vol. 20 (July 1909), pp. 569–606.

Kessels, S. H., "Is There a Highest Art?," *Music & Letters*, Vol. 12, No. 4 (October 1931), pp. 398–404.

Kim, Angela Y., "Authorizing Interpretation in Poetic Compositions in the Dead Sea Scrolls and Later Jewish and Christian Traditions," *Dead Sea Discoveries*, Vol. 10, No. 1, *Authorizing Texts, Interpretations, and Laws at Qumran* (2003), pp. 26–58.

King, Barbara J., "When Animals Mourn," *Scientific American*, Vol. 309, No.1 (July 2013), pp. 62–67.

Kinkeldey, Otto, "The Music of the Spheres," *Bulletin of the American Musicological Society*, Vol. 11/12/13 (September 1948), pp. 30–32.

Kirby, Percival R., *The Musical Instruments of the Indigenous People of South Africa* (Johannesburg: Wits University Press, 2013).

Kirby, Percival R., "The Trumpets of Tut-Ankh-Amen and Their Successors," *Man*, Vol. 49 (February 1949), p. 19.

Kitto, H. D. F., "The Greek Chorus," *Educational Theatre Journal*, Vol. 8, No. 1 (March 1956), pp. 1–8.

Kivilo, Maarit, *Early Greek Poets' Lives: The Shaping of the Tradition* (Boston, MA: E. J. Brill, 2010).

Klinghart, Matthias, "Prayer Formularies for Public Recitation. Their Use and Function in Ancient Religion," *Numen*, Vol. 46, No. 1 (1999), pp. 1–52.

Kramer, Samuel Noah, "Heroes of Sumer: A New Heroic Age in World History and Literature," *Proceedings of the American Philosophical Society*, Vol. 90, No. 2 (May 1946), pp. 120–130.

Kramer, Samuel Noah, "Immortal Clay: The Literature of Sumer," *The American Scholar*, Vol. 15, No. 3 (Summer 1946), pp. 314–326.

Krappe, Alexander H., "The Legend of Amphion," *The Classical Journal*, Vol. 21, No. 1 (October 1925), pp. 21–28.

Kuiper, Kathleen, *Ancient Egypt: From Prehistory to the Islamic Conquest* (New York, NY: Britannica Educational Publishing, 2011).

Kyle, Donald G., "Winning at Olympia," *Archaeology*, Vol. 49, No. 4 (July/August 1996), pp. 26–37.

Landels, J. G., "The Reconstruction of Ancient Greek *Auloi*," *World Archaeology*, Vol. 12, No. 3, *Archaeology and Musical Instruments* (February 1981), pp. 298–302.

Landels, John G., *Music in Ancient Greece and Rome* (New York, NY: Routledge, 1999).

Laweregren, Bo, and Gurney, O. R., "Sound Holds and Geometrical Figures: Clues to the Terminology of Ancient Mesopotamian Harps," *Iraq*, Vol. 49 (1987), pp. 37–52.

Lawergren, Bo, "Distinctions among Canaanite, Philistine, and Israelite Lyres, and Their Global Lyrical Contexts," *Bulletin of the American Schools of Oriental Research*, Vol. 309 (February 1998), pp. 41–68.

Lawergren, Bo, "The Origin of Musical Instruments and Sounds," *Anthropos*, Bd. 83, H. 1./3. (1988), pp. 31–45.

Lawler, Lillian B., *The Dance in Ancient Greece* (Middletown, CT: Wesleyan University Press, 1964).

Lawler, Lillian B., "The Maenads: A Contribution to the Study of the Dance in Ancient Greece," *Memoirs of the American Academy in Rome*, Vol. 6 (1927), pp. 69–112, pgs. 74–75.

Leibovitch, J., "The Statuette of an Egyptian Harper and String-Instruments in Egyptian Statuary," *The Journal of Egyptian Archaeology*, Vol. 46 (December 1960), pp. 53–59.

Lesley, Michael, "Illusions of Grandeur: The Instruments of *Daniel* 3 Reconsidered," in *Music in Antiquity: The Near East and Mediterranean*, edited by Joan Goodnick Westenholz, Yossi Maurey, Edwin Seroussi, and Joan Goodnick Westenholz (Boston, MA: Walter de Gruyter, 2014), pp. 201–202.

Ley, Graham, *The Theatricality of Greek Tragedy: Playing Space and Chorus* (Chicago, IL: The University of Chicago Press, 2007).

Leyland, John, "Musical Instruments as Works of Art," *The Decorator and Furnisher*, Vol. 12, No. 3 (June 1888), pp. 87–89.

Lönnroth, Lon, "Hjálmar's Death-Song and the Delivery of Eddic Poetry," *Speculum*, Vol. 46, No. 1 (January 1971), pp. 1–20.

Lonsdale, Steven H., "'Homeric Hymn to Apollo': Prototype and Paradigm of Choral Performance," *Arion: A Journal of Humanities and the Classics*, Third Series, Vol. 3, No. 1, *The Chorus in Greek Tragedy and Culture*, One (Fall 1994 – Winter 1995), pp. 25–40.

Lyne, R. O. A. M., "Horace Odes Book 1 and the Alexandrian Edition of Alcaeus," *The Classical Quarterly, New Series*, Vol. 55, No. 2 (December 2005), pp. 542–558.

Maas, Martha, "Polychordia and the Fourth-Century Greek Lyre," *The Journal of Musicology*, Vol. 10, No. 1 (Winter 1992), pp. 74–88.

Macchioro, Vittorio, "Orphism and Paulinism," *The Journal of Religion*, Vol. 8, No. 3 (July 1928), pp. 337–370.

Mackellar, Jo, *Event Audiences and Expectations* (Abingdon, United Kingdom: Routledge Press, 2018).

Mahrt, William Peter, "Gregorian Chant as a *Fundamentum* of Western Musical Culture: An Introduction to the Singing of a Solemn High Mass," *Bulletin of the American Academy of Arts and Sciences*, Vol. 33, No. 3 (December 1979), pp. 22–34.

Malm, William P., *Japanese Music and Musical Instruments* (Rutland, Vermont: Charles E. Tuttle Company, 1959).

Malone, Kemp, "Coming Back from the Mere," *PMLA* (i.e. *Publications of the Modern Language Association*), Vol. 69, No. 5 (December 1954), pp. 1292–1299.

Marconi, Clemente, "Early Greek Architectural Decoration in Function," in *KOINE: Mediterranean Studies in Honor of R. Ross Holloway*, edited by Derek B. Counts and Anthony S. Tuck (Oxford, United Kingdom: Oxbow Books, 2009), pp. 4–17.

Marlow, A. N., "Orpheus in Ancient Literature," *Music & Letters*, Vol. 35, No. 4 (October 1954), pp. 361–369.

Mazar, Amihai, "Ritual Dancing in the Iron Age," *Near Eastern Archaeology*, Vol. 66, No. 3, *Dance in the Ancient World* (September 2003), pp. 126–127, pg. 126.

McCasland, Vernon S., "Gabriel's Trumpet," *Journal of Bible and Religion*, Vol. 9, No. 3 (August 1941), pp. 159–161.

McDermott, John M., "Hilary of Poitiers: The Infinite Nature of God," *Vigiliae Christianae*, Vol. 27, No. 3 (September 1973), pp. 172–202.

Menaker, Daniel, "Watching Sports," *Grand Street*, Vol. 7, No. 1 (Autumn 1987), pp. 208–213.

Mesopotamia: The World's Earliest Civilization, edited by Kathleen Kuiper (New York, NY: Rosen Educational Services, 2011).

Messenger, Ruth Ellis, "The Descent Theme in Medieval Latin Hymns," *Transactions and Proceedings of the American Philological Association*, Vol. 67 (1936), pp. 126–147.

Miles, Clement, *Christmas Customs and Traditions: Their History and Significance* (New York, NY: Dover Publications, 2011).

Miller, James E., "Ancient Greek Demythologizing," in *Myth and Scripture: Contemporary Perspectives on Religion, Language, and Imagination*, edited by Dexter E. Callender (Atlanta, GA: Society for Biblical Literature Press, 2014), pp. 213–229.

Miller, Malcolm, "Ancient Symbols, Modern Meanings the Use of the Shofar in Twentieth- and Twenty-First-Century Music," in *Qol Tamid: The Shofar in Ritual, History, and Culture*, edited by Jonathan L. Friedmann and Joel Gereboff (Claremont, CA: Claremont Press, 2017), pp. 165–220.

Miller, Stephen G., and Christesen, Paul, *Arete: Greek Sports from Ancient Sources* (Berkeley, CA: The University of California Press, 2012).

Miller, Terry, "Appropriating the Exotic: Thai Music and the Adoption of Chinese Elements," *Asian Music*, Vol. 41, No. 2 (Summer/Fall 2010), pp. 113–148.

Mitchell, Jack, "Literary Quotation as Literary Performance in Suetonius," *The Classical Journal*, Vol. 110, No. 3 (February–March 2015), pp. 333–355.

Montagu, Jeremy, "One of Tut'ankhamūn's Trumpets," *The Journal of Egyptian Archaeology*, Vol. 64 (1978), pp. 133–134.

Montagu, Jeremy, "The Conch in Prehistory: Pottery, Stone and Natural," *World Archaeology*, Vol. 12, No. 3, *Archaeology and Musical Instruments* (February 1981), pp. 273–279.

Montagu, Jeremy, *Horns and Trumpets of the World: An Illustrated Guide* (New York, NY: Rowman and Littlefield, 2014).

Montagu, Jerry, "One of Tutankhamon's Trumpets," *The Galpin Society Journal*, Vol. 29 (May 1976), pp. 115–117.

Montgomery, James A., "Stanza-Formation in Hebrew Poetry," *Journal of Biblical Literature*, Vol. 64, No. 3 (September 1945), pp. 379–384.

Moore, Christopher, *Calling Philosophers Names: On the Origins of a Discipline* (Princeton, NJ: Princeton University Press, 2020).

Morris, Ian, "The Use and Abuse of Homer," *Classical Antiquity*, Vol. 5, No. 1 (April 1986), pp. 81–138.

Müller, Hildegund, "Challenges to Classical Education in Late Antiquity: The Case of Augustine of Hippo," in *A Companion to Ancient Education*, edited by W. Martin Bloomer (Chichester, West Sussex: Wiley Blackwell and Sons, 2015), pp. 358–373.

Muñoz, Daniel Sanchez, "The South Face of the Helicon: Ancient Egyptian Musical Elements in Ancient Greek Music," in *Current Research in Egyptology 2016: Proceedings of the Seventeenth Annual Symposium*, edited by Julia Chyla, Joanna Debowska-Ludwin, and Carl Walsh (Philadelphia, PA: Oxbow Books, 2017), pp. 173–186.

Myers, Robert Manson, "Neo-Classical Criticism of the Ode for Music," *PMLA* (i.e. *Publications of the Modern Language Association*), Vol. 62, No. 2 (June 1947), pp. 399–421.

Myers, Walter N., "Ancient and Medieval Latin Hymns," *The Classical Weekly*, Vol. 20, No. 20 (28 March 1927), pp. 155–161.

Nagano, Kent, and Kloepfer, Inge, *Classical Music: Expect the Unexpected*, translated by Hans-Christian Oeser (Chicago, IL: McGill Queen's University Press, 2019).

Nervegna, Sebastiana, "Staging Scenes or Plays? Theatrical Revivals of 'Old' Greek Drama in Antiquity," *Zeitschrift für Papyrologie und Epigraphik*, Bd. 162 (2007), pp. 14–42.

Newman, John Kevin, *The Classical Epic Tradition* (Madison, WI: The University of Wisconsin Press, 1986).

Nightingale, Andrea Wilson, "On Wandering and Wondering: '*Theôria*' in Greek Philosophy and Culture," *Arion: A Journal of Humanities and the Classics*, Third Series, Vol. 9, No. 2 (Fall 2001), pp. 23–58.

Nist, John, "Beowulf and the Classical Epics," *College English*, Vol. 24, No. 4 (January 1963), pp. 257–262.

Nortwick, Thomas Van, *Somewhere I have Never Travelled: The Hero's Journey* (New York, NY: Oxford University Press, 1996).

Novak, Michael Anthony, "The 'Odes of Solomon' as Apocalyptic Literature," *Vigiliae Christianae*, Vol. 66, No. 5 (2012), pp. 527–550.

Nuckolls, Janis B., "The Case for Sound Symbolism," *Annual Review of Anthropology*, Vol. 28 (1999), pp. 225–252.

Ohrt, F., "Abracadabra," *The Journal of the Royal Asiatic Society of Great Britain and Ireland*, Vol. 1 (January 1922), pp. 86–88.

Olsen, Dale A., *World Flutelore: Folktales, Myths and Other Stories of Magical Flute Power* (Chicago, IL: The University of Illinois Press, 2013).

Ostwald, Martin, *Language and History in Ancient Greek Culture* (Philadelphia, PA: The University of Pennsylvania Press, 2009).

Otten, Willemien, "Christianity's Content: (Neo)Platonism in the Middle Ages, Its Theoretical and Theological Appeal," *Numen*, Vol. 63, No. 2/3, *Special Issue: Divine Word and Divine Work: Late Platonism and Religion* (2016), pp. 245–270.

Palti, Kathleen, "Singing Women: Lullabies and Carols in Medieval England," *The Journal of English and Germanic Philology*, Vol. 110, No. 3 (July 2011), pp. 359–382.

Pasnau, Robert, "Epistemology Idealized," *Mind*, Vol. 122, No. 488 (October 2013), pp. 987–1021.

Paxson, Thomas D., "Art and Paideia," *The Journal of Aesthetic Education*, Vol. 19, No. 1, *Special Issue: Paestum and Classical Culture: Past and Present* (Spring 1985), pp. 67–78.

Pennisi, Elizabeth, "The First Language?," *Science, New Series*, Vol. 303, No. 5662 (February 27, 2004), pp. 1319–1320.

Perlove, Nina, "Inherited Sound Images: Native American Exoticism in Aaron Copland's Duo for Flute and Piano," *American Music*, Vol. 18, No. 1 (Spring 2000), pp. 50–77.

Perry, E. D., "Greek Literature," *The Classical Weekly*, Vol. 5, No. 23 (20 April 1912), pp. 178–182.

Pickard-Cambridge, A. W., *Dithyramb, Tragedy and Comedy*, revised by T. B. L. Webster (Cambridge, United Kingdom: Cambridge University Press, 1962).

Pinker, Steven, *How the Mind Works* (New York, NY: W.W. Norton and Co., 1997).

Poetry and Drama: Literary Terms and Concepts, edited by Katherine Kuiper (New York, NY: Britannica Educational Publishing, 2012), pg. 17.

Pomeroy, Sarah, "Plato and the Female Physician (Republic 454d2)," *The American Journal of Philology*, Vol. 99, No. 4 (Winter 1978), pp. 496–500.

Porter, John R., "Aristophanes, *Acharnians*. 1118–1121, 151," *Greece & Rome*, Vol. 51, No. 1 (April 2004), pp. 21–33.

Potter, John, and Sorrell, Neil, *A History of Singing* (New York, NY: Cambridge University Press, 2012).

Pound, Louise, "The Ballad and the Dance," *PMLA*, Vol. 34, No. 3 (1919), pp. 360–400.

Power, Timothy, "Vergil's *Citharodes*: Cretheus and Iopas Reconsidered," *Vergilius* (1959), Vol. 63 (2017), pp. 93–124.

Proulx, Donald A., *A Sourcebook of Nasca Ceramic Iconography: Reading a Culture through its Art* (Iowa City, IA: The University of Iowa Press, 2006), pg. 14.

Pulver, Jeffrey, "The Music of Ancient Egypt," *Proceedings of the Musical Association 48th Sess.* (1921–1922), pp. 29–55.

Racy, Ali Jihad, "A Dialectical Perspective on Musical Instruments: The East-Mediterranean Mijwiz," *Ethnomusicology*, Vol. 38, No. 1 (Winter 1994), pp. 37–57.

Ramsey, John T., "Cicero Pro Murena 29: The Orator as Citharoedus. The Versatile Artist," *Classical Philology*, Vol. 79, No. 3 (July 1984), pp. 220–225.

Rand, Edward Kennard, "Prudentius and Christian Humanism," *Transactions and Proceedings of the American Philological Association*, Vol. 51 (1920), pp. 71–83.

Rao, M. S. Nagaraja, "Survival of Certain Neolithic Elements among the Boyas of Tekkalakota," *Anthropos*, Bd. 60, H. 1./6. (1965), pp. 480–486.
Rawlins, F. I. G., "Episteme and Techne," *Philosophy and Phenomenological Research*, Vol. 10, No. 3 (March 1950), pp. 389–397.
Rayor, Diane J., *The Homeric Hymns: A Translation, with Introduction and Notes* (Berkley, CA: The University of California Press, 2014), pg. 16.
Redfield, James, "The *Proem* of the Iliad: Homer's Art," *Classical Philology*, Vol. 74, No. 2 (April 1979), pp. 95–110.
Reynolds, Robert D., "Textless Choral Music," *The Choral Journal*, Vol. 41, No. 2 (September 2000), pp. 19–34.
Reznik, Jan, "The Essence of Sport," in *Reflecting on Modern Sport in Ancient Olympia: Proceedings of the 2016 Meeting of the International Association for the Philosophy of Sport at the International Olympic Academy*, edited by Heather L. Reid and Eric Moore (Parnassos Press, Fonte Aretusa, 2017), pp. 95–104.
Richardson, Elaine, "(Dis)inventing Discourse: Examples from Black Culture and Hip-Hop Rap Discourse," in *Disinventing and Reconstituting Languages*, edited by Prof. Sinfree Makoni and Prof. Alastair Pennycook (Buffalo, NY: Multilingual Matters, Ltd., 2017), pp. 196–215.
Richardson-Hay, Christine, "Dinner at Seneca's Table: The Philosophy of Food," *Greece & Rome*, Second Series, Vol. 56, No. 1 (April 2009), pp. 71–96.
Rogers, Richard A., *Petroglyphs, Pictographs and Projections: Native American Rock Art in the Contemporary Landscape* (Salt Lake City, UT: The University of Utah Press, 2018).
Ruiz, Anna, *Spirit of Ancient Egypt* (New York, NY: Algora Publishing, 2001).
Rutherford, Ian, "*Et Hominum Et Deorum ... Laudes* (?): A Hypothesis about the Organisation of Pindar's 'Paean'," *Zeitschrift für Papyrologie und Epigraphik*, Bd. 107 (1995), pp. 44–52.
Ryan, Edwin, "Medieval Latin in the Secondary School," *The Classical World*, Vol. 52, No. 5 (February 1959), pp. 144–147.
Sachs, Curt, *The History of Musical Instruments* (New York, NY: Dover Publications, 1940).
Sachs, Curt, "The Mystery of the Babylonian Notation," *The Musical Quarterly*, Vol. 27, No. 1 (January 1941), pp. 62–69.
Sachs, Curt, *The Rise of Music in the Ancient World* (New York, NY: Dover Publications, 1971).
Samama, Leo, *The Meaning of Music* (Amsterdam: Amsterdam University Press, 2016).
Saville, M. H., "The Musical Bow in Ancient Mexico," *American Anthropologist*, Vol. 11, No. 9 (September 1898), pp. 280–284.
Schmidt, Michael, *Gilgamesh: The Life of a Poem* (Princeton, NJ: Princeton University Press, 2019).
Schrade, Leo, "Music in the Philosophy of Boethius," *The Musical Quarterly*, Vol. 33, No. 2 (April 1947), pp. 188–200.
Scodel, Ruth, *Listening to Homer: Tradition, Narrative and Audience* (Ann Abor, MI: The University of Michigan Press, 2009).

Scott, Allen J., *The Cultural Economy of Cities* (London: Sage Publications, 2000), pg. 2.

Segerman, Ephraim, "A Short History of the Cittern," *The Galpin Society Journal*, Vol. 52 (April 1999), pp. 77–107.

Seller, O. R., "Intervals in Egyptian Music," *The American Journal of Semitic Languages and Literatures*, Vol. 41, No. 1 (October 1924), pp. 11–16.

Sellers, Ovid R., "Musical Instruments of Israel," *The Biblical Archaeologist*, Vol. 4, No. 3 (September 1941), pp. 33–47.

Senn, Frank C., *Embodied Liturgy: Lessons in Christian Ritual* (Minneapolis, MN: Augsburg Fortress Publishers, 2016).

Shepherd, Louis T., and Simons, Gene M., "Music Training for the Visually Handicapped," *Music Educators Journal*, Vol. 56, No. 6 (February 1970), pp. 80–81.

Sherrat, Susan, "Homeric Epic and Contexts of Bardic Creation," in *Archaeology and Homeric Epic*, edited by Susan Sherratt and John Bennet (Philadelphia, PA: Oxbow Books, 2017), pp. 35–53.

Shewell, Christina, *Voice Work: Art and Science in Changing Voices* (Chichester, West Sussex: John Wiley and Sons, 2009).

Simonett, Helena, "Envisioned, Ensounded, Enacted: Sacred Ecology and Indigenous Musical Experience in Yoreme Ceremonies of Northwest Mexico," *Ethnomusicology*, Vol. 58, No. 1 (Winter 2014), pp. 110–132.

Smith, J. A., "The Language of Primitive Man," *The Hebrew Student*, Vol. 2, No. 7 (March 1883), pp. 193–200.

Smith, John Arthur, *Music in Ancient Judaism and Early Christianity* (New York, NY: Routledge, 2011).

Song, Bang-Song, "The Korean Pip'a and Its Notation," *Ethnomusicology*, Vol. 17, No. 3 (September 1973), pp. 460–493.

Spilker, John D., "'Oh My Son!': The Musical Origins and Function of King David's Lamentation," *College Music Symposium*, Vol. 49/50 (2009/2010), pp. 427–450.

Stahl, William Harris, *Martianus Capella and the Seven Liberal Arts, Vol. 1, The Quadrivium of Martianus Capella* (New York, NY: Columbia University Press, 1971), 21.

Staver, Ruth Johnson, *A Companion to Beowulf* (Westport, CT: Greenwood Press, 2005).

Steafel, Harold, "Jew's Harp," *The Galpin Society Journal*, Vol. 29 (May 1976), pp. 122–123.

Stephens, Susan A., "Linus Song," *Hermathena*, Vol. 173/174, *Studies in Hellenistic Poetry* (Winter 2002 and Summer 2003), pp. 13–28.

Stephens, Wade C., "Descent to the Underworld in Ovid's Metamorphoses," *The Classical Journal*, Vol. 53, No. 4 (January 1958), pp. 177–183.

Stewart, Susan, "What Praise Poems Are For," *PMLA*, Vol. 120, No. 1, *Special Topic: On Poetry* (January 2005), pp. 235–245.

Stibbe, Arran Stibbe, "Abracadabra, Alakazam: Colonialism and the Discourse of Entertainment Magic," *Soundings: An Interdisciplinary Journal*, Vol. 88, No. 3/4 (Fall/Winter 2005), pp. 413–425.

Stoffelen, Veerle, "Vergil's Circe: Sources for a Sorceress," *L'Antiquité Classique*, T. 63 (1994), pp. 121–135.
Strangways, A. H. Fox, "The Pipes of Pan," *Music & Letters*, Vol. 10, No. 1 (January 1929), pp. 58–64.
Straub, Sandra Helene, *101: A Workbook for Educating and Healing* (Amityville, NY: Baywood Publishing Company, 2002).
Suderman, W. Derek, and Sandoval, Timothy J., *Wisdom, Worship, and Poetry: Fortress Commentary on the Bible Study Edition* (Minneapolis, MN: Augsburg Fortress Publishing, 2016).
Sweeney, Emmet, *Empire of Thebes, or Ages of Chaos Revisited* (New York, NY: Algora Publishing, 2000).
The Literature of Ancient Sumer, translated and edited by Jeremy Black, Graham Cunningham, Eleanor Robson, and Gabor Zólyomi (New York, NY: Oxford University Press, 2004).
"The Ocarina," *The Scientific American*, Vol. 51, No. 14 (October 4, 1884), p. 216.
"The Sound of Arabian Music," *Music Educators Journal*, Vol. 49, No. 5 (April–May 1963), pp. 89–92.
Theunte, Mary Helen, *Memory Ireland: History and Modernity*, Vol. 1, (Syracuse, NY: Syracuse University Press, 2011).
Thomas, Carol G., and Webb, Edward Kent. *Persuasion: Greek Rhetoric in Action*, edited by Ian Worthington (New York, NY: Routledge, 1994), pp. 3–26.
Thornton, M. K., "Julio-Claudian Building Programs: Eat, Drink, and Be Merry," *Historia: Zeitschrift für Alte Geschichte*, Bd. 35, H. 1 (1st Qtr., 1986), pp. 28–44.
Thorpe, W. A., "The Comparison of Vocal Communication in Animals and Man," in *Non-Verbal Communication*, edited by Robert A. Hinde (New York, NY: Cambridge University Press, 1979), pp. 27–49.
Tomka, Steve A., "The Adoption of the Bow and Arrow: A Model Based on Experimental Performance Characteristics," *American Antiquity*, Vol. 78, No. 3 (July 2013), pp. 553–569.
Tomlinson, Richard Alan, "Theaters (Greek and Roman), Structure," Entry," in *The Oxford Classical Dictionary*, 4th Edition, edited by Simon Hornblower and Antony Spawforth (New York, NY: Oxford University Press, 2012).
Tong, Kin-Woon, "Shang Musical Instruments: Part Two," *Asian Music*, Vol. 15, No. 1 (1983), pp. 102–184.
Tracy, H. L., "The Epic Tradition," *The Classical Journal*, Vol. 42, No. 2 (November 1946), pp. 78–81.
Troxell, Edward L., "The Thumb of Man," *The Scientific Monthly*, Vol. 43, No. 2 (August 1936), pp. 148–150.
Turpin, E. H., *Proceedings of the Musical Association 15th Sess.* (1888–1889), pp. 19–34.
Ulrich, Roger B., and Quenemoen, Caroline K., *A Companion to Roman Architecture* (Hoboken, NJ: John Wiley and Sons, 2013).
Underhill, Roy, *Woodwright's Shop: A Practical Guide to Traditional Woodcraft* (Chapel Hill, NC: The University of North Carolina Press, 1981).

Urban, Hugh B., *New Age, Neopagan, and New Religious Movements: Alternative Spirituality in Contemporary America* (Oakland, CA: The University of California Press, 2015).

Versnel, H. S., "The Poetics of the Magical Charm: An Essay on the Power of Words," in *Magic and Ritual in the Ancient World*, edited by Paul Mirecki and Marvin Meyer (Boston, MA: E. J. Brill, 2002), 105–159.

Vorreiter, Leopold, "The Swan-Neck Lyres of Minoan-Mycenean Culture," *The Galpin Society Journal*, Vol. 28 (April 1975), pp. 93–97.

Votaw, Clyde Weber, "The *Septuagint* Greek Version of the Old Testament," *The Biblical World*, Vol. 16, No. 3 (September 1900), pp. 186–198.

Wallace, John, and McGrattan, Alexander, *The Trumpet* (New Haven, CT: Yale University Press, 2011).

Wasserman, Emma, *Apocalypse as Holy War: Divine Politics and Polemics in the Letters of Paul* (New Haven, CT: Yale University Press, 2018).

Waugh, Robin, "Literacy, Royal Power, and King-Poet Relations in Old English and Old Norse Compositions," *Comparative Literature*, Vol. 49, No. 4 (Autumn 1997), pp. 289–315.

Wegst, Ulrike G. K., "Wood for Sound," *American Journal of Botany*, Vol. 93, No. 10 (October 2006), pp. 1439–1448.

Wellesz, Egon, "Byzantine Music," *Proceedings of the Musical Association, 59th Sess.* (1932–1933), pp. 1–22.

Werner, Eric, "Musical Aspects of the Dead Sea Scrolls: For Curt Sachs on his Seventh-Fifth Birthday," *The Musical Quarterly*, Vol. 43. No. 1 (January 1957), pp. 21–37.

Wheeler, Graham, "Sing, Muse …: The Introit from Homer to Apollonius," *The Classical Quarterly*, Vol. 52, No. 1 (2002), pp. 33–49.

Winnington-Ingram, R. P., "Aristoxenus and the Intervals of Greek Music," *The Classical Quarterly*, Vol. 26, No. 3/4 (July–October 1932), pp. 195–208.

Woodward, Holly, "A Moirologist's Notes," *Chicago Review*, Vol. 40, No. 4 (1994), pp. 71–74.

Wulstan, David, "The Earliest Musical Notation," *Music & Letters*, Vol. 52, No. 4 (October 1971), pp. 365–382.

Wurm, Stefan, "Tonal Languages in New Guinea and the Adjacent Islands," *Anthropos*, Bd. 49, H. 3./4. (1954), pp. 697–702.

Yates, Frances, *The Art of Memory* (London: Routledge, 1966).

Zenter, Marcel, "Homer's Prophecy: an Essay on Music's Primary Emotions," *Music Analysis*, Vol. 29, No. 1/3, *Special Issue on Music and Emotion* (March–October 2010), pp. 102–125.

Zheng, Cao, and Knobloch, Yohana, "A Discussion of the History of the Gu zheng," *Asian Music*, Vol. 14, No. 2, *Chinese Music History* (1983), pp. 1–16.

Zinck, Alexandra, and Newen, Albert, "Classifying Emotion: A Developmental Account," *Synthese*, Vol. 161, No. 1 (March 2008), pp. 1–25.

Zulkader, Siddiqui Kazi, "The Problem of Similarities in Ancient Near Eastern Religions: A Comparison of the Hymn to Aton and Psalm 104," *Islamic Studies*, Vol. 40, No. 1 (Spring 2001), pp. 67–88.

Index

Abyssinian shepherds, 33
acapella singing, 128, 136
Achilles, 58
Aeschylus, 105
aesthetics, xiii
Aeterne Rerum Conditor, 127
Agamemnon, 105
agon, 102
agonistic festivals, 102–3
Akhenaton, Pharaoh, 11
Albright, William, 12
Alcaeus, 58
Alexander, Michael, 84
Ambrose, Saint, 126–27
American Sign Language, 1
Amphion, 56–58
Andean panpipes, 33
An die Freude, 16
animal communication, 3
anthems, 72
Antiphon, 13–14
Antiquity, 39, 75, 81, 106, 121, 128, 132, 136
Apollo, 35, 52–55, 76, 104–5, 107, 121
arete, 103
Aristophanes, 105
Aristotle, 27, 102
Aristoxenus, 40
Armana Letters, 12

arrowheads, 24
art, functional theory of, xix–xx
Artemis *Chelitis*, 55
The Art of Ancient Music, 142
arts, 23–24; of eloquence, 70
Asian music, 61–62
Asklepios, 15
Augustine of Hippo, Saint, 75, 136
auletrides, 59
aulos/auloi/tibia, 34
authentic epics, 73

Babylonian musical notation system, 39
Bacchae, 99–101
bad music, xiii
ballad, 77–78; in Roman world, 78
Bantu peoples, 31
bard (s), 85–86; defined, 78; distinction between bards and, 85
barritus, 83
beat-boxing, 5
Beatles, 82, 144
Beethoven's Ninth Symphony, 16
Beowulf, 83–85
Bible, 26, 28, 58; *nebel*, 56; *Psalm* 78, 75; trumpets mentioned in, 36
Biblical festivals, 97–98; dancing, 99
bird callers, 4
biwa, 61, 77

Blind Bard. *See* Homer
blind musicians, 77
blind poets, 76–77
Boethius, 133–34, 136; *The Fundamentals of Music*, 134
bone pendants, 27
Book of Acts, 112
Book of Praises, 13
Book of Psalms, 13
Book of Psalms Sepher Tillihim, 13
Book of the Dead, 10
Borges, Jorge Luis, 77
"bow of music," 62
Bowra, C. M., 73
Boyas of Tekkalakota, 10
Bradley, Richard, xix
Bromius, 100–101
Burnet, James, 4

Callimachus, 53
Cappella, Martianus, 132–33, 136; *Regarding the Marriage of Philology and Mercury*, 132–33
Celestine I, Pope, 123
Celtic culture, 86
Celtic poets, 82–83
Celtic Romanticism, 85
ceremonial knife, 10
chanting, 9–10, 17; uses, 10
Charlemagne, 130–32
chelys lyre, 54–55
chipping, 24
choral recitations, 105
choregos, 101
choruses, 101
Christian iconography, 129–30
Christianity, 119–21
Christian worship, 132
Chrysostom, John, 121; *On the Incomprehensible Nature of God*, 129
Church music, 119–21, 135–37; prejudices against, 121–22
cithara, 54–56
citharoedus, 54–55

Clement of Alexandria, 129
Clio, 81
clothing fashions, xvii
Collingwood, RG, xiv
communications, 2; animal, 3
conch trumpets, 36
Confessions, 75
Congreve, William, 33; "The Mourning Bride," 33
country talk-ballads, 5
crafts, 23–24; definition, xiv
creativity, xix
Creativity in Human Evolution and Prehistory, xix
Cretheus, 79
culture: music and, xvii–xviii; symbiotic relationship between society and, xvii

Daniel, 37
Dardanelles, 55
Dardanos tombs, 55
David, King, 28, 56
Dead Sea Scrolls, 14
Dido, Queen, 79
Dijve Babe Cave, 26
Dionysus, 107
dithyramb, 102
Donatus, Aelius, 78
"Don't Do It" mandate, 80
Doric mode, 40
double-reed sound production, 35
Druidic bards, 86
Druids, 85
Duillius, Gaius, 108

Ecclesiastes, 99
Eclogues, 78
edda, 83
Egypt, 25
electronic music, 23
epic, 72; of Gilgamesh, 73; hero, 73–74
epistemology, xv
Erasmus, 49
ethical Monotheism, 12

Euripides, 105; *Alcestis*, 105; *Medea*, 107
Eurydice, 79–80
Exodus 39, 28

Fender Telecasters, 23
festivals, 95; agonistic, 102–3; in ancient Egypt, 97; Biblical, 97–98; dancing, 98–99; Dionysian rites, 99–101; *dithyramb*, 102; nature of, 96; parties and banquets, 107–8; of prehistory, 96; role in history and music, 112–13; Roman, 108; theater spaces, 106–7
festive music, 107
Fine Arts, xiv, xviii, 1–2, 16, 25, 81, 95, 101, 103, 113
First Epistle to Thessalonians, 128
First Punic War, 108
flute, 29–31, *30*; American/Pre-Columbian, 29; in Japan, 29; ocarina, 31; producing sound in, 30–31
flute girls, 59
Ford, Andrew, 27
For Murena (Pro Murena), 54
Frazer, Sir James George, 96; *The Golden Bough*, 96
Freud, Sigmund, 7–8

Gadeira, 109
Galba-mocking song, 82
Genesis, 26
Germanic storytelling cultures, 82–84
Gilgamesh's epic, 73
Gospel of Matthew, 128
Great Flood, 8
Great Schism, 122
Greco-Roman theaters, 111
Greece, 25
Greek amphora, 55
Greek mythology, 103
Greek pipes of pan, 31–33, *32*
Greek system of musical notation, 39–40

Greek theaters, 106
Greek tradition of music and sports, 108–9
Gregory the Great, Pope, 127–28
Guardians, 76
Gumà, Jesús Salia, xviii
guzheng, 61
Gypsy musicians, 85

Habakkuk, 13
Handel, George Frederick, 14
Harley Lullaby, 7
Harmony, 133
harps, 49–51, 61, *87*; in Bible, 56; in Christian iconography, 129–30; tuning of, 55–56
healthy musical culture, xiii
Hebrew Bible, 13
Hermes, 52–54
Herodotus, 26, 103
heroic epics, 73–74
Hesiod, 72; *Theogony*, 11
Hilary of Poitiers, 124–25
hip-hop, 5
Hippotharus, 34
Homer, 76–77, 84, 107; *Iliad*, 58, 74, 82; *Odyssey*, 26, 74, 79, 82
Homeric Hymns, 15–16
Hopewell Indian Mounds of New Castle Indiana, 33
Horace, 16, 59
Horatian Odes, 16
horns, 35–37; metallurgy and, 37–38
Hosea, 37
human needs, xviii–xix; music for, xv–xvi
hymns, 32, 53, 72; of ancient Egypt, 11–12; antiphonal, 13–14; building, 12; definition, 11; distinction between ancient "chant" and, 11; Homeric, 15–16; Latin, 122–27, 136; Mesopotamian, 12; Prudentius's, 126; royal, 12; of Second Temple Period, 14
Hymn to Aton, 11

Iliad, 26
imitating animal sounds, 4
incantations, 9; Mesopotamian or Egyptian, 8
Industrial Revolution, 24
inspiration, 81–82
Ionian mode, 40
Ionic mode, 40
Ion of Chios, 53
Iopas, 53
Iopas's music, 79
Irish Bard, 86

Jeremiah, 37
Jerome, Saint, 123
jewelry, 26
Jew's Harp, 49
Joel (prophet), 36
Jokes and their Relation to the Subconscious, 8
Joyce, James, 77
Judaism, 14
Judge Ehud, 36

Keat, John, 16
khalil, 35
kinetic dancing, 99
kinnor, 56
knowing music, xv
knowledge, xiv
kymbala (cymbals), 29
kytheris, 54

laccifer laca, 54
Landini, Francesco, 132
languages, 5–6
larynx, 2
Latin Christianity, 122–23
Latin hymns, 122–27, 136
Latin music, 128
Lebanese *mijwiz*, 35
The Legend of Zelda: Ocarina of Time, 31
Lesbian Lyre, 58
Lesbos, 58

Libanius, 122
Life of Vergil, 78
Linus of Thrace, 58
Listening to Homer: Tradition, Narrative and Audience, 72
literary epics, 73
lithophones, 27
lullabies, 7–8; ancient, 8–9; chanting, 9–10
lute-type instrument, 52
Lydian mode, 40
lyres, 34, 49–51, *57*, *71*, 87–88; advantages, 50–51; in Bible, 56; Bronze Age period, 53; carvings of, 51; in Christian iconography, 129–30; fancy, 53–54; features, 51; gilded (*cithara aurata*), 53; Greek, 53; phorminx-style of, 53–54; principle difference between harp and, 49; tortoise *chelys* lyre, 55; tuning of, 55–56
lyrics, 72

maenads, 99
Magdalenian Cave, 29
magic words, 9
mammalian sounds, 5
marching-band lyres, 49–50
Marsyas, 35
Martin guitars, 23
Masonquo, 34
McCartney, Paul, 82
membranphones, 27
Mesopotamian hymn, 12
Mesopotamian musical traditions, 35
metallurgy, 37–38
metonymy, 81
Milton, John, 77; *Paradise Lost*, 129
mimetic poetry, 74–75
mnemotechnics, 75
moderation, 76
modes, 40–41
monodic, 58
Moses, 36
Mouth Harp, 49

Müller, G. E., 74
muses, 80–81; inspiration and, 81–82
music, xiv, xix–xx, 141–43; in ancient theater, 105–6; as an art, xiv–xv; culture and, xvii–xviii; defined, xi; as a discipline, 75–76; for human needs, xv–xvi; myths related to, 26; as part of cultural wars, 121–22; society and, xvi–xvii
musical instruments, xii, 1, 40–41; animals and, 33–34; *aulos/auloi/ tibia*, 34; Church, 128–29; conch trumpets, 36; horns, 35–37; making of, 23; reed instruments, 34–35; rhythm instruments, 27–28; stringed instruments, 41, 47; for summoning people, 36; tools and, 25–26; tuning instruments, 38; use of brass for, 35–36
musical notation, 39, 41; Greek system of, 39–40
Music of the Spheres, 134–35
Mycenaean Age, 26
Myth of Arion, 103–4
myth of "dying and reviving god," 96

Nascan process of "slip painting," 33
Native American Exoticism, 29
nebel, 56
Nero, Emperor, 59–60, 78, 82, 108
Neruda, Pablo, 16; *Oda a los calcetines*, 17; *Oda a un gran atún en el marcado*, 17; *Odas Elementales (Elemental Odes)*, 17
newborns' sense of hearing, 8
Nicomachean Ethics, xiv
Niebelungenlied (Song of the Niebelungen), 83
nofre, 51
noises, xi
nonsense rhymes or phrases, 7
nonsensical syllabic sounds, 7
Nostoi, 82

Ocarinas, 31

ode, 16–17
Odeon theaters, 111
Odysseus, 79
Old English *hearpe*, 49
Olsen, Dale A., 29
Olympics, 81
orchestra, 106
organs, 130–32, *131*
orientalism, 61
Orpheus, 79–80
Orphic musical traditions, 80
Orphism, 80
orthios nomos hymns, 104–5
Ovid's *Metamorphoses*, 80

paean, 15
pagans, 121–22
"Paleo-Byzantine" Christianity, 14
pandura, 51
Papacy, 81
paper/papyri, 39
parasites, 85–86
parties and banquets, 107–8
Pausanias, 57
percussion, xii
phonic games, 8
phorminx, 53–54
Phrygian mode, 40
Pindar, 15–16, 55, 107
"Pindaric Odes," 16
Pinker, Steven, xvi
pipa, 61
Plato, 76, 105; ideal state, 74; *Republic*, 35, 74; *Symposium*, 59, 107
pleasure, significance of, xii–xiv
Pliny, 75
Plotinus, 76
poetry, 86–88; as a discipline, 75–76; music and, 70–72; rhetoric in, 70
poet storytellers, 72
Polygnota of Thebes, 59
Polymnia, 11
popular songs, 82
Proverbs, 12
Prudentius's hymns, 126

Psalm 104, 11
Psalm 139, 12
Psalms of the Bible, 11, 13
Pseudo-Herodotus, 76
punk rock, xiii
Pythagoras, 38, 40
Pythagorean Theorem, 38

Quadrivium, 133
quijongo, 61

Ramses IV, 12
rap, 5
rattlers, 27–28
reed instruments, 34–35
reenactments, 96
Rekhmire's tomb, 51
Renaissance Italy, 25
rhetoric, 70
rhythm, 74
rhythm instruments, 27–28
ringing rocks, 27
ritual religious dances, 98–99, *100*
Roman emperors, 109; patronage and public works, 109; support for banquets and feasting, 110
Roman festivals, 108
Roman Triumph, 108
Rousseau, Jean Jacques Louis, 4

Sachs, Curl, 39
sacred stories, 86
Saint Mark's Scroll of Isiah, 14
Sappho, 58
scales, 6, 31, 41; *Aeolian* Scale, 40; diatonic, 40; "Major Scale" of Modern Western Music, 40; pentatonic, 31; seven-note, 39
Schumann, Frederick, 74
science, xiv
Scipio, L., 75
Scodel, Ruth, 72
scole, 112
scops, 84–85
Scribes, 73

Scythians, 34
secondary tools, 25
Second Temple Period, hymn of, 14
Se (instrument), 61
Seneca, 105
Seneca the Elder, 75
Septuagint, 13
Seven Liberal Arts, 132–33
seven-string lyre, 53
sexual sensations, 6
shakers, 27–28
Shambukaw, 34
Shang dynasty, 31
shofar, 36
siglum CBS 10966, 39
Silver Lyre of Ur, 54
singing, 2, 4–6, 17
singsong rhythms, 9
sistrum, 28–29, 99, *100*
six-string guitar, 53
skene, 107
societies, xvi–xviii
Solomon, King, 56
Solomon Islands, 4
Sophocles, 105
sounds, xi; nonsensical syllabic, 7; production of, xviii; shared responses to, 6
Spartans, 55
Staver, Ruth Johnson, 84
Steinway Grand Piano, 25
Steinway pianos, 23
Stone Age, xix, 29
stonecutters, 24
Stonehenge, xix
storytelling: history of, 69; relationship between music and, 69, 86–88; storytellers as characters in stories, 79
Stradivarius violins, 23
stringed instruments, 41, 47, 62–63; bowing effect, 48–49; bridge on, *50*; early, 51–52; in Japan, 61; materials used in, 52; in pre-Columbian American societies, 60–61;

relationship between archery and, 47–48. *See also* harps
Sufi Islam, 10
Sumerian Hymnal, 12
swan's song, 104–5
Symposium, 107

"talk-singing" style of performing, 5
Ten Commandments, 36
Terpnus, 60
tertiary tools, 25
Theater of Balbus, 111
Theater of Marcellus, 111
theaters: Greek origin of, 112; Roman, 110–12; spaces, 106–7
A Thousand and One Tales of the Arabian Nights, 9
thriambos, 108
timbrel, 28–29
Titus, Emperor, 60
Tomb of Nnkht, 51
tonal languages, 6
tones, 6
tools, 24–25; musical instruments and, 25–26; secondary, 25; tertiary, 25
Triton, 36

The Trivium: The Liberal Arts of Logic, Grammar and Rhetoric, xiv
trumpet-tube instruments, 36
tuning instruments, 38
tympanum, 28

Unas, 12

verbal and nonverbal communication, xvi
Vergil, 36, 53, 78, 85; *Aeneid*, 78–79
Vespasian, Emperor, 60
Virgil's *Aeneid*, 10, 15
visual arts, xiv
Vitruvius, 112
vocal music, 17
vocal sounds, 4
voices, xi; apparatus, 2–4; human, 1–2, 17–18; before language, 4; used during hunting, 4
Vulgate, 123, 136

wind instruments, 28–31

Yates, Frances, 74; *The Art of Memory*, 74–75
Yoreme tribe, 61

About the Author

David Leinweber is an associate professor of history at Oxford College of Emory University. He has logged many years of successful teaching in the college classroom, offering European history and Western Civ survey courses. He has won many awards for his teaching and service. Dr. Leinweber has traveled extensively, benefiting enormously from seeing other parts of the world. He also speaks frequently at academic, civic, and community functions. He has published a wide variety of articles, reviews, and reference entries. A proud Detroit native, Leinweber has a PhD from Michigan State University. He is a lifelong musician who frequently performs at festivals, concert venues, and other settings.

www.ingramcontent.com/pod-product-compliance
Lightning Source LLC
Chambersburg PA
CBHW050907300426
44111CB00010B/1416